ENGINEERING CHEMISTRY

ENGINEERING CHEMISTRY

A Textbook for B.Tech. 1st Semester

AVNISH GAUR
(M.Sc., Ph.D.) *Sr. Lecturer*
Tagore Engineering College, Kuchaman City, (Rajasthan)

•

RENU SHARMA
(M.Sc., Ph.D.) *Lecturer*
Department of Chemistry, JIET, Jodhpur (Rajasthan)

•

SATPAL YADAV
M.Sc. M.Phil, (Ph.D. Pursuing) *Sr. Lecturer*
Sribalaji College of Engineering & Technology, Jaipur (Rajasthan)

•

DR. RAJEEV MEHTA
(Ph.D.) *Assistant Professor & Head*
Department of Chemistry
Institute of Technology & Management, Bhilwara (Rajasthan)

•

SUSHIL KUMAR SHARMA
(Pursuing Ph.D.) *Lecturer*
Government Engineering College, Jhalawar (Rajasthan)

AN ISO 9001:2008 CERTIFIED COMPANY

VAYU EDUCATION OF INDIA

2/25, Ansari Road, Darya Ganj, New Delhi-110 002

Engineering Chemistry

ISBN: 978-93-80712-50-5

First Edition: 2010

Rs. 160.00

Printed & bound in India

Published by:

AN ISO 9001:2008 CERTIFIED COMPANY

VAYU EDUCATION OF INDIA

2/25, Ansari Road, Darya Ganj, New Delhi-110 002

Ph.: 91-11-47236600, 41564445

Fax: 91-11-41564440

E-mail: vei@veiindia.com

Web: www.veiindia.com

Dedicated

to

Our Parents

PREFACE

Engineering Chemistry *deals with the application of chemistry, to the process of converting raw materials or chemicals into more useful or valuable forms. Engineering Chemistry largely involves the design, improvement and maintenance of processes involving chemical or biological transformations for large-scale manufacture. It ensures that the processes operated are safe, sustainable and economical.*

Engineering Chemistry is applied in the manufacture of a wide variety of products. The chemical industry has a large scope, manufacturing inorganic and organic industrial chemicals, cement, lubricant, ceramics, fuels and petrochemicals, agrochemicals (fertilizers, insecticides, herbicides), plastics and elastomers, explosives, detergents (soap, shampoo, cleaning fluids), fragrances and flavors, additives, dietary supplements and pharmaceuticals. Closely allied or overlapping disciplines include wood processing, food processing, environmental technology including water treatment and the engineering of petroleum, glass, paints and other coatings, inks, adhesives and refractories.

Present book is designed for the first year engineering undergraduate students of Rajasthan Technical University, Kota. The chapters are divided unit wise as per the new syllabus of R.T.U., Kota. As the subject matter is written in easy and simple language, we hope that the students will find this book useful for studying and preparing for the examinations.

Efforts have been made to present the subject in correct and error free form, but even then some errors might have left. The authors invite further suggestions and corrective criticism for improvement of this book in forthcoming editions.

August, 2010 **Authors**

ACKNOWLEDGEMENTS

First of all we would like to thank specially to Great Almighty who was with us at every step. We wish to acknowledge our profound sense of reverence and gratitude towards Mr. Dhananjay Singh (Chairman, Tagore Engineering College, Kuchaman City), Mr. Pooran Singh Ranwa (Director, Tagore Balika Shiksha Samiti, Kuchaman City), Dr. Virendra Singh Kumpawat (Director, JIET Group of Institutions, Jodhpur), Dr. N. K. Srivastava (Dean Sciences, JIET Group of Institutions, Jodhpur) and Dr. R. Mehra (Head, Deptt. of Applied Chemistry, MDS University, Ajmer) for the encouragement and moral support.

We also want to express our heartfelt thanks to Dr. Aditi Soni, Dr. Rekha Israni, Dr. Meenakshi Pancholi, Dr. Pawan Swarnkar, Dr. Sudesh Nyol, Dr. Prashant Kriplani, Dr. Kirti Saraswat, Dr. Shahnawaz Khan, Dr. Sangeeta Gautum, Mr. Sandeep Mitharwal, Mr. Abhishek Gehlot, Mr. Hitesh Jaiman and Mr. Mahendra Singh Saharan , Dr. S.L.Kakani, Executive Director, ITM Bhilwara. Mrs Preeti Mehta, Ms Rakhi Goyal, Dr. Mukesh Paliwal, Lecturer ITM Bhilwara, Mrs Menka Surana, Lecturer, Mewar University, Chittoregarh for their valuable suggestions.

We also want to express our grateful thanks to Dr. R. K. Jain (Managing Director, Vayu Education of India, New Delhi). Our thanks are to Mr. Vijay Kumar Saini (Production Manager), and other production team members of Vayu Education of India, New Delhi and Sanjay Sharma (New Wave Computer); those published our book within a quite short duration.

The recallable, consistent moral encouragement and zeal added by our parents and other family members is unforgettable. Again, we iterate a word of thanks to all those hands that helped us in some way or the other in pursuing this elusive task.

Authors

Engineering Chemistry

According to Prescribed Syllabus
for
B.Tech. Ist Semester
of
Rajasthan Technical University, Kota

SYLLABUS

Engineering Chemistry

B.Tech. Ist Semester

Maximum Marks = 100

[Mid-term (20) and End-term (80)]

Duration = 3 Hours

Unit I

Water

- Common Impurities of water
- Hardness of water: Determination of hardness by Clark's test and complex metric (EDTA) method, Degree of hardness
- Numerical based on hardness and EDTA method
- Municipal Water Supply: Requisites of drinking water, Steps involved in purification of water, Sedimentation, coagulation, Filtration and Sterilization, Break point chlorination

Unit II

Water Treatment

- Softening of water: Lime-Soda Method, Permutit (Zeolite) Method and Deionization or Demineralization Method
- Boiler troubles their causes, disadvantages and prevention: Formation of solids (Scale and Sludge), Carry over (Priming and Foaming), Corrosion and Caustic Embrittlement
- Numerical problems based on Lime-Soda and Zeolite softening methods

Unit III

Polymers

- Different methods of classification and constituents of polymers
- Plastics: Themosets and Thermoplasts
- Preparation, Properties and uses of polyethylene, Bakelite, Terylene and Nylon
- Elastomers – Natural rubber, vulcanization, Synthetic Rubbers viz. Buna-S, Buna-N, Butyl and neoprene rubbers

Unit IV

Cement

- Definition, Composition, basic constituents and their significance, Manufacturing of Portland cement by Rotary Kiln Technology
- Chemistry of setting and hardening of cement and role of gypsum

Glass

- Definition, Properties, Manufacturing of glass
- Types of silicate glasses and their commercial uses
- Importance of annealing in glass making

Unit V

Refractories

- Definition, classification, properties, Requisites of good refractory and manufacturing of refractory
- Detailed study of silica and fire clay refractory and their uses
- Seger's (Pyrometric) Cone Test and RUL Test

Lubricants

- Introduction, classification and uses of lubricants.
- Types of lubrication.
- Viscosity & viscosity index, flash and fire point, cloud and pour point, steam emulsification number, precipitation number and neutralization number

ENGINEERING CHEMISTRY LAB-I

S.No.	List of Experiments (Any 7 experiments are to be performed)
1.	To determine the hardness of water by HCL method.
2.	To determine the hardness of water by EDTA method.
3.	Determination of CO2 in a water sample.
4.	To determine free chlorine in a given water sample.
5.	To determine the viscosity of a given lubricating oil by Redwood viscometer.
6.	Measurement of residual chlorine in water.
7.	To determine the flash and fire point of a given lubricating oil.
8.	Measurement of dissolves oxygen in water.
9.	To determine cloud and pour point of a given oil.
10.	Measurement of nitrate in water.

CONTENTS

UNIT-I

UNIT-II

UNIT-III

UNIT-VI

UNIT-VI

Unit - 1
WATER

Water is an essential part of our life. It is not only necessary for survival of living organisms but also play a key role in chemical and industrial processes. In industry, generally it is used for steam generation. Various chemical and industrial applications of water are affected by its different physical and chemical properties. Hardness of water is one of them. In this chapter, we discuss about hardness of water, its determination and purification of water.

1.1 SOURCES OF WATER

There are two main sources of water: Surface water and Underground water

1. Surface Water: Water present on the earth's surface is known as surface water. It may be of two types. Flowing water and Still Water.

(A) Flowing water: It includes following sources of water:

Rain Water: Rain water is obtained by evaporation of the surface water through water cycle. It is considered as the purest from of the natural water. But rain water during its downward path to the earth dissolves considerable amount of gases (e.g. CO_2, SO_2, NO_3, NO_2, etc.) and suspended solid particles presents in the atmosphere.

River water: The sources of river water are rains, snow and springs. As it flows over the earth surface, dissolves soluble minerals of the soil (like chloride, sulphate, sodium, calcium, magnesium, iron etc.) and several other soluble substances. River water also contains organic products (from decomposition of plants and animals) and small particles of sand and rock in suspension.

Sea water: This is the impure form of the water. Continuous evaporation increases the dissolved impurity content in it, which further increased by the impurity thrown by rivers as they join sea.

(B) Still water: It involves lakes, ponds and reservoirs. Lake water is less contaminated than river water. It contains lesser amount of dissolved and suspended impurities in it, the main impurities are organic matter.

2. Underground Water: The water which gets stored under the surface of earth is known as underground water. This water is generally safe and pure, because it undergoes natural filtration during the percolation through the soil pores or small holes of soil. Moreover, these waters are less likely to be contaminated by bacteria. However, these are rich in dissolve salts, minerals, gases etc. thus, water from these sources has more hardness. The main sources of underground water are tube wells, deep springs and wells.

The various sources of water available can be classified into the following:

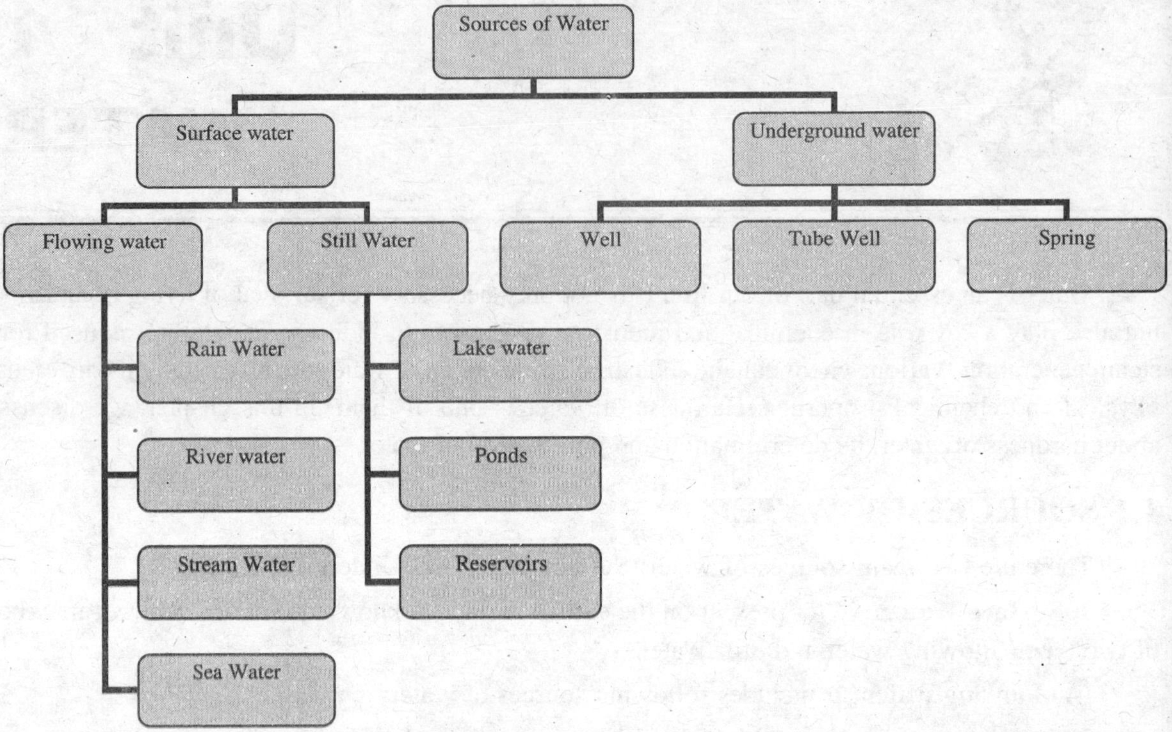

Fig 1.1: Sources of Water

1.2 COMMON IMPURITIES PRESENT IN WATER

The common impurities present in natural water may be classifies as follows:

(1) Dissolved impurities: Natural water may contain following dissolved impurities-

(A)Inorganic salts

(a) Cations: Ca^{+2}, Mg^{+2}, Na^{+}, K^{+}, Fe^{+2}, Al^{+3} etc.

(b) Anions: CO_3^{-2}, HCO_3^{-}, Cl^{-}, SO_4^{-2}, NO_3^{-} etc.

(b) Dissolved Organic substances:

(c) Dissolved gases: CO_2, O_2, H_2S, SO_2, NH_3 and oxides of nitrogen.

(2) Suspended impurities: There are two types of suspended impurities, which are:

(A) Inorganic: like Clay and sand

(B) Organic: Oil globules, vegetable and animal matter.

(3) Colloidal impurities: Fine particles of Silica and Clay, organic waste products, proteins, amino acids etc. are dispersed in colloidal form in water.

(4) Micro-organism: Various type of pathogenic bacteria, algae, fungi and viruses may present in natural water.

Adverse effects of impurities: These different types of impurities contaminate water by changing its physical, chemical and biological properties. Metallic substances like salts of iron, manganese and other industrial effluents impart colour to water. However, it is not harmful unless not associated with toxic substances. Disagreeable odour in water may be caused by living organisms like bacteria, algae, fungi and also due to presence of small amount of sulphides, suspended materials may impart turbidity to the water, presence of dissolved salts make the water hard whereas excess quantities of metals and dissolved gases makes it corrosive. Bacteriological impurities due to pathogenic bacteria make water unfit for drinking or domestic purposes. Hence, the water from any source has to be treated before it is used.

1.3 HARDNESS OF WATER

1.3.1 Hard Water

A sample of water which produces lather readily with soap is called soft water and if it does not produce lather readily with soap, it is said to be hard water. In other words, we may say that hardness of water is its soap consuming capacity. Soaps are the sodium salts of higher fatty acids like sodium stearate. When soap is added to soft water the sodium salt is dissolved in water and gives lather. However, when soap is added to hard water (which contains calcium and magnesium salts), it is precipitated as insoluble salt, hence no lather is produced until all calcium and magnesium ions are consumed.

$$\underset{\text{Sodium Stearate}}{2C_{17}H_{35}COONa} + CaCl_2 \xrightarrow{\Delta} \underset{\text{Precipitate of calcium soap}}{(C_{17}H_{35}COO)Ca\downarrow} + 2NaCl$$

Disadvantages of hard water:

The hard water has following disadvantage

- It is not useful for various domestic purposes like washing, bathing, drinking etc.
- It is not suitable for steam generation in boiler because it cause different problems in boiler like caustic embrittlement, scale and sludge formation, boiler corrosion, priming and foaming etc.
- It imparts colour and shades when used in textile industry.
- The hardness causing ions interfere in various reactions during laboratory analysis.

1.3.2 Types of hardness of water

Hardness of water may be classified in two categories:

(i) Temporary or carbonate hardness: It is due to the presence of carbonates and bicarbonates of calcium and magnesium in water. It can be removed by boiling. On boiling bicarbonates are decomposed into insoluble carbonates or hydroxides which can be easily filtered off or may settle down at bottom of vessel.

$$\underset{\text{Calcium bicarbonate}}{Ca(HCO_3)_2} \xrightarrow{\Delta} \underset{\text{Calcium carbonate}}{CaCO_3\downarrow} + H_2O + CO_2$$

(ii) Permanent or non-carbonate hardness: it is due to the presence of sulphates, chlorides and nitrates of calcium, magnesium and other heavy metals present in water and can not be easily removed by boiling. It requires special treatments.

Table 1.1: Comparison between Soft water and Hard water

S.N.	Soft Water	Hard Water
1.	Produce lather easily with soap. Hence, soap is not wasted during washing and bathing.	Does not produce lather with soap easily but forms a white curd. So soap is wasted during washing and bathing.
2.	It does not contain dissolved Ca and Mg salts.	It contains dissolved Ca and Mg salts impurities.
3.	Less fuel and time are required for cooking and steam generation.	The boiling point of water is increased due to the presence of dissolved salts. Hence, more fuel and time are required for cooking and steam generation.
4.	Has good taste for drinking.	Not suitable for drinking.

1.3.3 Degree of Hardness

As the type and concentration of hardness causing substances can vary from sample to sample, it is necessary to express the hardness of water in a suitable term. The degree of hardness of water is usually expressed in terms of equivalent amount of $CaCO_3$. For this, the concentrations of hardness causing substances are converted in terms of their respective equivalent weight of $CaCO_3$. The reason for expressing hardness of water as $CaCO_3$ equivalent is due to two reasons: (i) its molecular weight is 100 and equivalent weight is 50 (hence, easy for calculation) (ii) it is the most insoluble salt that can be precipitated during water treatment.

The equivalent of $CaCO_3$ for hardness producing substance can be calculated by following formula:

$$CaCO_3 \text{ equivalence} = \frac{\text{Weight of hardness producing Substance (in mg/L)} \times \text{Chemical equivalent of } CaCO_3 \text{ (i.e. 50)}}{\text{Chemical equivalent of hardness producing substance}}$$

Or

$$CaCO_3 \text{ equivalence} = \text{Weight of hardness producing Substance (in mg/L)} \times \text{multiplication factor}$$

where

$$\text{Multiplication factor} = \frac{\text{Molecular weight of } CaCO_3}{2 \times \text{Equivalent weight of hardness producing substance}}$$

Equivalent weight of a substance can be calculated by following general formula:

$$\text{Equivalent weight} = \frac{\text{Molecular weight of substance}}{\text{Acidity or basicity of that substance (oxidation no. of cation)}}$$

For e.g.

Molecular weight of $CaCO_3$ = Ca + C + (3 × O)
Molecular weight of Ca = 40, C = 12 and O = 16
Hence, molecular weight of $CaCO_3$ = 40 + 12 + 48
= 100
Oxidation state of Ca in $CaCO_3$ is 2

Hence, equivalent weight of $CaCO_3 = \frac{100}{2}$

Equivalent weight of few hardness causing substances are listed in table 1.2

Table 1.2: Equivalent of few compounds

S.N.	Substance	Molecular weight	Equivalent weight	Multiplication factor
1.	$Ca(HCO_3)_2$	162	81	100/162
2.	$Mg(HCO_3)_2$	146	73	100/146
3.	$CaCl_2$	111	55.5	100/111
4.	$MgCl_2$	95	47.5	100/95
5.	$CaSO_4$	136	68	100/136
6.	$MgSO_4$	120	60	100/120
7.	$Ca(NO_3)_2$	164	82	100/164
8.	$Mg(NO_3)_2$	148	74	100/148
9.	CO_2	44	22	100/44
10.	HCl	36.5	36.5	100/73
11.	H_2SO_4	98	49	100/98
12.	$Al_2(SO_4)_3$	342	57	3 × (100/342) = 100/114
13.	$NaAlO_2$	82	82	100/164
14.	$FeSO_4 \cdot 7H_2O$	278	139	100/278

1.3.4 Units of hardness and their inter-relationship

Followings are units in which hardness of water is expressed:

(i) Parts per million (*ppm*): It is defined as the number of parts of hardness by weight of $CaCO_3$ equivalent present in one million (10^6) parts by weight of water, that is:

$1ppm = 1$ part of $CaCO_3$ equivalent hardness in 10^6 parts of water

(ii) Milligram per litre (*mg/L*): It is defined as the number of milligrams of hardness by $CaCO_3$ equivalent present in one litre of water, that is:

$1mg/L = 1$ mg of $CaCO_3$ equivalent hardness in 1 litre of water

Density of water at room temperature is 1 kg/m^3

Hence, $1L = 1kg = 1000$ g or 1000×1000 mg $= 10^6$ mg

$mg/L = 1$ mg of $CaCO_3$ equivalent hardness in 1 litre of water

$= 1$ mg of $CaCO_3$ equivalent hardness in 10^6 mg of water

$= 1$ part of $CaCO_3$ equivalent hardness in 10^6 parts of water $= ppm$

i.e. $mg/L = ppm$

(iii) Degree Clark (*°Cl*): It is defined as the parts of $CaCO_3$ equivalent hardness present in 70000 parts of water or number of grains present in one gallon that is:

$1°Cl = 1$ grain of $CaCO_3$ equivalent hardness in one gallon of water

$= 1$ part of $CaCO_3$ equivalent hardness in 70000 parts of water

One grain = lb/70000,

One gallon = 10 lbs or 70000 grains

(iv) Degree French (*°Fr*): It is defined as the parts of $CaCO_3$ equivalent hardness present in 10^5 parts of water, that is:

$1°Fr = 1$ part of $CaCO_3$ equivalent hardness in 10^5 parts of water

Relationship between different units of hardness:

$1ppm = 1$ part of $CaCO_3$ equivalent hardness in 10^6 parts of water

$1mg/L = 1$ mg of $CaCO_3$ equivalent hardness in 1 litre of water $= ppm$

$1°Cl = 1$ part of $CaCO_3$ equivalent hardness in 70000 parts of water

$1°Fr = 1$ part of $CaCO_3$ equivalent hardness in 10^5 parts of water

Hence, $10^6\ ppm = 10^6\ mg/L = 70000\ °Cl = 10^5\ °Fr$

$100\ ppm = 100\ mg/L = 7\ °Cl = 10\ °Fr$

$1\ ppm = 1\ mg/L = 0.07\ °Cl = 0.1°Fr$

SOLVED EXAMPLE BASED ON HARDNESS OF WATER

Example 1 : A sample of water contains 204 mg of $CaSO_4$ per litre. Calculate the hardness in terms of $CaCO_3$ equivalent. **[R.T.U. 2010]**

Sol. : $CaSO_4 = CaCO_3$

Mol. mass 136 g/mol = 100g/mol

or 136 mg/lit of $CaSO_4$ = 100 mg/lit of $CaCO_3$

or 102 mg/lit of $CaSO_4 = \frac{100 \text{ mg/lit of } CaCO_3 \text{ eq.}}{136} \times 204$

$= 150$ mg/lit of $CaCO_3$ eq.

Hence hardness = 150 mg/lit or ppm

Example 2 : A sample of hard water has hardness 620 ppm. Express the hardness in terms of °Clark and °French.

Sol. : 1 ppm = 0.1° French

1 ppm = 0.07° Clarke

620 ppm = 620 × 0.1° French = 62° French

620 ppm = 620 × 0.07° Clark

= 43.4° Clark

Example 3 : A sample of hard water has hardness 500 ppm. Calculate the hardness in °French and °Clrak units.

Sol. 1 ppm = 0.1 °F = 0.07°Cl

Thus 500 ppm = 50 × 0.1°Fr = 500 × 0.07°Cl

=50 °Fr = 35°Cl

Hardness in °French = 50°Fr

Hardness in °Clarke = 35°Cl

Example 4 : A sample of water contains 408 mg of $CaSO_4$ per litre. Calculate the hardness in terms of $CaCO_3$ equivalents.

Sol. Hardness = [Mass of Hardness Producing substance in mg/L

$$\times \frac{\text{Chemical eq. of } CaCO_3}{\text{Chemical eq. of hardness producing subs.}}]$$

$$= \frac{408 \text{ mg/L} \times 50}{68}$$

= 300 mg/L = 300 ppm.

Hence hardness of water sample = 300mg/L $CaCO_3$ equivalent.

Example 5 : A sample of water has following analytical data :

$Ca(HCO_3)_2 = 23.16°\,Fr, SiO_2 = 1.43°\,Fr, MgSO_4 = 5.72°\,Fr$

$CaSO_4 = 2.86°\,Fr, MgCl_2 = 1.43°\,Fr.$

Calculate the temporary and permanent hardnes in °Clark and ppm scale.

Sol. We know that

$1°\,Fr = 0.7°\,Cl = 10\,ppm$

On Clarke scale	**On ppm scale**
$MgCl_2 = 1.43°\,Fr = 1.43 \times 0.7°\,Cl = 1.001°\,Cl$	$= 1.43° \times 10 = 14.3\,ppm$
$SiO_2 = 1.43°\,Fr = 1.43 \times 0.7 = 1.001°\,Cl$	$= 1.43 \times 10 = 14.3$ ppm
$MgSO_4 = 5.72°\,Fr = 5.72 \times 0.7 = 4.004°\,Cl$	$= 5.72 \times 10 = 57.2\,ppm$

$CaSO_4 = 2.86°Fr = 2.86 \times 0.7 = 2.002°Cl$ $= 2.86 \times 10 = 28.6 ppm$

$Ca(HCO_3)_2 = 23.16°Fr = 23.16 \times 0.7 = 16.212°Cl$ $= 23.16 \times 10 = 231.6$ ppm

SiO_2 does not produce any hardness therefore not considered.

The hardness in $CaCO_3$ equivalent can be expressed in °Clarke in calculation.

$$MgCl_2 = 1.001 \times \frac{100}{95} = 1.054°Cl$$

$$MgSO_4 = 4.004 \times \frac{100}{120} = 3.337°Cl$$

$$CaSO_4 = 2.002 \times \frac{100}{136} = 1.472°Cl$$

$$Ca(HCO_3)_2 = 16.212 \times \frac{100}{162} = 10.007°Cl$$

Thus, temporary hardness is due to only $Ca(HCO_3)_2$ in Clarke scale = 10.007°Cl equivalent of $CaCO_3$

Permanent hardness in °Clark scale

$= (MgCl_2 + MgSO_4 + CaSO_4)$

$= (1.054 + 3.337 + 1.472)$ °Clark of $CaCO_3$ equivalent

= 5.863 °Cl of $CaCO_3$ equivalent

The hardness in $CaCO_3$ equivalent

The hardness in $CaCO_3$ equivalent

$$MgCl_2 = 14.3 ppm \times \frac{100}{95} = 15.033 ppm \text{ of } CaCO_3 \text{ eq.}$$

$$MgSO_4 = 57.2 ppm \times \frac{100}{120} = 47.667 ppm \text{ of } CaCO_3 \text{ eq.}$$

$$CaSO_4 = 28.6 \times \frac{100}{136} = 21.029 \text{ of ppm of } CaCO_3 \text{ eq.}$$

$$Ca(HCO_3)_2 = 231.6 \times \frac{100}{162} = 142.963 \text{ ppm of } CaCO_3 \text{ eq.}$$

Thus temporary hardness in ppm scale = 142.963 ppm of $CaCO_3$ equivalent.

Permanent hardness

$= (MgCl_2 + MgSO_4 + CaSO_4)$ ppm of $CaCO_3$ equivalent

$= (15.053 + 47.667 + 21.029)$ ppm of $CaCO_3$ equivalent

$= 83.749$ ppm of $CaCO_3$ equivalent

Temporary hardness = 143.963 ppm
Permanent hardness = 83.749 ppm

Example 6 : A water sample on analysis gives the following data.

$Mg(HCO)_3 = 83mg / L; Ca(HCO_3)_2 = 134$ mg/L; $CaSO_4 = 124$mg/L;

$MgCl_2 = 84$ mg/L; $CaCl = 94$mg / L; NaCl = 54mg / L. Calculate the temporary and permanent hardness in degree Clark.

Sol. Calculation of $CaCO_3$ equivalents

Constituent	Quantity mg / L	Multiplication Factor	$CaCO_3$ Equivalents (mg / L)
$Mg(HCO_3)_2$	83	100/146	56.8
$Ca(HCO_3)_2$	134	100/162	82.7
$CaSO_4$	124	100/136	91.2
$MgCl_2$	84	100/95	88.4
$CaCl_2$	94	100/111	84.7
NaCl	50	Does not produce hardness	

Temporary hardness = Hardness due to $Mg(HCO_3)_2 + Ca(HCO_3)_2$
$= 139.5$ mg/L = 139.5 ppm
$= 139.5 \times 0.07° Cl = 9.77°Cl$

Permanent hardness = Hardness due to $\{CaSO_4 + MgCl_2 + CaCl_2\}$
$= 264.3$ mg/L = 264.3 ppm
$= 264.3 \times 0.07°Cl = 18.50°Cl$

Example 7 : A sample of water contains following impurities

$Mg(HCO_3)_2 = 14.6$mg/L, $MgCl_2 = 19$mg/L
$Mg(NO_3)_2 = 29.6$mg/L, $CaCO_3 = 10$mg/L
$MgSO_4 = 36$mg/L, NaCl = 29mg/L

Calculate temporary, permanent and total hardness of water sample in ppm and °Clark.

Sol. NaCl does not impart hardness to water conversion into $CaCO_3$ equivalents.

Sol. NaCl does not impart hardness to water conversion into $CaCO_3$ equivalents.

S. No.	Substance	Amount(inmg / L) Orppm	Multiplication factor	$CaCO_3$equivalent (mg / L)
1.	$Mg(HCO_3)_2$	14.6	$\frac{100}{146}$	$14.6\times\frac{100}{146}=10$
2.	$MgCl_3$	19	$\frac{100}{95}$	$19\times\frac{100}{95}=20$
3.	$Mg(NO_3)_2$	29.6	$\frac{100}{148}$	$29.6\times\frac{100}{148}=20$
4.	$CaCO_3$	10	$\frac{100}{100}$	$10\times\frac{100}{100}=10$
5.	$MgSO_4$	36	$\frac{100}{120}$	$36\times\frac{100}{120}=30$

Temporary hardness due to $Mg(HCO_3)_2$ and $CaCO_3$

= (10 + 10) mg/L of $CaCO_3$ eq.

= 20 mg/L of $CaCO_3$ eq.

On ppm scale

Since 1mg/L = 1ppm = 0.07 Clark

Temporary hardness = 20 × 1 = 20 ppm

Temporary hardness in °Clark = 20 × 0.07 = 1.40°Cl

Permanent hardness $=\left(MgCl_2+Mg\left(NO_3\right)_2+MgSO_4\right)$

$=\left(20+20+30\right)$ mg/L of $CaCO_3$ eq.

= 70 mg/L of $CaCO_3$ eq

Permanent hardness in ppm = 70 ppm of $CaCO_3$ eq.

Permanent hardness in °Clark = 70 × 0.07 °Clark

= 4.90 °Clark

Example 8 : Calculate the total hardness of a water sample having following analytical data in ppm. $CaCO_3$ = 20°Cl; $MgSO_4$ = 4°Cl, $CaSO_4$ = 2°Cl; Fe_2O_3 = 0.04°Cl, $MgCl_2$ = 4°Cl; SiO_2 = 0.09°Cl.

Sol.

Constituent	Amount (°Cl)	Multiplication Factor	$CaCO_3$ equivalent (°Cl)
$CaCO_3$	20	$\frac{100}{100}$	20
$CaSO_4$	2	$\frac{10}{136}$	1.47
$MgCl_2$	4	$\frac{100}{95}$	4.21
$MgSO_4$	4	$\frac{100}{120}$	3.33
Fe_2O_3	0.04	–	–
SiO_2	0.0	–	–

Fe_2O_3 and SiO_2 do not impart hardness

Total hardness of water sample = 29.01°Cl

= 29.01 × 14.3 ppm = 414.84 ppm

Example 9 : How many grams of $FeSO_4$ dissolved per litre gives 210.5 ppm of hardnes? (Fe = 56, S = 32, O = 16, Ca = 40, C = 12).

Sol. $FeSO_4 \equiv CaCO_3$

$\therefore$ 100 ppm of hardness $\equiv$ 136 ppm of $FeSO_4$

or 210.5 ppm of hardness $= \frac{136 \times 210.5}{100} = 286.3$ ppm or $FeSO_4$

= 286.3 mg/L or 0.2863 g/L of $FeSO_4$

Hence, 0.2863g of $FeSO_4$ dissolved per litre gives 210.5 ppm of hardness

Example 10 : Calculate the total hardness of water in °Fr and °Cl from the following analytical data of water sample

$$Mg(HCO_3)_2 = 20.8 mg/L; Mg(NO_3)_2 = 28.8 mg/L; MgCl_2 = 21.0 mg/L;$$

$$MgSO_4 = 20.4 mg/L; CaCO_3 = 21.2 mg/L; KCl = 73.2 mg/L$$

Sol. Calculation of $CaCO_3$ equivalents.

Salt	Amount Mg/L	Multiplication Factor	Equivalentsof $CaCo_3$ mg/L
$Mg(HCO_3)_2$	20.8	$\frac{100}{143}$	14.2
$Mg(NO_3)_2$	28.8	$\frac{100}{148}$	19.45
$MgCl_2$	21.0	$\frac{100}{95}$	22.10
$MgSO_4$	20.0	$\frac{100}{120}$	16.67
$CaCO_3$	21.2	$\frac{100}{100}$	21.2
KCl	73.2	–	–
			Total Hardness = 93.62mg/L

KCl does not impart hardness

Total hardness = 93.62 mg/L

= 93.62 × 0.1 °Fr

= 9.362 °Fr

Total Hardness in °Cl = 93.62 × 0.07°Cl

= 6.55 °Cl

Example 11 : A sample of water contain : Ca $(HCO_3)_2$ = 4 mg/L; $Mg(HCO_3)_2$ = 6mg/L; $CaSO_4$ = 8 mg/L; $MgSO_4$ = 10 mg/L. Calculate the temporary, permanent and total hardness of water in ppm, °Fr and °Cl. [Mol. of $Ca(HCO_3)_2$ = 162; $Mg(HCO_3)_2$ = 146; $CaSO_4$ = 136, $MgSO_4$ = 120]

Sol. Conversion into $CaCO_3$ equivalents :

Constituent	Multiplication	$CaCO_3$ equivalent
$Ca(HCO_3) = 4mg/L$	$\frac{100}{162}$	$4\times\frac{100}{162} = 2.469mg/L$
$Mg(HCO_3)_2 = 6mg/L$	$\frac{100}{146}$	$6\times\frac{100}{146} = 4.110mg/L$
$CaSO_4 = 8mg/L$	$\frac{100}{136}$	$8\times\frac{100}{136} = 5.882mg/L$
$MgSO_4 = 10mg/L$	$\frac{100}{120}$	$10\times\frac{100}{120} = 8.333mg/L$

Temporary hardness due to $Ca(HCO_3)_2$ and Mg $Mg(HCO_3)_2$

$$= (2.469 + 4.110)mg/L = 6.579mg/L = 6.579ppm.$$

$= 6.579 \times 0.1\ ^\circ F = 0.6579\ ^\circ Fr$
$= 6.579 \times 0.07^\circ Cl = 0.4605\ ^\circ Cl$

Permanent hardness due to $CaSO_4$ and $MgSO_4$

$= (5.882 + 8.333)$ mg/L = 14.215 mg/L = 14.215 ppm.
$= 14.215 \times 0.1\ ^\circ Fr = 1.42156^\circ Fr$
$= 14.215 \times 0.07^\circ\ Cl = 0.9950^\circ Cl$

Total hardness = (6.579 + 14.215) ppm = 20.794 ppm.
$= 20.794 \times 0.1^\circ F = 2.0794^\circ Fr$
$= 20.794 \times 0.07^\circ Cl = 1.4556^\circ Cl.$

Example 12 : Calculate the temporary hardness and permanent hardness of a sample of water containing : $Mg(HCO_3)_2$ = 7.3 mg/L; $Ca(HCO_3)_2$ = 16.2 mg/L; $MgCl_2$ = 9.5 mg/L; $CaSO_4$ = 13.6 mg/L.

Sol. Conversion into $CaCO_3$ equivalents :

Constituent	Multiplication	$CaCO_3$equivalent
$Mg(HCO_3)_2$	$\frac{100}{146}$	$7.3 \times \frac{100}{146} = 5mg/L$
$Ca(HCO_3)_2 = 16.2mg/L$	$\frac{100}{162}$	$16.2 \times \frac{100}{162} = 10mg/L$
$MgCl_2 = 9.5mg/L$	$\frac{100}{95}$	$9.5 \times \frac{100}{95} = 10mg/L$
$CaSO_4 = 13.6mg/L$	$\frac{100}{136}$	$13.6 \times \frac{100}{136} = 10mg/L$

$\therefore$ Temporary hardness, due to $Mg(HCO_3)_2$ and $Ca(HCO_3)_2$

= (5 + 10) mg/L = 15 mg/L or 15 ppm.

Permanent hardness, due to $MgCl_2$ and $CaSO_4$

= (10 + 10) mg/L =20 mg/L or 20 ppm.

1.4 DETERMINATION OF HARDNESS OF WATER

1.4.1 EDTA method / Complexometric method

This method is more accurate as compared to other methods used for determination of hardness of water. In this method complexometric titration is performed between EDTA and water sample using Eriochrome black-T as indicator.

EDTA (Ethylene Diamine Tetra Acetic acid): It is a strong complexing agent. Its structure is-

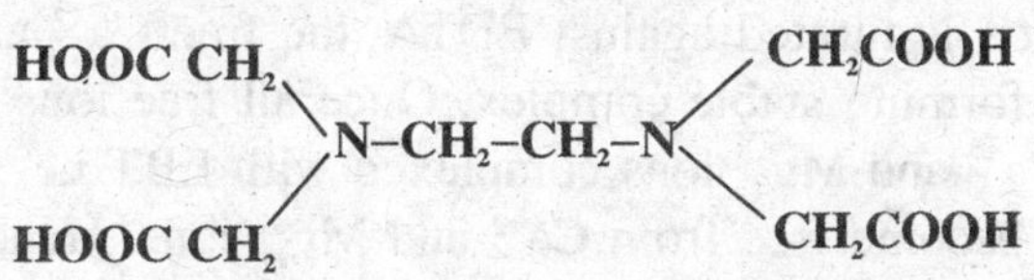

Fig 1.2: Structure of EDTA

EDTA is a hexadentate ligand and can form dative bonds with Ca^{+2} and Mg^{+2} ions present in hard water. As EDTA is not soluble in water, its disodium salt which is soluble in water is used for titration.

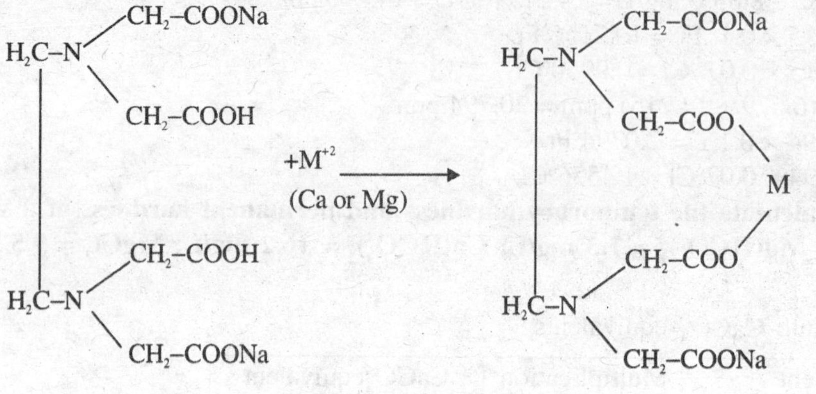

Fig 1.3: Complex of EDTA with metal ion

Eriochrome Black-T (EBT): It is capable of forming soluble wine-red complex with Ca^{+2} and Mg^{+2} ions. In titration, it is found in two forms:

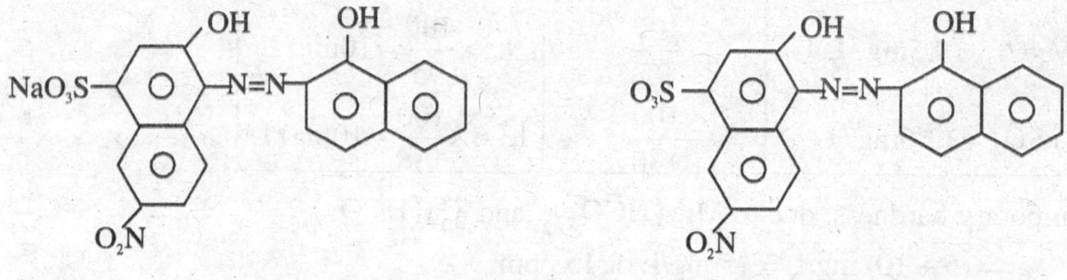

Fig 1.4: (a) Blue Coloured (unionized form) (b) Wine red coloured (ionized form) Sodium (1-hydroxy 2-naphthylazo 6-nitro 2-naphthol 4-sulphonate)

Principle of titration: Determination of hardness by EDTA method is based upon following principle:

The indicator EBT (blue Coloured) forms unstable complex with Ca^{+2} and Mg^{+2} ions (wine red coloured) present in water sample at pH = 9 to10.

$$\underset{\text{Blue Coloured}}{Ca^{+2} / Mg^{+2} \text{ ions} + EBT} \xrightarrow{\text{pH}= 9 \text{ to } 10} \underset{\text{Wine-red coloured complex}}{Ca^{+2} / Mg^{+2} - EBT}$$

When this solution is titrated against EDTA, the free Ca^{+2} and Mg^{+2} ions present in water combines with EDTA forming stable complex. Once all free ions are complexed with EDTA, it forms complex with Ca^{+2} and Mg^{+2} ions complexed with EBT i.e. it replaces Ca^{+2} and Mg^{+2} ions from EBT. Now EBT become free from Ca^{+2} and Mg^{+2} ions. Hence, solution turns blue. At this point all Ca^{+2} and Mg^{+2} ions present in water samples are consumed. Thus, amount of EDTA used corresponds to the total hardness of water.

$$Ca^{+2} / Mg^{+2} \text{ ions}^{-}EBT + EDTA \longrightarrow Ca^{+2} / Mg^{+2}\,^{-} EDTA + EBT$$

Wine-red coloured complex — Blue Coloured solution

The temporary hardness is removed by boiling and precipitates are removed by filtration. Above mentioned titration is repeated with filtrate sample and amount of EDTA consumed corresponds to permanent hardness. Temporary hardness can be calculated by taking difference between total and permanent hardness.

Procedure: The experimental procedure includes following steps-

(A) Preparation of solutions:

(i) Preparation of standard hard water: The solution of known concentration/strength is called as standard solution (in present case it is solution of known hardness). Dissolve one gram of pure and dry $CaCO_3$ in minimum quantity of dilute HCl and boil it. The solution is evaporated to dryness to remove excess of HCl and CO_2. The residue is dissolved in distilled water and make up the solution up to one litre. The hardness of this solution is 1g/L or 1mg/mL or 1000 *ppm*.

(ii) Preparation of EDTA solution: As EDTA forms 1:1 complex with the metal ions, 0.01M EDTA solution is prepared by dissolving 3.7 g of its disodium salt (Molecular weight = 272.25) in distilled water to make up one litre.

(iii) Preparation of buffer solution: EDTA and EBT both are pH sensitive. Hence, a constant pH of 9 to 10 has to be maintained. For this purpose, a buffer solution is prepared by dissolving 67.5 g of NH_4Cl in 570 mL of concentrated ammonia solution (NH_4OH) and the solution is diluted upto one litre with distilled water.

(iv) Preparation of indicator solution: Dissolve 0.5 g of Eriochrome Black-T in 100 mL of alcohol.

(B) Titration:

(i) Standardization of EDTA solution: To find out exact strength of EDTA solution, it is titrated against standard hard water. Fill up the burette with EDTA solution after washing and rinsing. Pipette out 50 mL of unknown water sample into a conical flask. Add 10 mL of buffer solution (pH = 9 to 10) and 2-3 drops of EBT indicator. Colour of this solution is wine red. Now this solution is titrated with EDTA solution until colour changes to blue. Let the volume of EDTA consumed (burette reading) is V_1 mL.

(ii) Determination of total hardness: The titration mentioned above is repeated with 50 mL unknown water sample (replacing standard hard water). Let the volume of EDTA consumed (burette reading) is V_2 mL.

(iii) Determination of permanent hardness: Take 250 mL of the water sample in a 500 mL beaker and boil it till the volume of water sample is reduced to 50 mL. Due to boiling temporary hardness is removed and water sample contains only permanent hardness. Filter the sample after boiling and make up it upto 250 mL with distilled water. Take 50mL of this boiled water sample and titrate it against EDTA solution. Let the volume of EDTA consumed (burette reading) is V_3 mL.

Observation:

Volume of the sample taken each time = 50 mL

Volume of EDTA consumed when titrated against Std. Hard water = V_1 mL

Volume of EDTA consumed when titrated against Sample water = V_2 mL

Volume of EDTA consumed when titrated against boiled sample water = V_3 mL

Calculations:

Step I: Standardization of EDTA soludion:

Hardness of Standard hard water = 1 mg/mL

i.e. 1 mL of Std. hard water contains 1 mg of $CaCO_3$ equivalent

50 mL of Std. hard water contains 50 mg of $CaCO_3$ equivalent

Volume of EDTA consumed when titrated against 50 mL of Std. Hard water = V_1 mL

V_1 mL of EDTA solution = 50 mL of Std. Hard water

Or

V_1 mL of EDTA solution = 50 mg of $CaCO_3$ equivalent

1 mL of EDTA solution = $(50/V_1)$ mg of $CaCO_3$ equivalent

Step II: Calculation of Total hardness

Volume of EDTA consumed when titrated against 50 mL of Sample water = V_2 mL

50 mL of Sample water = V_2 mL of EDTA solution

Since, 1 mL of EDTA solution = $(50/V_1)$ mg of $CaCO_3$ equivalent

Hence, 50 mL of Sample water = $V_2 \times (50/V_1)$ mg of $CaCO_3$ equivalent

1 mL of Sample water $= \dfrac{(V_2)\times 50}{(V_1)\times 50}$ mg of $CaCO_3$ equivalent

1000 mL of Sample water $= \dfrac{(V_2)\times 50}{(V_1)\times 50} \times 1000$ mg of $CaCO_3$ equivalent

Total hardness of Sample water $= \dfrac{(V_2)}{(V_1)} \times 1000$ mg/L or *ppm*

Step III: Calculation of Permanent hardness

Volume of EDTA consumed with 50 mL of boiled Sample water = V_3 mL

50 mL of boiled sample water = V_3 mL of EDTA solution

Since, 1 mL of EDTA solution = $(50/V_1)$ mg of $CaCO_3$ equivalent

Hence, 50 mL of boiled sample water = $V_3 \times (50/V_1)$ mg of $CaCO_3$ equivalent

1 mL of boiled sample water $= \dfrac{(V_3)\times 50}{(V_1)\times 50}$ mg of $CaCO_3$ equivalent

1000 mL of boiled sample water $= \dfrac{(V_3)\times 50}{(V_1)\times 50} \times 1000$ mg of $CaCO_3$ equivalent

Permanent hardness of Sample water $= \dfrac{(V_3)}{(V_1)} \times 1000$ mg/L or *ppm*

Step IV: Calculation of temporary hardness

Temporary hardness = Total hardness – Permanent hardness

Temporary hardness of Sample water $=\left(\frac{V_2}{V_1}\times 1000\right)-\left(\frac{V_3}{V_1}\times 1000\right)mg/L$

Temporary hardness of Sample water $=\frac{(V_2-V_3)}{(V_1)}\times 1000\ mg/L$

SOLVED NUMERICAL BASED EDTA METHOD

Example 1 : One gram of $CaCO_3$ was dissolved in diluted HCl and the solution diluted to 1 litre, 50 ml of this solution required 45 ml of EDTA solution while 50 ml of hard water sample required 18 ml of EDTA solution. On the other hand, 50 ml of the boiled sample of hard water when titrated against EDTA consumed 9ml of the solution. Find out temporary, permanent and total hardness and express it in ppm of $CaCO_3$ equivalents.

Sol. 1000 ml of standard water = 1 g of 1000 mg of $CaCO_3$ **[RTU 2008]**

1 ml of standard water = 1 mg of $CaCO_3$

45 ml of EDTA solution = 50 ml of standard water

= 50 × 1 mg of $CaCO_3$

1 ml of EDTA solution = 50/45 of $CaCO_3$

Further, 50 ml of sample water = 18 ml of EDTA solution

= (50/45) × 18 mg of $CaCO_3$

Hardness is expressed in ppm = Hardness present in one litre

∴ 1000 ml of sample of water = (50/45) × 18 × 1000/50

= 400 mg of $CaCO_3$

∴ Total hadness = 400 mg of $CaCO_3$ /litre

50 ml of boiled sample of water = 9 ml of EDTA solution (where temporary hardness is removed on boiling)

$=(50/45)\times 9$ mg of $CaCO_3$

1000 ml of boiled water = (50/45) × 9 × (1000/50)

= 200 mg of $CaCO_3$ /litre

This is residual hardness, which is remaining after boiling; this is equal to permanent hardness,

Permanent hardnes = 200 mg of $CaCO_3$ /litre = 200 ppm

Temporary hardness = Total hardness - Permanent hardness

= 400 – 200 = 200 ppm

Example 2 : 50 ml of standard hard water containing 1mg of pure $CaCO_3$ per ml consumed 25ml of EDTA. 50 ml of a water sample consumed 25 ml of the same. EDTA solution using EBT as indicator, find oute the total hardness of water sample in mg/L.

Sol. Step (i) : Standardizaton of EDTA solution

Given, 1ml of standard hard water contains 1mg of $CaCO_3$

Now, 25 ml of EDTA = 50 ml of EDTA = 50 ml of standard hard water

= 50 mg of $CaCO_3$ eq. hardness

Hence, 1 ml of EDTA = 50/25 = 2 mg of $CaCO_3$ eq. hardness

Step (ii), Determination of total hardness of water sample

50 ml of sample water = 25 ml of EDTA

= 25 × 2 = 50mg of $CaCO_3$ eq. hardness

Hence, 1 litre of sample water $=\frac{50}{50}\times1000=1000$ mg of $CaCO_3$ eq. hardness

Thus, total hardness of water = 1000 mg/L

Example 3 : A standard hard water contains 15g $CaCO_3$ per litre. 20 ml of this standard to hardwater required 25 ml of EDTA solution. 100ml of sample water required 18 ml of EDTA solution. After boiling, the sample required 12 ml of EDTA solution. Calculate the temporary hardness of the given sample of water in terms of ppm.

Sol. Step (i) : Standardization of EDTA solution:

Given, 1 litre of stanard hard water cotains 15g $CaCO_3$

1 ml of standard hard water cotains 15 mg $CaCO_3$

25 ml of EDTA = 20 ml of standard hard water

= 20 × 15 = 300 mg of $CaCO_3$

1 ml of EDTA = 300/25

= 12 mg of $CaCO_3$ equivalent hardness

Step (ii) Determination of total hardness of water

100 ml of sample water = 18 ml of EDTA

= 18 × 12 = 216 mg of $CaCO_3$ eq. hardness

∴ 1litre of sample water = 2160 mg of $CaCO_3$ eq hardness

Hence total hardness = 2160 ppm

Step (ii) Determination of permanent hardness:

100 ml of boiled water = 12 ml of EDTA

= 12 × 12 = 144 mg of $CaCO_3$ eq. hardness

∴ 1 litre of boiled water = 1440 mg of $CaCO_3$ eq. hardness

Hence, permanent hardness of water = 1440 ppm

Step (iv) Determination of temporary hardness:

Temporary hardness = Total hardness - Permanent hardness

= 2160 - 1440 = 720 ppm

∴ Temporary hardness = 720 ppm

Example 4 : 0.28g of $CaCO_3$ wad dissolved in HCl and the solution was made to 1 litre with distilled water. 100 ml of this solution required 28 ml of EDTA solution on titration. 100 ml of the hard water sample required 35 ml of the same EDTA solution on titration. After boiling 100ml of this water, required 10 ml of EDTA solution. Calculate the temporary and pemanent hardness of water in terms of ppm.

Sol. Step (i) Standardization of EDTA solution

Given, 1 litre of standard hard water contains 0.28g $CaCO_3$. Hence, each ml of standard hard water contains 0.28 mg $CaCO_3$.

As, 28 ml of EDTA = 100 ml standard hard water

$= 100 \times 0.28 = 28$ mg of $CaCO_3$

$\therefore$ 1 ml of EDTA = 28/28 = 1 mg $CaCO_3$ ....(i)

Step (ii) Determination of total hardness of water

Given, 100ml of unknown hard water sample = 35 ml of EDTA

$= 35 \times 1 = 35$ mg $CaCO_3$ (by using (i))

1000 ml (or 1 litr) of unknown hard water sample

$$= \frac{35}{100} \times 1000$$

= 350 mg of $CaCO_3$ eq. hardness

Hence, total hardness = 350 ppm

Step (iii) Determination of permanent hardness

100 ml of boiled water = 10 ml of EDTA

$= 10 \times 1 = 10$ mg of $CaCO_3$ eq. hardness

1000 ml (or 1 litre) of boiled water $= \frac{10}{100} \times 1000$

= 100 mg of $CaCO_3$ eq. hardness

Step (iv) Determination of temporary hardness

Temporary hardness = Total hardness - Permanent hardness

$\Rightarrow$ Temporary hardness = 250 ppm

Example 5 : A sample of water contains the following impurities:

$Mg(HCO_3)_2$ = 73 mg/L; $Ca(HCO_3)_2$ = 162 mg/L; $CaSO_4$ = 136 mg/L; $MgCl_2$ = 95 mg/L; $CaCl_2$ = 111 mg/L and NaCl = 100 mg/L. Calculate the temporary and permanent hardness.

Sol. First the concentration of the impurities have to be converted to $CaCO_3$ equivalent of hadness.

Salt		$CaCO_3$ equivalent
$Mg(HCO_3)_2$	$=73\times(100/146)=50mg/L$	$=50ppm$
$Ca(HCO_3)_2$	$=162\times(100/162)=100mg/L$	$=100ppm$
$CaSO_4$	$=136\times(100/136)=100mg/L$	$=100ppm$
$MgCl_2$	$=95\times(100/95)=100mg/L$	$=100ppm$
$CaCl_2$	$=111\times(100/111)=100mg/L$	$=100ppm$

NaCl doesn't contribute to hardness and hence, it is omitted from the calculation of hardness.

Temporary hardness = hardness due to $Mg(HCO_3)_2$ + hardness due to $Ca(HCO_3)_2$

= 50 + 100 = 150 mg/L

Permanent hardness = hardness due to $CaSO_4$ + hardness due to $MgCl_2$ + hardness due to $CaCl_2$

= 100 + 100 + 100 = 300 mg/L

Total hardness = Temporary hardness + permanent hardness

= 150 + 300 = 450 mg/L

Example 6 : The standard hard wate solution is prepared by dissolving 10 grams of pure and dried $CaCO_3$ in 1000 ml of distilled water. 20 ml of this when titrated, consumed 21 ml of EDTA solution. When 100 ml of hard water sample titrated with EDTA, it required 22 ml of EDTA solution. The same hard water sample after boiling consumed 16 ml of EDTA soluton. Find out all types of hardness of the given water sample in terms ppm.

Sol. Step 1 : Standardization of EDTA solution :

1000 ml of standard hard water = 10 grams of $CaCO_3$

or 1 ml of standad hard water = 10 mg of $CaCO_3$ equivalent

20 ml of standard hard water = 21 ml of EDTA solution

i.e. 21 ml of EDTA solution = 20 ml of standard hard water sample

= (20 × 10) mg of $CaCO_3$ equivalent

(As1 ml of standard hard water = 10 mg of $CaCO_3$ equivalent)

= 200 mg of $CaCO_3$ equivalent

Therefore 1 ml EDTA $=\frac{200}{21}$ mg of $CaCO_3$ equivalent

= 9.52 mg of $CaCO_3$ equivalent

Determination of total hardness

100 ml of hard water = 22 ml EDTA

= 22 × 9.52 mg of $CaCO_3$ equivalent

(As 1 ml EDTA = 9.52 mg of $CaCO_3$ equivalent)

100 ml of hard water = 9.52 mg of $CaCO_3$ equivalent

1000 ml of hard water = 9520 mg of $CaCO_3$ equivalent

Total hardness = 9520 mg of $CaCO_3$ equivalent

= 9520 ppm

Determination of Permanent hardness

100 ml of boiled water = 16 ml of EDTA

(As the temporay hardness is removed on boiling)

= (16 × 9.52) mg of $CaCO_3$ equivalents

Therefore,

100 ml of hard water sample = 152.32 mg of $CaCO_3$ equivalent

1000 ml of hard water sample = 1523.2 mg of $CaCO_3$ equivalent

thus, permanent hardness = 1523.2 mg of $CaCO_3$ equivalent

= 1523.2 ppm

Determination temporary hardness

Temporary hardness = Total hardness - Permanent hardness

= (9520 – 1523) ppm

= 7997 ppm

Hence,

Total hardness = 9520 ppm

Permanent hardness = 1523 ppm

Temporary hardness = 7997 ppm

Example 7 : The standard water was prepared by dissolving 1.0 gm of pure and dry $CaCO_3$ in 1 litre distilled water. 50 ml of this required 46 ml of EDTA solution while 50 ml of given hard water sample consumed 20 ml of EDTA solution. Boiled sample of hard water consumed 10 ml of EDTA soluton. Determine the each type of hardness in ppm.

Sol .

Standardization of EDTA solution:

1000 ml of standard hard

water sample = 1 g (1000mg) of $CaCO_3$

1 ml of standard hard water = 1 mg of $CaCO_3$

46 ml of EDTA solution = 50 ml of standard hard water sample

= 50 × 1 mg of $CaCO_3$

1 ml of EDTA solution $= \frac{50}{46}$ mg of $CaCO_3$

= 1.0869 mg of $CaCO_3$ equivalent

Total hardness:

50 ml of a given hard water sample = 20 ml of EDTA solution

$$=\frac{50}{46}\times 20 \text{ mg of } CaCO_3$$

$$=21.7391 \text{ mg}$$

$$1000 \text{ ml of sample of hard water} = \left(\frac{50}{46}\right)\times 20\times\frac{1000}{50}$$

$$= 434.78 \text{ mg of } CaCO_3$$

Total hardness = 434.78 mg of $CaCO_3$

= 434.78 ppm

Permanent hardness:

50 ml of boiled given sample of hard water

= 10 ml of EDTA solution

(As temporary hardness is removed on boiling)

$$=\frac{50}{46}\times 10 \text{ mg of } CaCO_3$$

1000 ml of boiled hard water sample

$$=\left(\frac{50}{46}\right)\times 10\times\frac{1000}{50} \text{ mg } CaCO_3 \text{ equivalent}$$

= 217.39 mg $CaCO_3$ equivalent

Permanent hadness of hard water sample

= 217.39 mg of $CaCO_3$

= 217.39 ppm

Temporary hardness = Total hadness - permanent hardness

= 434.78 - 217.39

= 217.39 ppm

Example 8 : 100 ml of a sample of water required 20 ml of 0.01 M EDTA for titration using EBT. After boiling, 100 ml of the sample required 10 ml of 0.01M EDTA. Determine

(i) the total hardness,

(ii) permanent hardness,

(iii) and temporary hardness.

Sol. Since EDTA forms 1:1 complex with the metal ions

Hence, 1 molar solution of EDTA reacts with 1 mole of $CaCO_3$

or 1000 ml of 1M EDTA reacts with = 100 g of $CaCO_3$

$$1 \text{ ml of 1M EDTA reacts with} = \frac{100}{1000}\times 1000 \text{ mg of } CaCO_3$$

$= 100$ mg of $CaCO_3$

1 ml of 0.01M EDTA reacts with $\frac{100}{100} = 1$ mg of $CaCO_3$

Strength of the given EDTA solution = 1 mg/ml

(i) Total hardness :

Since, 1 ml of EDTA is required for = 1 mg of $CaCO_3$

20 ml of EDTA is required for = 20 mg of $CaCO_3$

Hence, 100 ml of sample hard water contains = 20 mg of $CaCO_3$

1000 ml of sample hard water contains = $\frac{20}{100} \times 1000 = 200$ mg of $CaCO_3$

$\therefore$ Total hardness = 200 mg/litre = 200 ppm

(ii) Permanent hardnes

10 ml of 0.01M EDTA is required for = 1 × 10 mg of $CaCO_3$

Hence, 100ml of boiled sample hard water contains = 10 mg of $CaCO_3$

1000 ml of boiled sample hard water contains = 10 mg of $CaCO_3$

$\therefore$ Total hardness = 100 mg/litre = 100 ppm

(iii) Temporary hardness

Total hardness - permanent hardness = 200 - 100 = 100 ppm

1.4.2 Soap Titration Method / Clark's Method

When soluble soap (sodium or potassium salt of higher fatty acids) is added to hard water, it does not produce lather, until a sufficient amount of soap is added to precipitate all the hardness causing substances. Further addition of soap gives lather. The volume of soap that is consumed at this point is taken as a measure of hardness of water.

$$\underset{\text{Sodium Stearate}}{2C_{17}H_{35}COONa} + CaCl_2 \longrightarrow \underset{\text{Precipitate of calcium soap}}{(C_{17}H_{35}COO)Ca} + 2NaCl$$

$$\underset{\text{Sodium Stearate}}{2C_{17}H_{35}COONa} + MgCl_2 \longrightarrow \underset{\text{Precipitate of magnesium soap}}{(C_{17}H_{35}COO)Mg} + 2NaCl$$

Procedure:

(i) Preparation of standard hard water: The solution of known concentration/strength is called as standard solution (in present case it is solution of known hardness). Dissolve one gram of pure and dry $CaCO_3$ in minimum quantity of dilute HCl and boil it. The solution is evaporated to dryness to remove excess of HCl and CO_2. The residue is dissolved in distilled water and make up the solution up to one litre. The hardness of this solution is 1g/L or 1mg/mL or 1000 *ppm*.

(ii) Preparation of Soap solution: 100 g of pure and dry soap is dissolved in 800 mL of alcohol and 200 mL of distilled water.

(iii) Standardization of Soap solution: Fill up the burette with soap solution after washing and rinsing. Pipette out 50 mL of standard hard water sample into a glass stoppered bottle. Soap solution is added to this solution drop by drop. After each drop content of bottle is shaked vigorously until lather formation starts which persists at least for 2 minutes. Let the volume of soap solution consumed (burette reading) is V_1 mL.

(iv) Lather Factor: it is amount of standard soap solution required to produce lather (which persists for 2 minutes) with distilled water (of zero hardness). 50 mL of distilled water is taken in stoppered bottle and is titrated with soap solution. Volume of the soap solution is noted when lather persists for 2 minutes. This volume is known as lather factor (V mL). This volume is to be subtracted from all titre values.

(v) Determination of total hardness: The titration mentioned above is repeated with 50 mL unknown water sample (replacing standard hard water). Let the volume of soap solution consumed (burette reading) is V_2 mL.

(iii) Determination of permanent hardness: Take 250 mL of the water sample in a 500 mL beaker and boil it till the volume of water sample is reduced to 50 mL. Due to boiling temporary hardness is removed and water sample contains only permanent hardness. Filter the sample after boiling and make up it upto 250 mL with distilled water. Take 50 mL of this boiled water sample and titrate it against soap solution. Let the volume of soap solution consumed (burette reading) is V_3 mL.

Observation:

Volume of the sample taken each time = 50 mL

Lather factor = V mL

Volume of soap consumed when titrated against Std. Hard water = $(V_1 - V)$ mL

Volume of soap consumed when titrated against Sample water = $(V_2 - V)$ mL

Volume of soap consumed when titrated against boiled sample water = $(V_3 - V)$ mL

Calculations:

Step I: Standardization of soap solution:

Hardness of Standard hard water = 1 mg/mL

i.e. 1 mL of Std. hard water contains 1 mg of $CaCO_3$ equivalent

50 mL of Std. hard water contains 50 mg of $CaCO_3$ equivalent

Volume of soap consumed when titrated against 50 mL of Std. Hard water = $(V_1 - V)$ mL

$(V_1 - V)$ mL of soap solution = 50 mL of Std. Hard water

Or

$(V_1 - V)$ mL of soap solution = 50 mg of $CaCO_3$ equivalent

1 mL of soap solution = $(50/(V_1 - V)$ mg of $CaCO_3$ equivalent

Step II: Calculation of Total hardness

Volume of soap consumed when titrated against 50 mL of Sample water = $(V_2 - V)$ mL

50 mL of Sample water = $(V_2 - V)$ mL of soap solution

Since, 1 mL of soap solution = $(50/(V_1 - V))$ mg of $CaCO_3$ equivalent

Hence, 50 mL of Sample water = $(V_2 - V) \times (50/(V_1 - V))$ mg of $CaCO_3$ equivalent

1 mL of Sample water = $= \dfrac{(V_2 - V)\times 50}{(V_1 - V)\times 50}$ mg of $CaCO_3$ equivalent

1000 mL of Sample water = $= \dfrac{(V_2 - V)\times 50}{(V_1 - V)\times 50} \times 1000$ mg of $CaCO_3$ equivalent

Total hardness of Sample water = $= \dfrac{(V_2 - V)}{(V_1 - V)} \times 1000$ mg/L or *ppm*

Step III: Calculation of Permanent hardness

Volume of soap consumed with 50 mL of boiled Sample water = $(V_3 - V)$ mL

50 mL of boiled sample water = $(V_3 - V)$ mL of soap solution

Since, 1 mL of soap solution = $(50/(V_1 - V))$ mg of $CaCO_3$ equivalent

Hence, 50 mL of boiled sample water = $V_3 \times (50/(V_1 - V))$ mg of $CaCO_3$ equivalent

1 mL of boiled sample water = $= \dfrac{(V_3 - V)\times 50}{(V_1 - V)\times 50}$ mg of $CaCO_3$ equivalent

1000 mL of boiled sample water = $= \dfrac{(V_3 - V)\times 50}{(V_1 - V)\times 50} \times 1000$ mg of $CaCO_3$ equivalent

Permanent hardness of Sample water = $= \dfrac{(V_3 - V)}{(V_1 - V)} \times 1000$ mg/L or *ppm*

Step IV: Calculation of temporary hardness

Temporary hardness = Total hardness − Permanent hardness

Temporary hardness of Sample water = $= \dfrac{(V_2 - V)}{(V_1 - V)}\times 1000 - \dfrac{(V_3 - V)}{(V_1 - V)} \times 1000$ mg/L

Temporary hardness of Sample water = $= \dfrac{(V_2 - V_3)}{(V_1 - V)} \times 1000$ mg/L

NUMERICAL EXERCISES BASED ON DETERMINATION OF HARDNESS BY CLARK'S METHOD

Example 1. Soap titration method is used for determination of hardness for a sample of water. 50 mL of water sample of each time of titration against soap solutions gave the following results :

(i) Lather factor = 0.3 mL

(ii) Volume of soap with sample water = 9.3 mL

(iii) Volume of soap with boiled water = 3.1 mL

(iv) Standard hard water containing 400 mg of $CaCO_3$ per litre = 18.3 mL

Calculate total, permanent and temporary hardness in ppm.

Sol. $V = 0.3 \text{ mL}, V_1 = 18.3 \text{ mL}, V_2 = 9.3 \text{ mL}, V_3 = 3.1 \text{ mL}$

1 litre of standard hard water contains 400 mg of $CaCO_3$ equation.

50 mL of standard hard water contains $= \dfrac{400}{1000} \times 50 \text{ mg of } CaCO_3 = 20$ mg of $CaCO_3$ eq.

Volume of soap consumed with standard hardwater $(V_1 - V) = (18.3 - 0.3) \text{ mL} = 18$ mL

50 mL of standard hard water = 18 mL of soap solution

or 18 ml of soap solution = 20 mg of $CaCO_3$ eq.

1 mL of soap solution $= \dfrac{20}{18}$ mg of $CaCO_3$ eq.

50 mL of sample water $= (V_2 - V)$ mL of soap solution

$= (9.3 - 0.3)$ mL of soap solution

$= 9$ mL

Since 1mL of soap solution $= \dfrac{20}{18}$ mg of $CaCO_3$ eq.

hence 50 mL of sample water $= 9 \times \dfrac{20}{18}$ mg of $CaCO_3$ eq.

1 mL of sample water $= \dfrac{9}{50} \times \dfrac{20}{18}$ mg of $CaCO_3$ eq.

$$1000 \text{ mL(or 1L) sample water } = \frac{9}{50} \times \frac{20}{18} \times 1000 \text{ mg } CaCO_3 \text{ eq.}$$

$$\text{Total hardness } = \frac{9 \times 20}{50 \times 18} \times 1000 \text{ mg/L}$$

$$= 200 \text{ mg/L}$$

Permanent hardness

$$50 \text{ mL of boiled water } = (V_3 - V) \text{ mL of soap solution}$$

$$50 \text{ mL of boiled water} = (3.1 - 0.3) \text{ mL of soap solution}$$

$$50 \text{ mL of boiled water} = 2.8 \text{ mL of soap solution}$$

$$50 \text{ mL of boiled water } = 2.8 \times \frac{20}{18} \text{ mg of } CaCO_3 \text{ eq.}$$

$$1 \text{ mL of boiled water } = \frac{2.8 \times 20}{50 \times 18} \text{ mg of } CaCO_3 \text{ eq.}$$

$$1 \text{ mL of boiled water } = \frac{2.8 \times 20}{50 \times 18} \text{mg} \times 1000 \text{ mg of } CaCO_3 \text{ eq.}$$

Permanent hardness = 62.22 mg/L

Temporary hardnes = Total – Permanent

= (200 – 62.22) mg/L

= 137.78 mg/L

Example 2. Determine the hardness of a water sample from the following data using clark's method, when 50 ml of water sample is titrated with soap solution :

Lather factor = 0.5 mL, volume of soap with std. hardwater= 40.5 mL, volume of soap with sample water = 15.5 mL, Volume of soap with boiled water = 12.5 mL.

Sol. Since 1 L of standard hard water contain = 200 mg of $CaCO_3$

$$50 \text{ mL of SHW contain } = 200 \times \frac{50}{1000} \text{ mg of } CaCO_3 \text{ eq.}$$

Now 50 mL SHW = 10 mg of $CaCO_3$ eq. = 40.5 – 0.5 mL of soap solution.

40 mL of soap solution = 10 mg of $CaCO_3$ eq.

$$1 \text{ mL of soap solution } = \frac{10}{40} CaCO_3 \text{ eq.}$$

$= 0.25$ mg of $CaCO_3$ eq.

(i) Calculation of total hardness

50 mL of hard water sample = (15.5 – 0.5) mL of soap solution

$= 15 \times 0.25$ mg of $CaCO_3$ eq.

$= 3.75$ mg of $CaCO_3$ eq.

1 L of hard water sample $= \frac{3.75}{50} \times 1000$ mg of $CaCO_3$ eq.

$= 75.00$ mg of $CaCO_3$ eq.

(ii) Calculation of permanent hardness

50 mL of boiling hard water sample

$= (12.5 - 0.5)$ mL of soap solution.

$= 12 \times 0.25$ mg of $CaCO_3$ eq.

$= 3.00$ mg of $CaCO_3$ eq.

1 L of boiling hard water sample

$= \frac{3 \times 1000}{50}$ mg of $CaCO_3$ eq.

$= 60.00$ mg/L or 60 ppm

(iii) Hence temporary hardness = (75 – 60) = 15 ppm

1.5 MUNICIPAL WATER OR DRINKING WATER

Water is an essential compound for human and all other living organisms. Quality of drinking water can be characterized by its physical, chemical and biological parameters. Government and non government agencies like WHO, ICMR etc. are involved in characterization of safe drinking water. According to Word Health Organization (WHO) safe drinking water may be defined as water of sufficiently high quality, which can be used without risk of immediate or long term harm on living organisms. The Water Quality Standards as set by Union Health Ministry are listed in Table 1.3

Table 1.3: Quality standars for drinking water

PHYSICAL STANDARDS			
S.N.	**Characteristics**	**Acceptable***	**Cause for Rejection***
1	Turbidity (units on J.T.U. scale)	2.5	10
2	Colour (units on platinum-cobalt scale)	5.0	25
3	Taste and odour	Unobjectionable	Unobjectionable

S.N.	Characteristics	Acceptable*	Cause for Rejection*
	CHEMICAL STANDARDS		
1	pH	7.0-8.5	6.5-9.2
2	Total dissolved solids (mg/l)	500	1500
3	Total hardness (as $CaCo_3$) (mg/l)	200	600
4	Chlorides (as Cl) (mg/l)	200	1000
5	Sulphates (as So_4) (mg/l)	200	400
6	Fluorides (as F) (mg/l)	1.0	1.5
7	Nitrates (as No_3) (mg/l)	45	45
8	Calcium (as Ca) (mg/l)	75	200
	Magnesium (as Mg) (mg/l)	>30	150
9	Iron (as Fe) (mg/l)	0.1	1.0
10	Manganese (as Mn) (mg/l)	0.05	0.5
11	Copper (as Cu) (mg/l)	0.05	1.5
12	Zinc (as Zn) (mg/l)	5.0	15.0
13	Phenolic compounds (as phenol) (mg/l)	0.001	0.002
14	Anionic detergents (as MBAS) (mg/l)	0.2	1.0
15	Mineral oil (mg/l)	0.01	0.3
16	Arsenic (as As) (mg/l)	0.05	0.05
17	Cadmium (as Cd) (mg/l)	0.01	0.01
18	Chromium (as hexavalent Cr) (mg/l)	0.05	0.05
19	Cynides (as CN) (mg/l)	0.05	0.05
20	Lead (as Pb) (mg/l)	0.1	0.1
21	Selenium (as Se) (mg/l)	0.01	0.01
22	Mercury (total as Hg) (mg/l)	0.001	0.001
23	Polynuclear aromatic hydrocarbons (PAH) (μg/l)	0.2	0.2
24	Gross alpha activity (pCi/l)	3	3
25	Gross beta activity (pCi/l)	30	30

Note - The figures indicated under the column 'acceptable' are the limits up to which the water is generally acceptable to the consumers.

*Figures in excess of those mentioned under 'acceptable' render the water not acceptable, but still may be tolerated in the absence of alternative and better source up to the limits indicated under column 'cause for rejection' above which the supply will have to be rejected.

BACTERIOLOGICAL STANDARDS

Water in the distribution system shall satisfy these three criteria.

(i) E.Coli count in 100 ml of any sample should be zero.

(ii) Coliform organisms not more than 10 per 100 ml shall be present in any sample.

(iii) Coliform organisms should not be detectable in 100 ml of any two consecutive samples or more than 50 percent of the samples collected for the year.

1.5.1 Characteristics of Drinking Water

In general, drinking water must poses following characteristics:

Physical Characteristics:

1. It should be colourless.
2. It should be pleasant in taste.
3. It should be odourless.
4. It should be perfectly cool.
5. Its turbidity should not exceed 10 ppm.

Chemical Characteristics:

1. It should be free from dissolved harmful gases.
2. It should be free from toxic elements like Pb, As, Mn, Cr.
3. Chlorides and Sulphates must be less than 250 ppm.
4. Total hardness and TDS should be less than 500 ppm.
5. Flourides should be lees than 1 to 5 ppm.
6. Its alkalinity should not be high. Its pH should be 7 to 8.5

Biological Characteristics:

1. It should be free from diseases producing bacteria and other pathogenic micro-organisms.
2. Coliform bacteria should be under permissible limits.

1.5.2 Purification of Drinking Water

Natural water contains various impurities in it. Hence, it is not suitable for drinking purposes as it is. It requires special treatments. The treatment of water for domestic supply will depend upon the quality of the source water. A typical treatment plant for surface water might include the following sequence of steps:

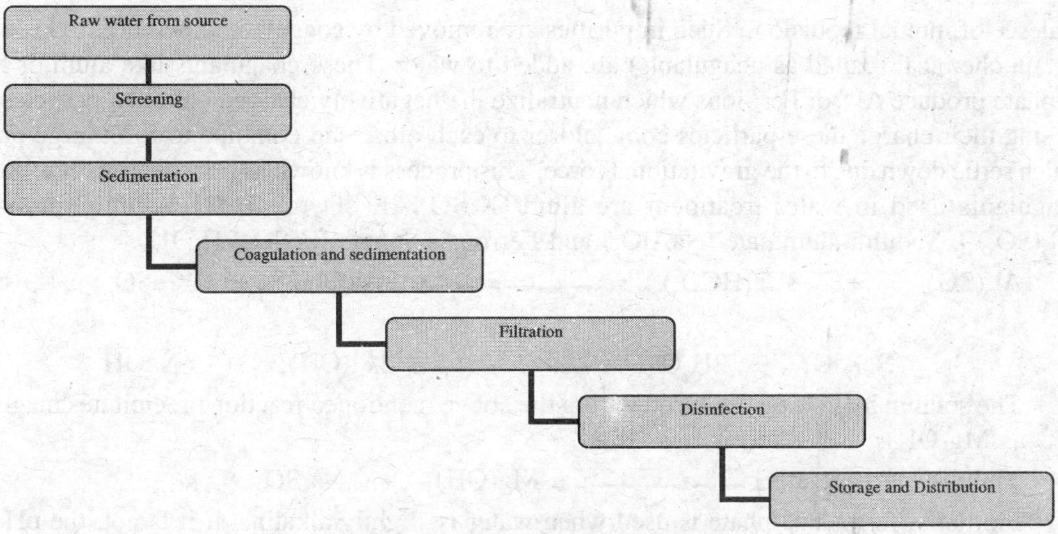

Fig. 1.5 : Purification of Water

(i) Screening:

Screening is the process of removal of floating materials like wood pieces, leaves etc. from water. Raw water is allowed to pass through a screen, having a large number of holes, which hold back the floating matter and allow the water to pass.

(ii) Sedimentation:

Sedimentation is the process of removal of suspended impurities by allowing the water to stand undisturbed for 2-6 hours in big tanks. Under the gravitational force, most of the suspended particles settle down at the bottom and they are removed. Sedimentation removes only 70-75% of the suspended matter.

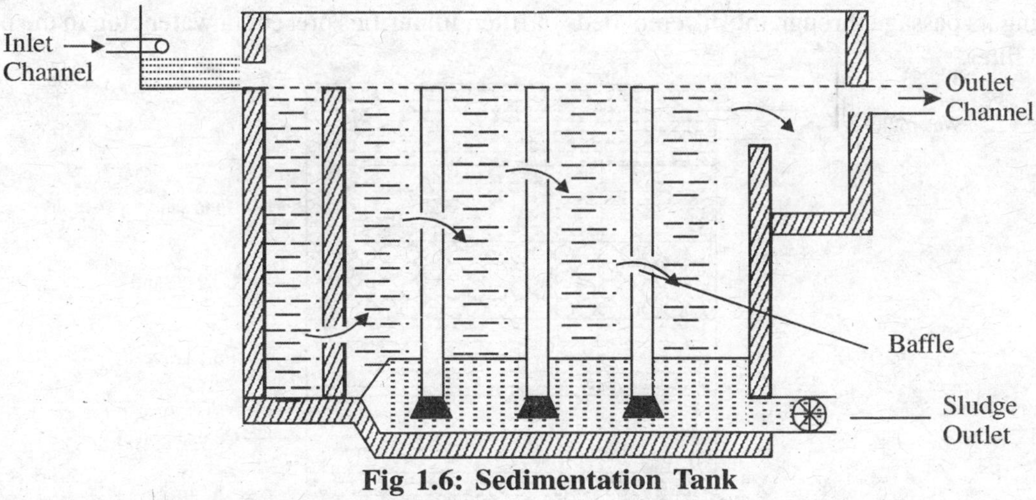

Fig 1.6: Sedimentation Tank

(iii) Sedimentation with coagulation:

Finely divided silica, clay etc. do not settle down easily, and hence, cannot be removed by sedimentation. Most of these are in colloidal from and are negatively charged and hence do not coalesce of mutual repulsion. Such impurities are removed by coagulation method. In this method certain chemical (called as coagulants) are added to water. These coagulants like alum or ferrous sulphate produce Al^{+3} or Fe^{+2} ions which neutralize the negatively charged colloidal particles. After loosing their charge these particles come closer to each other and combine to form large particles which settle down due to the gravitational force. This process is known as flocculation. Few common coagulants used in water treatment are alum $[K_2SO_4.Al_2(SO_4)_3.24H_2O]$, Aluminum sulphate $[Al_2(SO_4)_3]$, Sodium aluminate ($NaAlO_2$) and Ferrous sulphate $[FeSO_4.7H_2O]$.

$$Al_2(SO_4)_3 + 3Ca(HCO_3)_2 \longrightarrow 2Al(OH)_3 + 3CaSO_4 + 6CO_2$$

$$NaAlO_2 + 2H_2O \xrightarrow{pH = 5.5 \text{ to } 8.5} 2Al(OH)_3 + NaOH$$

The sodium hydroxide produced during the above mentioned reaction precipitates magnesium salts as $Mg(OH)_2$.

$$MgSO4 + 2NaOH \longrightarrow Mg(OH)_2 + Na_2SO_4$$

Similarly, ferrous sulphate is used when water is slightly alkaline, if it is not, the pH of the water must be raised by adding lime $Ca(OH)_2$.

$$FeSO_4 + Mg(HCO_3)_2 \longrightarrow Fe(OH)_2 + MgSO_4 + 2CO_2$$

$$Fe(OH)_2 + 2H_2O + O_2 \longrightarrow 4Fe(OH)_3$$

(iv) Filtration: This process involves the removal of colloidal impurities and few micro-organisms by passing water through a sand filter. The sand filter is a porous medium consiting of beds of find sand, coarse sand and gravels respectively. Two types of filters are used in water treatment (i) gravity filters and (ii) pressure filters

(i) Gravity Filters : This type of filter consist of thick beds of fine sand (at the top), coarse sand, find gravel and coarse gravel (at the bottom). This type of filtration is carried out under gravitational force. When water passes through the filter, it flows downward due to the gravity. During its passage through the different beds of filter, impurities present in water clog in the pores of sand filter.

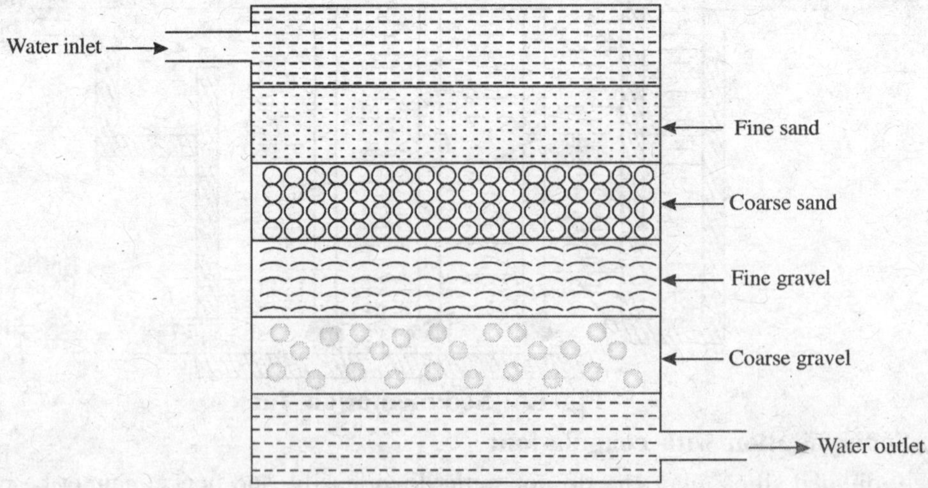

Fig. 1.7 : Sand Filter

(ii) Pressure filters : In this type of filter, water is forced through filter bed under pressure. There filters may be installed in water supply system to avoid repumping of filtered water.

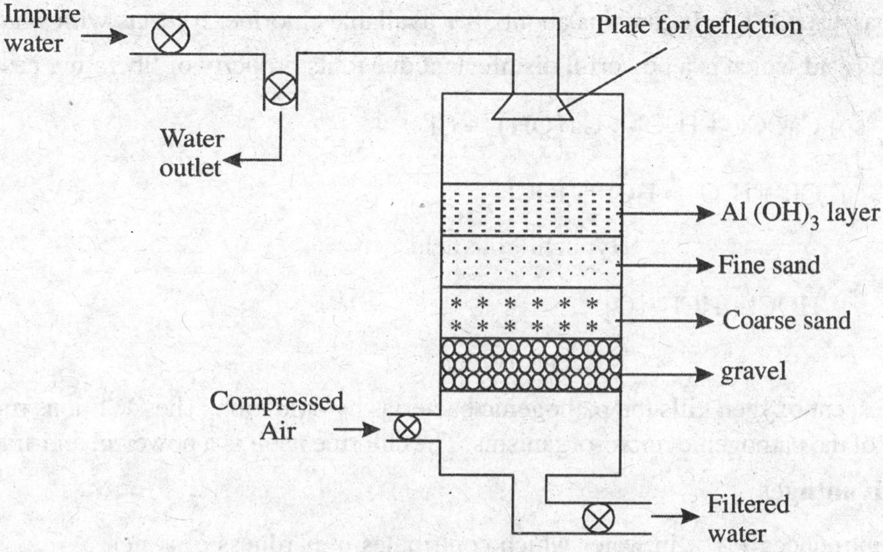

Fig. 1.8 : Pressure Filter

(v) Disinfection : After screening, sedimentation, coagulation and filtration processes the raw water still contain small quantity of pathogenic bacterias and other micro-organisms. For supply of safe drinking water, it is necessary to remove these disease producing pathogenic bacterias. The process of removal pathogenic bacterias and other micro-organisms from water is called as disinfection and the chemicals used for this purposes are known as disinfection. An ideal disinfectant should has following properties :

(i) It should be cheap.

(ii) It should be effective for killing bacterias at room temperature.

(iii) It should be non-toxic.

(iv) It should retain its effect during storage of water.

The disinfection process may be carried out using following methods :

(i) By boiling of water

(ii) Addition of Bleaching powder

(iii) Ozonolysis process

(iv) By adding chloramine

(v) By chlorination

(i) By Boiling of Water

The disease producing bacterias can be destroyed by boiling of water for 15-20 minutes. It is also known as sterlisation.

It is an expensive method and is not suitable for manicipal supply. However, this method can be used in individual cases.

(ii) Addition of Bleaching Powder

The composition of bleaching powder is $Ca(OCl_2).CaCl_2.Ca(OH)_2.2H_2O$ but it is generally represented as $Ca(OCl_2)$. It contains about 30% available chlorine. It reacts with water to produce hypochlorous acid which is a powerful disinfectant due to its property of liberating nascent oxygen.

$$CaOCl_2 + H_2O \rightarrow Ca(OH)_2 + Cl_2$$

$$Cl_2 + H_2O \rightarrow HCl + \underset{\text{Hypochlorous acid}}{HOCl}$$

$$HOCl + HCl + \underset{\text{Nascent oxygen}}{[O]}$$

The nescent oxygen kills the pathogenic bacterias by oxidation. The OCl^- ions rupture the cell membranes of the pathogenic micro-organisms. The chlorine itself is a powerful anti-microbal agent.

Disadvantages

(a) It introduces Ca^{++} in water which contributes in hardness of water.

(b) Excess of bleaching powder, imparts disagreeable odor and bad taste in water. Hence, calculated quantity of beaching powder should be used for disinfection purposes.

Before addition of bleaching powder its chlorine content should be analyzed due to its continuous decomposition during storage.

(c) Ozonolysis Process

Ozone is produced by passing silent electric discharge through cold and dry oxygen.

$$3O_2 \xrightarrow[\text{disch arge}]{\text{silent electric}} 2O_3$$

Because of its high oxidation potential (2.076 V), ozone is a powerful disinfectant than chlorine (13.6V). Ozones enters in the cell membrones of microbes and oxidizes the organic substance in the microbes cell in order to kill it.

Ozone is highly unstable and it liberates nascent oxygen after break down.

$$O_3 \rightarrow O_2 + \underset{\text{Nascent oxygen}}{[O]}$$

The nascent oxygen is also a good oxidizing agent and destroys all bacteria and organic matter present in water. Disinfection of water ozone is carried out in ozone sterilizer which is shown in fig.1.9.

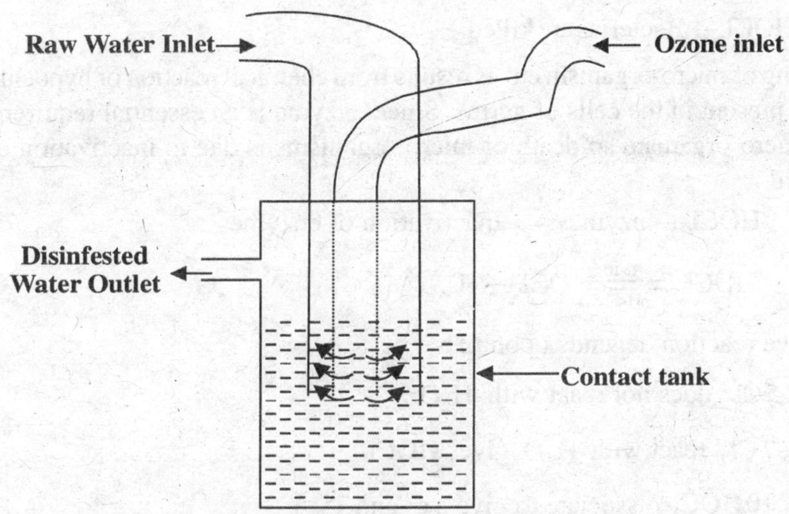

Fig. 1.9 : Ozone Sterilizer

In this process, ozone is introduced into the water to come in contact in a sterilizing tank for 10-15 minutes. The disinfected water is removed from the outlet from the top of the sterilizer. The disinfected water is colorless, odorless and tasteless.

(iv) By adding Chloramine

This method involves addition of ammonia and chlorine to water which results in formation of mono and dichloramines; which destroy all the bacteria.

$$2NH_2 + Cl_2 \rightarrow NH_4Cl + NH_2Cl$$

$$2NH_3 + 3Cl_2 \rightarrow 2NH_4Cl + NHCl_2$$

Chloramine compounds have more batericidal action than chlorine because on hydrolysis in water it give $HOCl$, which is good disinfectant

$$NH_2Cl + H_2O \rightleftharpoons NH_3 + \underset{\text{Disinfectant}}{HOCl}$$

Chloramine process is mostely used method for disinfection of water, because its excess does not produce any irritating odour and it imparts a good taste to disinfected water.

(v) Chlorination Method

Chlorine is the most widely used disinfectant for water treatment. It can be used in liquid or gaseous form. Chlorine produces hypochlorous acid, which is a powerful germicide, and kills pathogens.

$$Cl_2 + H_2O \xrightarrow{pH<5} \underset{\text{Hypochlorous acid}}{HOCl} + HCl$$

$HOCl \rightarrow$ Bacterias are killed

The killing of micro-organism etc. is results from chemical reaction of hypochlorous acid (HOCl) with enzymes present in the cells of germs. Since enzyme is an essential requirement for metabolic activities of micro-organism so death of micro-organisms is due to inactivation of enzymes by hypochlorous acid.

$$HOCl + \text{enzymes} \rightarrow \text{Inactivation of enzymes}$$

$$HOCl \underset{pH<7}{\overset{pH>10}{\rightleftharpoons}} OCl^- + H^+$$

The above reaction depends upon pH

At $pH < 5\,Cl_2$ does not react with H_2O

$pH < 7\,Cl_2$ react with H_2O gives HOCl

$pH < 10\,HOCl$ dissociate to give H^+ and OCl^-

Apparatus used for chlorination is known an **chlorinator** which is a large vertical tower having a number of baffle plates. From the top of the tower, calculated dose of chlorine and water are introduced. They get throughly mixed during their passage. Disinfected water is taken drained out from outlet at the bottom of chlorinator.

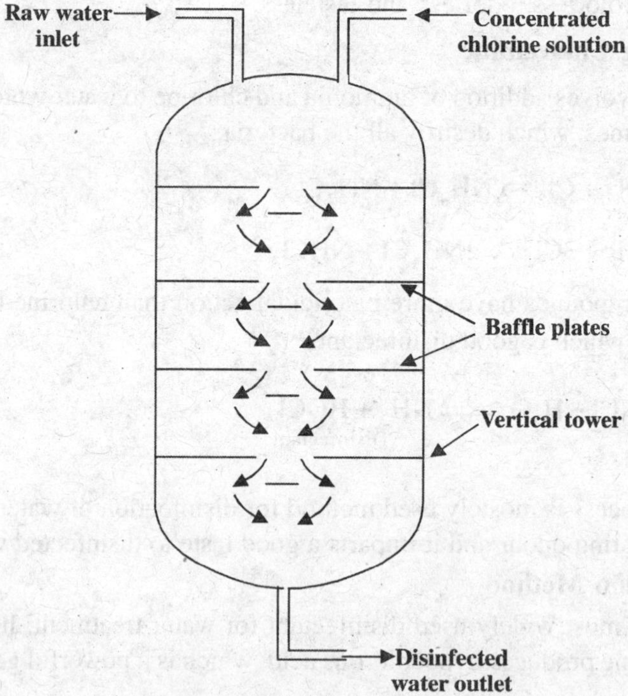

Fig. 1.10 Chlorinator

BREAK POINT CHLROINATION

"Break point chlorination is addition of sufficient amount of chlorine which not only oxidise organic material but also kill disease producing pathogenic bacterieas."

When, chlorine is addd to water, it oxidise reducing substances, organic compounds and also free ammonia. Remaining chlroine possesses disinfecting action against pathogenic bacteria. It is also known as **free residual chlorination.**

Relationship between the amount of chlorine added to water and the free residual chlorine begins is shown in fig. 1.11.

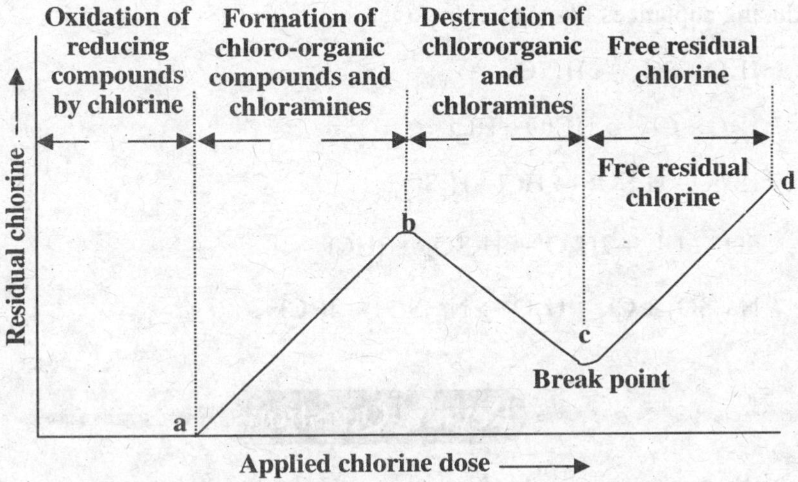

Fig. 1.11 : Break Point Chlorination Curve

The break point chlorination shows **four stages** of disinfection.

Stage 1 : Initially (for lower amount of Cl_2) all the chlorine added is consumed and there is no free residual chlorine due to the complete oxidation of reducing substances present in water.

Stage 2 : Further addition of Cl_2 show steady increase in the amount of residual chlorine. This stage corresponds to the formation of chloro organic compounds and chloramines without undergoing oxidation. Choramines have disinfectant properties and help in killing the micro-organisms.

Stage 3 : When the amount of Cl_2 is further increased, the oxidation of chlro-organic compounds and micro-organism takes place. Consequently, the amount of free residual chlorine also decrease and reaches point C or this point is known as **'break point"** where the oxidative destruction is complete.

Stage 4 : After break point, further added chlorine is not used in any reaction, Hence, the residual chlorine keeps on increasing in direct proportion to added chlorine. For effective distruction of micro-organisms, sufficient amount of chlorine has to be added and this is indicated by the break point in the break chlorination plot.

Advantages

(i) It oxidizes organic substances, ammonia and other reducing substance completely.

(ii) It kills (100%) all the pathogens.

(iii) It prevents water from the growth of weeds.

(iv) It removes bad odor and bad taste.

Dechlorination

The removal of excess chlorine from water is called as **dechlorination.** It is performed in such a manner that at the end of dechlorination process, some residual chlorine still remains in water to disinfect it when it is flowing through the distribution system. Water after break point chlorination is filtered through activated carbon which removes decomposition products as well as excess of chlorine remaining in water. The excess of chlorine can also be removed by the addition of small quantity of reducing subtances like SO_2, Na_2SO_3.

$$H_2O + SO_2 \rightarrow H_2SO_3$$

$$H_2O + Cl_2 \rightarrow HClO + HCl$$

$$HClO + H_2SO_3 \rightarrow HCl + H_2SO_4$$

$$SO_2 + Cl_2 + 2H_2O \rightarrow H_2SO_4 + 2HCl$$

$$Na_2SO_3 + Cl_2 + H_2O \rightarrow Na_2SO_4 + 2HCl$$

Review Questions

1. What is hardness of water? Explain EDTA Complexometric method of hardness determination in detail. ***[R.T.U. 2008, 2009]***
2. Why hardness is expressed in terms of equivalent amount of $CaCO_3$? Give units of Hardness and relation between them.
3. What do you understand by temporary and permanent hardness? ***[R.T.U. 2010]***
4. What are various impurities associated with natural water?
5. What is hardness of water? Distinguish between carbonate and non-carbonate hardness.
6. How is the degree of hardness of water expressed? Name the important methods used for the determination of water and describe one of them in detail.
7. Write structure and IUPAC name of indicator used in complexometric method of determination of hardness of water.
8. Discuss the Clark's method for determination of hardness of water. ***[R.T.U. 2010]***
9. What are the characteristics of drinking water? Explain the various processes involved in purification of raw water for domestic use. ***[R.T.U. 2007]***
10. Write a detailed note on purification of water for drinking purposes.
11. Explain 'Break point chlorination'. ***[R.T.U. 2008, 2009]***
12. Discuss various methods involved in disinfection of water.
13. Discuss dechlorination.
14. Differentiate hard and soft water.
15. Write information notes on the following :

(i) Sedimentation
(ii) Break point chlorination
(iii) Structure of EDTA and EBT *[R.T.U. 2010]*

16. Give the chemical reactions involved in determination of hardness by EDTA method. *[R.T.U. 2010]*

Numerical Problems

1. How many grams of $MgCl_2$ dissolved per litre gives 190 ppm of hardness?
[Ans. 0.1805 g/L]

2. How many grams of $FeSO_4$ dissolved per litre gives 210.5 ppm of hardness.
[Ans. 319.96 mg/L

3. A water sample contains 204 mg of $CaSO_4$ per litre. Calculate the hardness in terms of $CaCO_3$ equivalents. *[R.T.U. 2010]*
[Ans. 150 ppm]

4. A sample of water on analysis has been found to contain the following in ppm :

$Ca(HCO_3)_2 = 105\,ppm; CaCO_4 = 7.5\,ppm; MgSO_4 = 2.6\,ppm$

$Mg(HCO_3)_2 = 12.5\,ppm; CaCl_2 = 8.2\,ppm;$

Calculate the temporary and permanent hardness in degree French.
[Ans. Temporary = 1.504 and Permanent = 1.507 degree French]

5. A sample of water on analysis has been found to contain following salts :

$CaSO_4 = 13.6\,ppm; Ca(HCO_3)_2 = 16.2\,ppm; MgSO_4 = 6.0\,ppm$

$CaCl_2 = 8.0\,ppm; Mg(HCO_3)_2 = 29.2\,ppm; Na_2SO_4 = 10\,ppm$

Calculate the temporary, permanent and total hardness in degree French.
[Ans. Temporary hardness = 3.0 "French = 3.0, Permanent hardness = 2.22 °French, Tota hardness = 5.22 °French]

6. A sample of water on analysis was found to contain the following in ppm:

$Ca(HCO_3)_2 = 10\,ppm; Mg(HCO_3)_2 = 8.5\,ppm; CaSO_4 = 12\,ppm; MgSO_4 = 14\,ppm$

Calculate the temporary, permanent and total hardnes of water in Mg/L.
[Ans. Temporary 11.99 mg/L, Permanent = 20.49 mg/L, Total = 32.48 mg/L]

7. A standard hard water solution was prepared by dissolving 250 mg of dry $CaCO_3$ in 1 litre of distilled water. 50 mL of this solution consumed 17.2 mL of soap solution. 50 mL of distilled water consumed 0.6 mL of soap solution. The 50 ml of sample water consumed 7.6 ol of soap solution. Calculate the each type of hardness.
[Ans. Total hardness = 105.42 mg/L, Permanent hardness = 93.372 mg/L, Temporary hardness = 12.048 mg/L]

8. A sample of water is found to contain 40.5 mg/L of $Ca(HCO_3)_2$;45.6mg/Lof $Mg(HCO_3)_2$; 27.6mg/L of $MgSO_3$;32.1mg/Lof $CaSO_4$; and 22.45mg/L of $CaCl_2$. Calculate the total hardness of water. **[Ans.** 124.68 ppm]

9. 20 ml of standard hard water (containing 15 g $CaCO_3$ per litre) required 25 mL EDTA solution for end point. 100 mL of water sample required 18 ml EDTA solution, while same water after boiling required 12 mL EDTA solution. Calculate temporary and permanent hardness of water. **[Ans.** Temporary = 720 ppm
Permanent = 1440 ppm]

10. Find out permanent and temporary hardness in a given hard water sample. When 50 ml of standard hard water (containing 1 mg of $CaCO_3$ per ml), consumed 22 ml of EDTA solution. 50 ml of water sample after boiling, filteration etc. consumed 20 ml of EDTA solution.
[Ans. Permanent hardness = 909 ppm; Temporary hardness = 318 ppm]

11. A standard hard water was prepared by dissolving 1 gm of pure and dry $CaCO_3$ in 1 litre distilled water. 50 ml of this required 40 ml of EDTA solution while 50 ml of given hard water sample consumed 24 ml of EDTA solution. Afte boiling, hard water consumed 12 ml of EDTA solution. Estimate total, permanent and temporary hardness in ppm of $CaCO_3$ equivalent.
[Ans. Total hardness = 600 ppm; permanent hardnes = 300 ppm;
Temporary hardness ; = 300 ppm]

12. Hardness of standard hard water (A) in terms of $CaCO_3$ is 1000 mg/litre. 50.0 ml of hard water (A) required 50.0 ml of EDTA solution for titration, 50.0 ml of hard water (B), required 40.0 ml of EDTA solution of titration. In another titration, 50 ml of hard water (B) after boiling cooling and filtering, required 20.0 ml of EDTA solution. Calculate temporary and permanent hardness of hard water (B) in different units.
[Ans. Permanent hardness = 2 × 10' mg/L; Temporary hardness = 2 × 10' mg/L]

13. 0.5 g of $CaCO_3$ dissolved in HCl and the solution made upto 500 ml with distilled water. 50 ml of the solution required 48 ml of EDTA solution for titration. 50 ml of hard water sample required 15 ml of EDTA and after boiling and filtering required 10 ml of EDTA solution. Calculate the hardness.
[Ans. Total hardness = 312.5 ppm, Non-Carbonate = 208.3 ppm, Carbonate = 104.2 ppm]

14. If 50 ml of a sample of hard water consumed 15 ml of 0.01 M EDTA. What is the hardness of the water. **[Ans.** 300 ppm]

15. The standard water was prepared by dissolving 1.0 gm of pure and dry $CaCO_3$ in 1 litre distilled water. 50 ml of this required 46 ml of EDTA solution while 50 ml of given hard water sample consumed 20 ml of EDTA solution. After boiling sample of hard water consumed 10 ml of EDTA solution. Determine the total, permanent and temporary hardness in ppm of $CaCO_3$ equivalent.**[Ans.** Total hardness = 43.75 ppm; permanent hardnes = 271.39 ppm;
Temporary hardness = 217.3 ppm]

❑❑❑

Unit - 2
WATER TREATMENT

2.1 WATER SOFTENING METHODS

The process of removal of hardness producing substances/salts from hard water is known as softening of water. The hardness causing salts are converted into insoluble salts which ca be removed easily and thus water will be softened. The process of softening of hard water depends upon type of hardness (temporary or permanent).

2.1.1 Removal of temporary hardness

Temporary hardness of water is due to the presence of bicarbonates of calcium and magnesium, which on boiling are decomposed into insoluble carbonates of calcium and magnesium respectively. These insoluble carbonates can be easily removed by filtration. Thus, the water is softened.

$$\underset{\text{Calcium bicarbonate}}{Ca(HCO_3)_2} \xrightarrow{\Delta} \underset{\text{Calcium carbonate}}{CaCO_3} \downarrow + CO_2 + H_2O$$

$$\underset{\text{Magnesium bicarbonate}}{Mg(HCO_3)_2} \xrightarrow{\Delta} \underset{\text{Magnesium hydroxide}}{Mg(OH)_2} \downarrow + 2CO_2$$

This method is only effective for domestic purposes but it is not possible for the treatment of water on large scale.

2.1.2 Methods for removal of temporary and permanent hardness

In industry, mainly three methods are used for softening of hard water.

(a) Lime-Soda process

(b) Zeolite Process

(c) Ion-exchange process

These methods are also called as external methods because softening of water is done outside the boiler.

2.1.2 (a) Lime-Soda Process

In this process, the soluble hardness producing salts in water are chemically converted into insoluble compounds/precipitates, by addition of calculated amount of lime [$Ca(OH)_2$] and Soda [Na_2CO_3]. The insoluble precipitates are then filtered off.

$$\text{Hard water} \xrightarrow{\text{Lime/Soda}} \text{Insoluble ppt.} + \text{Soft water}$$

The reaction of lime and soda with various constituents present in water are as follows:

Temporary Hardness:

Due to calcium carbonate

$$\underset{}{Ca(HCO_3)_2} + \underset{\text{Lime}}{Ca(OH)_2} \rightarrow 2CaCO_3 + 2H_2O$$

Lime required is one in case of temporary calcium hardness.

Due to magnesium carbonate:

$$Mg(HCO_3)_2 + \underset{\text{Lime}}{Ca(OH)_2} \rightarrow MgCO_3 + CaCO_3 + 2H_2O$$

$$MgCO_3 + \underset{\text{Lime}}{Ca(OH)_2} \rightarrow Mg(OH)_2 + CaCO_3$$

In case of temporary magnesium hardness lime requirement is two.

Permanent Hardness:

Due to $CaCl_2$ or $CaSO_4$ or $Ca(NO_3)_2$ (permanent calcium hardness)

$$CaCl_2 + \underset{\text{Soda}}{Na_2CO_3} \rightarrow CaCO_3 + 2NaCl$$

$$CaSO_4 + \underset{\text{Soda}}{Na_2CO_3} \rightarrow CaCO_3 + Na_2SO_4$$

$$Ca(NO_3)_2 + \underset{\text{Soda}}{Na_2CO_3} \rightarrow CaCO_3 + 2NaNO_3$$

Soda requirement is one in each case of permanent calcium hardness.

Due to $MgCl_2$ or $MgSO_4$ or $Mg(NO_3)_2$ (permanent Magnesium hardness)

$$MgCl_2 + \underset{\text{Lime}}{Ca(OH)_2} \rightarrow Mg(OH)_2 + CaCl_2$$

$$CaCl_2 + \underset{\text{Soda}}{Na_2CO_3} \rightarrow CaCO_3 + 2NaCl$$

$$MgSO_4 + \underset{\text{Lime}}{Ca(OH)_2} \rightarrow Mg(OH)_2 + CaSO_4$$

$$CaSO_4 + \underset{\text{Soda}}{Na_2CO_3} \rightarrow CaCO_3 + Na_2SO_4$$

$$Mg(NO_3)_2 + \underset{\text{Lime}}{Ca(OH)_2} \rightarrow Mg(OH)_2 + Ca(NO_3)_2$$

$$Ca(NO_3)_2 + \underset{\text{Soda}}{Na_2CO_3} \rightarrow CaCO_3 + 2NaNO_3$$

For each case of permanent magnesium hardness one lime and one soda is required.

Coagulants:

Aluminium or iron salts may be present in water and they contribute to permanent hardness or they may be added as coagulants. Addition of a coagulant like alum helps in the faster sedimentation of sludge which can then be removed easily.

$$FeSO_4 + \underset{\text{Lime}}{Ca(OH)_2} \rightarrow Fe(OH)_2 + CaSO_4$$

$$CaSO_4 + \underset{\text{Soda}}{Na_2CO_3} \rightarrow CaCO_3 + Na_2SO_4$$

$$Al_2(SO_4)_3 + \underset{\text{Lime}}{3Ca(OH)_2} \rightarrow 2Al(OH)_2 + 3CaSO_4$$

$$CaSO_4 + \underset{\text{Soda}}{Na_2CO_3} \rightarrow CaCO_3 + Na_2SO_4$$

However, sodium aluminate gives OH^- with water which may combine with Ca^{+2} ions present in hard water and form Lime. This lime should be subtracted from amount of calculated lime to be added for softening of water.

$$\underset{\text{Sodium aluminate}}{NaAlO_2} + H_2O \rightarrow \underset{\text{(may produce lime)}}{Na^{+2} + OH^- + Al(OH)_3}$$

Dissolved gases and minerals:

$$CO_2 + \underset{\text{Lime}}{Ca(OH)_2} \rightarrow CaCO_3 + H_2O$$

$$H_2S + \underset{\text{Lime}}{Ca(OH)_2} \rightarrow CaS + H_2O$$

In each case lime required is one.

If H^+ present in water (free acids, like HCl, H_2SO_4 etc.), it requires one lime and one soda.

$$H^+ + \underset{\text{Lime}}{Ca(OH)_2} \rightarrow Ca^{+2} + 2H_2O$$

$$CaSO_4 + \underset{\text{Soda}}{Na_2CO_3} \rightarrow CaCO_3 + Na_2SO_4$$

$$HCO_3^- + \underset{\text{Lime}}{Ca(OH)_2} \rightarrow CaCO_3 + 2H_2O + \underset{\text{(may produce soda)}}{CO_3^-}$$

This may combine with Na^+ ions present in water and form soda. Thus, amount of this soda should be subtracted from total amount of calculated soda required. So in case of bicarbonates other than Ca and Mg (like $NaHCO_3$) lime required is 1 and soda is -1.

Total amount of lime required for treatment of hard water containing these salts is given by following formula:

$= \frac{74}{100}$ [Temp. Ca^{+2}+ [2 × Temp. Mg^{+2}]+ Permanent [Mg^{+2}+ Fe^{+2} +Al^{+3}] + CO_2 + H^+ + HCO_3^- – $NaAlO_2$ all in terms of $CaCO_3$ Equiv.]

where 74 is the molecular weight of $Ca(OH)_2$. To remove 100 parts of $CaCO_3$74 parts of $Ca(OH)_2$ are required,

Similarly, the amount of soda of soda required is

$= \frac{106}{100}$ [Permanent [Ca^{+2} + Mg^{+2}+ Fe^{+2} +Al^{+3}] + H^+ - HCO_3^- all in terms of $CaCO_3$ Equiv.]

where 106 is the molecular weight of Na_2CO_3.

Table 2.1: Amount o lime and soda for precipitation of various constituents

S.N.	Constituents	Required Lime(L)/ Soda(S)
1	$CaCO_3$, $Ca(HCO_3)_2$ (Temporary Ca hardness)	L
2	$MgCO_3$, $Mg(HCO_3)_2$ (Temporary Mg hardness	2L
3	$CaCl_2$ / $CaSO_4$ / $Ca(NO_3)_2$ (Permanent Ca hardness)	S
4	$MgCl_2$ / $MgSO_4$ / $Mg(NO_3)_2$ (Permanent Mg hardness)	L + S
5	$FeSO_4$	L + S
6	$Al_2(SO_4)_3$	L + S
7	$NaAlO_2$	–S
8	CO_2	L
9	H_2S	L
10	H^+	L + S
11	HCO_3^-	L – S

The lime soda process may be carried out either in cold or hot condition.

(1) Cold Lime- Soda process

In this process, calculated amount of lime and soda are mixed with hard water at room temperature. Since the precipitates formed are very fine and hence, they remain suspended in water and do not settle down easily. Therefore, they cannot be removed by filtration immediately. To make setting faster coagulants like sodium aluminate, aluminium sulphate or alum are added, These coagulates get hydrolysed to gelatinous precipitates of aluminum hydroxide which easily entrap the fine particles of solids and make them to settle down.

$$NaAlO_2 + 2H_2O \rightarrow NaOH + Al(OH)_3$$

$$Al_2(SO_4)_3 + 3Ca(HCO_3)_2 \rightarrow 2Al(OH)_3 + 3CaSO_4 + 6CO_2$$

The cold L-S process may be of two types:

(i) Batch process

(ii) Continuous process

(i) Batch process

This process is carried out in tanks provided with mechanical stirrers for thorough mixing. Calculated amount of lime and soda are added to the water tank and mixed thoroughly. Required amount of a coagulant is also added to facilitate setting down of the precipitate. It takes usually about 2 hours for the precipitate to settle down completely at the bottom of the tank when kept undisturbed.

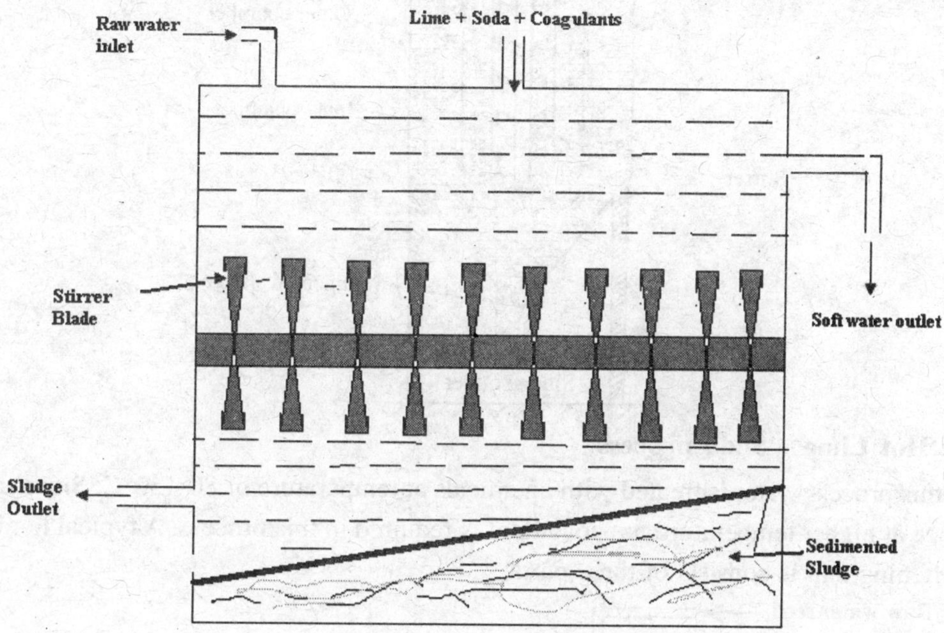

Fig 2.1: Batch Cold Lime Soda Process

The softened water from the top is drawn out using pumps and passed through sand filters. The sludge formed at the bottom is removed and cleaned up with water. The tank, is ready for another batch of operation.

(ii) Continuous Process

Water to be treated and calculated amount of lime, soda and coagulant are fed through the top into the inner toe inner the circular chamber fitted with rotating shafts having paddles. As the water flows down in the vertical chamber, there is thorough mixing and due to the various chemical reactions taking place in this process, softening is achieved. The softened water rises upwards through the outer coaxial chamber. The softened water is passed through a filtering medium to ensure complete removal of sludge. Filtered soft water flows out continuously through the outlet at the top. From the bottom, sludge is periodically removed.

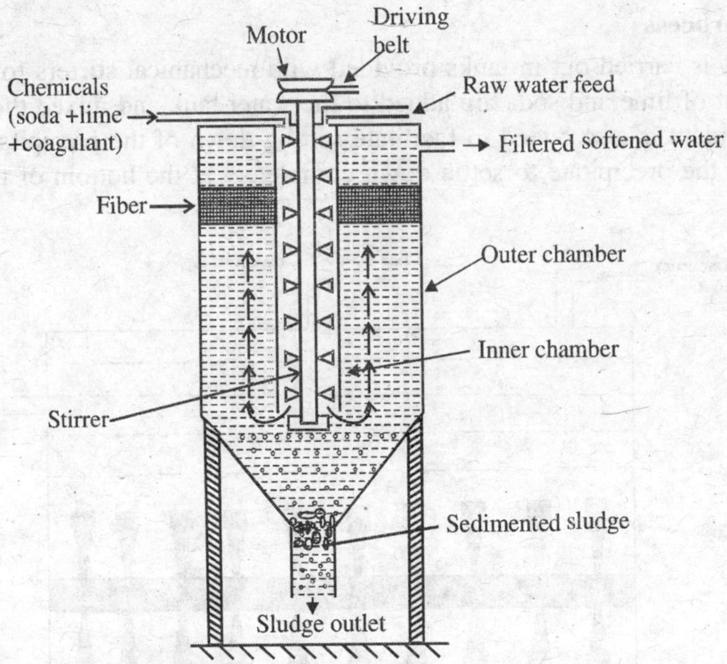

(2) Hot Lime – Soda process

In this process water is treated with chemicals at temperature of 80-150°C. Since the reaction takes place at higher temperature, no coagulant is required in this process. A typical hot lime –soda water softening unit is consists of three parts:

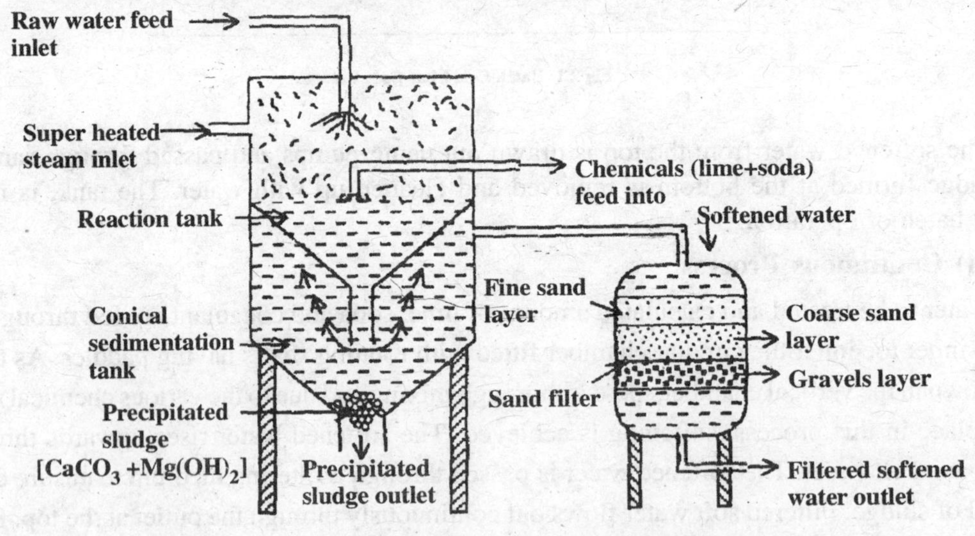

Fig.2.3 : Hot lime-soda process.

(1) Reaction Tank: This tank has three separate inlets, one each for raw water, chemicals and super- heated steam. These three are then thoroughly mixed inside the tank. The beginning and completion of reactions occur in reaction tank.

(2) Conical Sedimentation Tank: Form the reaction tank the contents go to the sedimentation tank so that sludge settles down.

(3) Sand Filter: It has layers of fine and coarse sand which acts as filter and ensures complete removal of sludge from the softened water.

Advantages:

(a) The process rate is increased and the softening reactions are completed in about 15 minutes.

(b) Sludge settles faster and the addition of coagulants is not required.

(c) Dissolved gases like CO_2 are expelled.

(D) Viscosity is decreased and so filtration is faster.

Table 2.2: Differences between Hot and Cold Lime-Soda process

S.N.	Cold Lime Soda Process	Hot Lime Soda Process
1	Calculated amount of lime and soda is mixed at room temperature (25-30°C).	This is done at comparatively higher temperature (80-150°C).
2	It is a slow process.	It is a fast process.
3	The precipitates formed are finely divided and cannot settle down. Hence, filtration is not easy.	The precipitates formed are like sludge, which settles down easily. Hence, filtration is easy.
4	Use of coagulant is necessary.	Coagulants are not required.
5	Softened water has residual hardness about 60 ppm.	Residual hardness is around 15-30 ppm.
6	Dissolved gases are not removed.	Dissolved gases are removed to some extent.

Advantages of Lime-Soda Process:

(1) Lime-Soda process is very economical.

(2) Treated water is alkaline and hence has less corrosion tendencies.

(3) It removes not only hardness causing salts but also minerals.

(4) The amount of pathogenic bacteria is considerably reduces in treated water since it is alkaline in nature.

(5) To some extent iron and manganese are also removed.

Disadvantages if Lime – Soda process:

(1) It requires careful operation and skilled supervision for economical and efficient softening.

(2) Sludge disposal is a problem.

(3) Water softened by this process contains appreciable concentrations of soluble salts and cannot be used in high pressure boilers.

SOLVED NUMERICAL BASED ON LIME SODA PROCESS

1. A sample of water contains following impurities:

CO_2 = 22 mg/L $Ca(HCO_3)_2$ = 20 mg/L $Mg(HCO_3)_2$ = 29.2 mg/L

$MgCl_2$ = 47.5 mg/L $CaSO_4$ = 34 mg/L $Al_2(SO_4)_3$ =57 mg/L

Calculate the quantity of lime and soda required for the softening of 60,000 litres of hard water. [RTU 2009]

S.N.	Substance	Amount of Substance	Multiplication factor	$CaCO_3$ Equivalence (mg/L)	Lime/soda
1	CO_2	22 mg/L	$\frac{100}{44}$	$\frac{100}{44}\times 22 = 50$	1L
2	$Ca(HCO_3)_2$	20 mg/L	$\frac{100}{162}$	$\frac{100}{162}\times 20 = 12.34$	1L
3	$CaSO_4$	34 mg/L	$\frac{100}{136}$	$\frac{100}{136}\times 34 = 25$	1S
4	$Mg(HCO_3)_2$	29.2 mg/L	$\frac{100}{146}$	$\frac{100}{146}\times 29.2 = 20$	2L
5	$MgCl_2$	47.5 mg/L	$\frac{100}{95}$	$\frac{100}{95}\times 47.5 = 50$	L + S
6	$Al_2(SO_4)_3$	57 mg/L	$\frac{100}{114}$	$\frac{100}{114}\times 57 = 50$	L + S

Lime Required =

$$\frac{74}{100}\,[CO_2 + Ca(HCO_3)_2 + 2 \times Mg(HCO_3)_2 + MgCl_2 + Al_2(SO_4)_3 \text{ as } CaCO_3 \text{ Equiv.}] \times \text{Vol. of Water}$$

$$= \frac{74}{100}\times\left[50 + 12.34(2\times 20) + 50 + 50\right]\frac{mg}{L}\times 60000\,\text{L}$$

$$= \frac{74}{100}\times 202.34\times 60000\ mg$$

$$= 8983896 \times 10^{-6} \text{ kg}$$

Lime Required = 8.98 kg

$$\text{Soda Required} = \frac{106}{100}\,[CaSO_4 + MgCl_2 + Al_2(SO_4)_3 \text{ as } CaCO_3 \text{ Equiv. }] \text{ Vol. of Water}$$

$$= \frac{106}{100} [50 + 25 + 50]\ 60000\ L$$

$$= \frac{106}{100} [125]\ 60000\ mg$$

$$= 7950000 \times 10^{-6}\ kg$$

$\boxed{\text{Soda Required} = 7.95\ kg}$

2. A water sample has the analytical report as under:

$MgCO_3$ = 84 mg/L **$CaCO_3$ = 40 mg/L** **$CaCl_2$ = 55.5 mg/L**

$MgNO_3$ = 37 mg/L **KCl = 20 mg/L**

Calculate the amount of lime (86% pure) and Soda (83% pure) needed for the treatment of 80,000 litres of water. **[RTU 2010]**

Ans.

S.N.	Substance	Amount of Substance	Multiplication factor	$CaCO_3$ Equivalence (mg/L)	Lime/soda
1	$CaCO_3$	40 mg/L	$\frac{100}{100}$	$\frac{100}{100}\times 40 = 40$	1L
2	$MgCO_3$	84 mg/L	$\frac{100}{84}$	$\frac{100}{84}\times 84 = 100$	2L
3	$CaCl_2$	55.5 mg/L	$\frac{100}{111}$	$\frac{100}{111}\times 55.5 = 50$	1S
4	$MgNO_3$	37 mg/L	$\frac{100}{148}$	$\frac{100}{148}\times 37 = 25$	L+S
6	KCl	20 mg/L	Does not impart hardness		

Lime required of given quality (i.e. 86% pure) for 80,000 litres water:

Lime Required =

$$\frac{74}{100} [CaCO_3 + 2 \times MgCO_3 + MgNO_3 \text{ as } CaCO_3 \text{ Equiv.}] \times \text{Vol. of Water} \times \%\ \text{purity}$$

$$= \frac{74}{100} \times [40 + (2\times 100) + 25] \frac{mg}{L} \times 8000\ L \times \frac{100}{86}$$

$$= 18241860.46\ mg$$

$$= 18241860.46 \times 10^{-6}\ kg$$

$\boxed{\text{Lime Required} = 18.24\ kg}$

Soda required of given quality (i.e. 83% pure) for 80,000 litres water

$$= \frac{106}{100} \text{ [CaCl}_2 + \text{MgNO}_3 \text{ as CaCO}_3 \text{ Equiv.] Vol. of Water} \times \text{\% purity}$$

$$= \frac{106}{100}[50+25]\frac{mg}{L} \times 80000\,L \times \frac{100}{83}$$

$= 7662650.60$ mg

$= 7662650.60 \times 10^{-6}$ kg

Soda Required = 7.66 kg

3. Calculate the amount of lime and Soda needed for the treatment of 50,000 litres of water containing the following salts per litre: $Ca(HCO_3)_2$ = 8.1 mg; $Mg(HCO_3)_2$ = 7.5 mg; $CaSO_4$ = 13.6 mg; $MgSO_4$ = 12 mg; $MgCl_2$ = 2 mg; NaCl = 4.7 mg.

Ans.

S.N.	Substance	Amount of Substance	Multiplication factor	$CaCO_3$ Equivalence (mg/L)	Lime/soda
1	$Ca(HCO_3)_2$	8.1 mg/L	$\frac{100}{162}$	$\frac{100}{162}\times 8.1 = 5$	1L
2	$Mg(HCO_3)_2$	7.5 mg/L	$\frac{100}{146}$	$\frac{100}{146}\times 7.5 = 5.1$	2L
3	$CaSO_4$	13.6 mg/L	$\frac{100}{136}$	$\frac{100}{136}\times 13.6 = 10$	1S
4	$MgSO_4$	12 mg/L	$\frac{100}{120}$	$\frac{100}{120}\times 12 = 10$	L+S
5	$MgCl_2$	2 mg/L	$\frac{100}{95}$	$\frac{100}{95}\times 2 = 2.10$	L + S
6	NaCl	4.7 mg/L	Does not impart hardness		

Lime Required =

$$\frac{74}{100} \text{ [Ca(HCO}_3)_2 + 2 \times \text{Mg(HCO}_3)_2 + \text{MgSO}_4 + \text{MgCl}_2 \text{ as CaCO}_3 \text{ Equiv.]}$$

$$\times \text{ Vol. of Water}$$

$$= \frac{74}{100} \times [5 + (2\times 5.1) + 10 + 2.1]\frac{mg}{L} \times 50000\text{ L}$$

$$= \frac{74}{100} \times 27.3 \times 50000\,mg$$

$= 1010100$ mg

$= 1010100 \times 10^{-6}$ kg

Lime Required = 1.01 kg

Soda Required = $\frac{106}{100}$ [$MgCl_2 + MgSO_4 + CaSO_4$ as $CaCO_3$ Equiv.] Vol. of Water

$= \frac{106}{100} [10 + 10 + 2.1]$ 50000 L

$= 1171300$ mg

$= 1171300 \times 10^{-6}$ kg

Soda Required = 1.17 kg

4. Analysis of water gave the following results: H_2SO_4 = 196 mg/L; $MgSO_4$ = 24 mg/L; $CaSO_4$ = 272 mg/L and NaCl = 25 mg/L. water is to be supplied to the town of the population of one lakh only. The daily consumption of water is 50 litres per head. Calculate the cost of lime soda required for the softening of hard water for the town for the month of April 2002. If the cost of lime is Rs. 5/- per kg and soda is Rs. 8/- per kg.

Ans.

S.N.	Substance	Amount of Substance (mg/L)	Multiplication factor	$CaCO_3$ Equivalence (mg/L)	Lime/soda
1	H_2SO_4	196	$\frac{100}{98}$	$\frac{100}{98} \times 196 = 200$	L+S
2	$MgSO_4$	24	$\frac{100}{120}$	$\frac{100}{120} \times 24 = 20$	L+S
3	$CaSO_4$	272	$\frac{100}{136}$	$\frac{100}{136} \times 272 = 200$	S
4	NaCl	25	Does not impart hardness		

Lime Required =

$= \frac{74}{100}$ [$H_2SO_4 + MgSO_4$ as $CaCO_3$ Equiv.] $\times$ Vol. of Water

$$= \frac{74}{100} \times [200 + 20] \frac{mg}{L} \times (50 \times 100000)\,\text{L}$$

$= 814 \times 10^6$ mg per day

$= 814 \times 10^6 \times 10^{-6}$ kg per day

$$\boxed{\text{Lime Required} = 814 \text{ kg per day}}$$

Soda Required $= \frac{106}{100}$ [$H_2SO_4 + MgSO_4 + CaSO_4$ as $CaCO_3$ Equiv.] Vol. of Water

$$= \frac{106}{100}[200 + 20 + 200] \frac{mg}{L} \times (50 \times 100000)\,\text{L}$$

$= 2226 \times 10^6$ mg per day

$= 2226 \times 10^6\ 10^{-6}$ kg per day

$$\boxed{\text{Soda Required} = 2226 \text{ kg per day}}$$

Cost of lime and soda for the month of April 2002 i.e. for 30 day:

Cost of lime = quantity of lime total days rate

$= 814 \times 30 \times 5$

$$\boxed{\text{Cost of lime} = \text{Rs. } 1,22,100}$$

Cost of Soda = quantity of soda total days rate

$= 2226\ \ 30\ \ 8$

$$\boxed{\text{Cost of soda} = \text{Rs.} 5,34,240}$$

5. Calculate the amount of lime (80% pure) and soda (90% pure) required to softening 50,000 litres of water which analyzed as follows: $Ca(HCO_3)_2$ = 40.5 mg/L; $Mg(HCO_3)_2$ = 73 mg/L; $CaSO_4$ = 34 mg/L; $CaCl_2$ = 27.5 mg/L; $MgSO_4$ = 60 mg/L and NaCl = 20 mg/L.

[RTU 2008]

Ans.

S.N.	Substance	Amount of Substance	Multiplication factor	$CaCO_3$ Equivalence (mg/L)	Lime/soda
1	$Ca(HCO_3)_2$	40.5 mg/L	$\frac{100}{162}$	$\frac{100}{162}\times 40.5 = 25$	1L
2	$Mg(HCO_3)_2$	73 mg/L	$\frac{100}{146}$	$\frac{100}{146}\times 73 = 50$	2L
3	$CaSO_4$	34 mg/L	$\frac{100}{136}$	$\frac{100}{136}\times 34 = 25$	1S
4	$MgSO_4$	60 mg/L	$\frac{100}{120}$	$\frac{100}{120}\times 60 = 50$	L+S
5	$CaCl_2$	27.5 mg/L	$\frac{100}{111}$	$\frac{100}{111}\times 27.5 = 24.77$	L + S
6	NaCl	20 mg/L	Does not impart hardness		

Lime Required =

$$\frac{74}{100}[Ca(HCO_3)_2 + 2 \times Mg(HCO_3)_2 + MgSO_4 \text{ as } CaCO_3 \text{ Equiv.}] \times \text{Vol. of Water } (\% \text{ purity})$$

$$= \frac{74}{100}\times[25+(2\times 50)+50]\frac{mg}{L}\times 50000 \text{ L}\times\frac{100}{80}$$

$$= \frac{74}{100}\times 175\times 50000\times\frac{100}{80} \text{ mg}$$

$= 8093750$ mg

$= 8093750 \times 10^{-6}$ kg

Lime Required = 8.094 kg

Soda Required =

$$= \frac{106}{100}[CaCl_2 + MgSO_4 + CaSO_4 \text{ as } CaCO_3 \text{ Equiv.}] \text{ Vol. of Water } (\% \text{ purity})$$

$$= \frac{106}{100}[24.77+50+25]\frac{mg}{L}\times 50000 \text{ L}\times\frac{100}{90}$$

$= 5875344.4$ mg

$= 5875344.4 \times 10^{-6}$ kg

Soda Required = 5.87 kg

6. Calculate the amount of lime (90% pure) and soda (98% pure) required to softening 1,00,000 litres of water containing the following: HCl = 7.3 mg/L; $Al_2(SO_4)_3$ = 34.2 mg/L; $MgCl_2$ = 9.5 mg/L; and NaCl = 29.25 mg/L. purity of lime is 90% and that of soda is 98%. 10% of chemicals are to be used in excess in order to complete the reaction quickly.

[RTU 2008]

Ans.

S.N.	Substance	Amount of Substance	Multiplication factor	$CaCO_3$ Equivalence (mg/L)	Lime/soda
1	HCl	7.3 mg/L	$\frac{100}{73}$	$\frac{100}{73} \times 7.3 = 10$	L + S
2	$Al_2(SO_4)_3$	34.2 mg/L	$\frac{100}{114}$	$\frac{100}{114} \times 34.2 = 30$	L + S
3	$MgCl_2$	9.5 mg/L	$\frac{100}{95}$	$\frac{100}{95} \times 9.5 = 10$	L + S
4	NaCl	20 mg/L	Does not impart hardness		

Lime Required =

$$= \frac{74}{100} \times [10 + 30 + 10] \frac{mg}{L} \times 100000 \text{ L}$$

Lime required of given quality (i.e. 90% pure) with 10% excess:

$$= \frac{74}{100} \times [10 + 30 + 10] \frac{mg}{L} \times 100000 \text{ L} \times \frac{100}{90} \times \frac{110}{100}$$

Lime Required = 4.552 kg

Soda Required =

$$= \frac{106}{100} [10 + 30 + 10] \frac{mg}{L} \times 100000 \text{ L}$$

Soda required of given quality (i.e. 98% pure) with 10% excess:

$$= \frac{106}{100} [10 + 30 + 10] \frac{mg}{L} \times 100000 \text{L} \times \frac{100}{98} \times \frac{110}{100}$$

Soda Required = 5.948 kg

7.A water sample is analyzed as follows: $Ca(HCO_3)_2$ = 48.6 ppm; $Mg(HCO_3)_2$ = 3.8 ppm; $CaSO_4$ = 54.4 ppm; $CaCl_2$ = 33.3 ppm; $MgSO_4$ = 48 ppm; Fe_2O_3 = 56.7 ppm and SiO_2 = 44.6 ppm.

This water is to be soften by lime soda process at the rate of 5000 litres of water per minute. For coagulation 13.9 ppm of commercial grade $FeSO_4.7H_2O$ is to be used. Calculate the quantity of lime and soda required per hour if the % purity of lime is 80 and that of soda is 98. [RTU 2008]

Ans.

S.N.	Substance	Amount of Substance (ppm)	Multiplication factor	$CaCO_3$ Equivalence (ppm)	Lime/soda
1	$Ca(HCO_3)_2$	48.6	$\frac{100}{162}$	$\frac{100}{162}\times 48.6 = 30$	1L
2	$Mg(HCO_3)_2$	29.6	$\frac{100}{146}$	$\frac{100}{146}\times 29.6 = 20.27$	2L
3	$CaSO_4$	54.4	$\frac{100}{136}$	$\frac{100}{136}\times 54.4 = 40$	1S
4	$CaCl_2$	33.3	$\frac{100}{111}$	$\frac{100}{111}\times 33.3 = 30$	1S
5	$MgCl_2$	3.8	$\frac{100}{95}$	$\frac{100}{95}\times 3.8 = 4$	L + S
6	$MgSO_4$	48	$\frac{100}{120}$	$\frac{100}{120}\times 48 = 40$	L+S
7	$FeSO_4.7H_2O$	13.9	$\frac{100}{278}$	$\frac{100}{278}\times 13.9 = 5$	L+S

Note: Fe_2O_3 and SiO_2 does not cause hardness.

$$\text{Lime Required} = \frac{74}{100}\,[30 + (2 \times 20.27) + 4 + 40 + 5] \times \text{Vol. of Water} \times (\%\ \text{purity})$$

$$= \frac{74}{100}\times[119.54]\,\frac{mg}{L}\times 500\ \text{L}\times\frac{100}{80}$$

= 552872.5 mg per minute

$= 552872.5 \times 10^{-6}$ kg/min.

$= 0.5528725 \times 60$ kg/hour

Line Required = 33.1723 kg/hr

Soda Required =

$$= \frac{106}{100}[40+30+4+40+5] \times \text{Vol. of Water} \times (\% \text{ purity})$$

$$= \frac{106}{100}[119]\frac{mg}{L} \times 5000 \text{ L} \times \frac{100}{98}$$

= 643571.4 mg per minute

= 643571.4×10^{-6} kg/min.

= 0.6435714×60 kg/hour

Soda Required = 38.61 kg/hr

8. A water sample on analysis gives the following data: Ca^{2+} = 20 ppm, Mg^{2+} = 25 ppm, CO_2 = 30 ppm, HCO_3^- = 150 ppm, K^+ = 10 ppm. Calculate the lime (87% pure) and soda (91% pure) required to soften 1 million litres of water sample. [RTU 2010]

Ans.

S.N.	Substance	Amount of Substance (ppm)	Multiplication factor	$CaCO_3$ Equivalence (ppm)	Lime/soda
1	Ca^{2+}	20	$\frac{100}{40}$	$\frac{100}{40} \times 20 = 50$	1S
2	Mg^{2+}	25	$\frac{100}{24}$	$\frac{100}{24} \times 25 = 104.17$	L + S
3	CO_2	30	$\frac{100}{44}$	$\frac{100}{44} \times 30 = 68.18$	L
4	HCO_3^-	150	$\frac{100}{122}$	$\frac{100}{122} \times 150 = 122.95$	L – S
5	K^+	10	Does not impart hardness		

Lime Required =

$$\frac{74}{100}[104.17 + 68.18 + 122.95] \times \text{Vol. of Water} \times (\% \text{ purity})$$

$$= \frac{74}{100}[295.3]\frac{mg}{L} \times 1000000 \text{ L} \times \frac{100}{87}$$

= 251.17×10^6 mg per minute

= $251.17\ 10^6 \times 10^{-6}$ kg/min.

Lime Required = 251.17 kg

Soda Required =

$$= \frac{106}{100}[104.17 + 50 - 122.95] \text{ Vol. of Water (\% purity)}$$

$$= \frac{106}{100}[31.05]\frac{mg}{L} \times 1000000 \text{ L} \times \frac{100}{91}$$

$= 36.17 \times 10^6$ mg per minute

$= 36.17 \times 10^6 \times 10^{-6}$ kg

Soda Required = 36.17 kg

Example 9 : Calculate the quantities of lime and soda needed for softening 2000 litres of hard water which analyzed as follows.

Analysis of raw water
Ca^{+2} = 160 ppm
Mg^{+2} = 72 ppm
HCO_3^- = 732 ppm
Dissolved CO_2 = 44 ppm
HCl = 73 ppm

Analysis of treated water
CO_3^{-2} = 30 ppm
OH^- = 17 ppm

[Raj. Univ. 2000]

Sol. Conversion to $CaCO_3$ equivalent

Constituent Raw water	Amount (ppm)	Multiplication factor	$CaCO_3$ equivalent (ppm)
Ca^{+2}	160	$\frac{100}{140}$	$160 \times \frac{100}{140} = 400$
Mg^{+2}	72	$\frac{100}{24}$	$72 \times \frac{100}{24} = 300$
HCO_3^-	732	$\frac{100}{122}$	$732 \times \frac{100}{122} = 600$
CO_2	44	$\frac{100}{44}$	$44 \times \frac{100}{44} = 100$
HCl	73	$\frac{100}{73}$	$7.3 \times \frac{100}{73} = 10$
Treated water			
OH^-	17	$\frac{100}{34}$	$17 \times \frac{100}{34} = 50$
CO_3^{-2}	30	$\frac{100}{60}$	$30 \times \frac{100}{60} = 50$

(A) Amount of lime required for raw water

$$=\frac{74}{100}\left[Mg^{+2}+HCO_3^-+CO_2+HCl\right]\times \text{Vol.of water}$$

$$=\frac{74}{100}[300+600+100+10]\times 2000$$

$$=\frac{74}{100}[1010\times 2000]$$

$$=1.495\times 10^6\,Mg=1.495\,Kg$$

Amount of lime required for excess of OH^- in treated water

$$=\frac{74}{100}[OH]^-\times \text{Vol of water}$$

$$=\frac{74}{100}\times 50\times 2000$$

= 74000 mg = .074 Kg

Total amount of lime = 1.495 + .074

= 1.569 Kg

(B) Soda Requires :

$$=\frac{106}{100}\left[Ca^{+2}+Mg^{+2}+HCl-HCO_3^-\right]\times \text{ Vol. of water}$$

$$=\frac{106}{100}[400+300+1-600]\times 2000$$

$$=\frac{106}{100}\times 110\times 2000$$

= 233200 Mg = 0.233 Kg

Amount of Soda required for excess OH^- and CO_3^{-2} ions in treated water

$$=\frac{106}{100}\left[OH^-+CO_3^{-2}\right]\times \text{Vol.of water}$$

$$=\frac{106}{100}[50+50]\times 2000$$

$$=\frac{106}{100}\times 100\times 2000$$

$$=21000\,Mg=0.212\,Kg$$

Total soda required = 0.233 + 0.212 Kg

= 0.445 Kg

Example 10 : Calculate the quantity of lime and sada required for softening 20,000 litres of hard water which analysed as follows

Analysis of raw water
Ca^{+2} = 400 ppm
Mg^{+2} = 288 ppm
HCO_3^- = 1586 ppm
CO_2 = 88 ppm
$FeSO_4$ $7H_2O$ = 139 ppm

Analysis of treated water
OH^- = 34 ppm
CO_3^{-2} = 30 ppm

Purity of lime is 94% and soda is 86%

Sol. Conversion to $CaCO_3$ equivalent

Substances	Amount (ppm)	Multiplication factor	$CaCO_3$equivalent
Ca^{+2}	400	$\frac{100}{140}$	$400\times\frac{100}{140}=1000$
Mg^{+2}	288	$\frac{100}{24}$	$288\times\frac{100}{24}=1200$
HCO_3^-	1586	$\frac{100}{122}$	$1586\times\frac{100}{122}=1300$
CO_2	88	$\frac{100}{44}$	$88\times\frac{100}{44}=200$
$FeSO_4\cdot 7H_2$	139	$\frac{100}{278}$	$139\times\frac{100}{278}=50$
Treated water			
OH^-	34	$\frac{100}{34}$	$34\times\frac{100}{34}=100$
CO_3^{-2}	30	$\frac{100}{60}$	$30\times\frac{100}{60}=50$

(A) Lime required : $\frac{74}{100}\left[Mg^{+2}+HCO_3^-+CO_2+FeSO_4\cdot 7H_2O\right]\times \text{Vol.of water}$

$$=\frac{74}{100}\times[1200+1300+200+50]\times 20,000$$

$$=\frac{74}{100}\times 2750\times 20,000$$

$= 40.70\,\text{Kg}$

Lime required for excess OH^- in treated water

$$= \frac{74}{100}[OH]^- \times \text{Vol.of water}$$

$$= \frac{74}{100} \times 100 \times 20000$$

$= 1.48$ Kg

Total amount of lime required = [40.70 + 1.48]

= 42.18 Kg

Total amount of line with purity 94% required for water

$$= 42.18 \times \frac{100}{94}$$

$= 44.87$ Kg

(B) Soda Required

$$= \frac{106}{100}\left[Ca^{+2} + Mg^{+2} + FeSO_4 \cdot 7H_2O - HCO_3^-\right] \times \text{Vol. of water}$$

$$= \frac{106}{100}[1000 + 1200 + 50 - 1300] \times 20000$$

$$= \frac{106}{100} \times 950 \times 20000$$

$= 20.14$ kg

Soda required for excess [OH^- and CO_3^{-2}] ions in treated water

$$= \frac{106}{100}\left[OH^- + CO_3^{-2}\right] \times \text{Vol.of water}$$

$$= \frac{106}{100}[100 + 50] \times 20000$$

$$= \frac{106}{100}[150] \times 20000$$

$= 3.18$ Kg

Total amount of soda requires = 20.14 + 3.18 = 23.32 Kg

Total amount of soda with purity 86% required

$$= 23.32 \times \frac{100}{86}$$

$= 27.12$ Kg

2.1.2 (b) Zeolite or permutit process

Zeolites are hydrated sodium alumino silicate minerals capable of exchanging (reversibly) its sodium ions for hardness producing cations present in hard water, The general formula of zelites is $Na_2O.Al_2O_3.xSiO_2.yH_2O$, where $x = 2$ to 10 and $y = 2$ to 6. Zeolites are also known as permutits. Zeolites are of two types:

(a) Natural zeolites: These are non porous and amorphous in nature. These are derived from green sands by washing, heating and treating with NaOH.

Example: Natrolite ($Na_2O.Al_2O_3.4SiO_2.2H_2O$)

(b) Synthetic zeolites: these are porous and posses a crystalline structure. They are prepared by heating together sodium carbonate (Na_2CO_3), alumina (Al_2O_3) and silica (SiO_2).

Principle:

Zeolite can be simply represented as Na_2Z where Z is the insoluble radical frame work. It holds sodium loosely. When hard water is passed through a bed of zeolite the hardness causing cations are exchanged with sodium of zeolite. So, sodium zeolite is converted to calcium and magnesium Zeolites. In the process, the water becomes free from hardness causing Ca and Mg ions.

$$CaCl_2 + Na_2Z \rightarrow CaZ + 2NaCl$$

$$MgCl_2 + Na_2Z \rightarrow MgZ + 2NaCl$$

$$CaSO_4 + Na_2Z \rightarrow CaZ + Na_2SO_4$$

$$MgSO_4 + Na_2Z \rightarrow MgZ + Na_2SO_4$$

When all sodium ions of sodium zeolite are exchanged with hardness causing cations of hard water then the zeolite bed loses its sodium exchange capacity and the Zeolite is said to be exhausted.

Regeneration of zeolite bed:

The regeneration is carried out by washing the bed with concentrated solution of sodium chloride (brine solution).

$$CaZ + 2NaCl \rightarrow Na_2Z + CaCl_2$$

$$MgZ + 2NaCl \rightarrow Na_2Z + MgCl_2$$

Process:

The hard water is percolated through the bed of zeolite housed in a cylindrical unit. The hardness causing cations Ca^{+2} and Mg^{+2} are retained by the zeolite as CaZ and MgZ and the outgoing water contains the sodium salts. When the zeolite is exhausted, it is regenerated using a 10% sodium chloride solution. Thus, the whole process involves alternate cycles of softening of water and the regeneration of zeolite bed. The regeneration involves backwashing, brining and rinsing before reuse. The residual hardness of water from this process is 0-15 ppm.

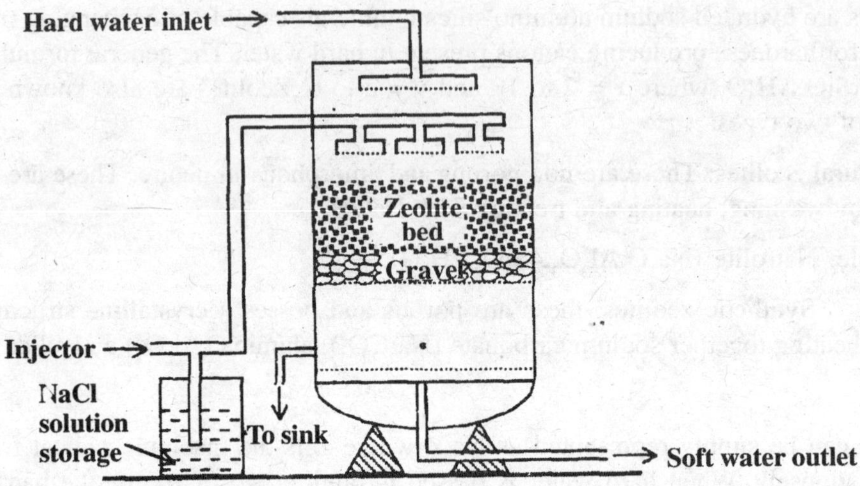

Fig.2.4 : Zeolite Process.

The amount of NaCl consumed for regeneration of exhausted zeolite and the hardness of water may be calculated using following formula:

$$\text{Hardness} = \frac{50 \times m \times V_2}{58.5 \times V_1}$$

where,

V_1 = Total volume of hard water to be softened in litres

V_2 = Total volume of NaCl used for regeneration in litres

m = Amount of NaCl present (g/L)

Advantages of Zeolite Process:

- o It is quite clean and rapid process which requires less time for softening.
- o The hardness is completely removed and water of about 10 ppm hardness is produced.
- o For maintenance and operations, less skill is required.
- o The equipment used is compact and occupies less space.
- o Impurities are not precipitated, hence there is no danger of sludge formation.

Limitation of Zeolite Process:

- The water to be softened should not be hot as the zeolite tends to dissolve in hot water.

- If the supplied water is turbid, the suspended matter must be removed before the water is fed to the zeolite bed. Otherwise, the pores of the zeolite bed will get clogged by the turbidity, thus making it inactive.
- If water contains large quantities of Mn^{+2}, they must be removed since these ions produce manganese and iron zeolites, which are very difficult to be regenerated.
- Mineral acids, if present, destroy the zeolite bed, and hence, must be neutralized before feeding the water into the zeolite bed.
- Anions are not removed by this process. Thus, the bicarbonates present in hard water get converted to $NaHCO_3$ which further dissociates to NaOH and CO_2 as follows:

$$NaHCO_3 \rightarrow NaOH + CO_2$$

Since NaOH causes caustic embrittlement and CO_2 makes the water acidic and corrosive, the temporary hardness should be removed before treatment.

- The higher cost of the plant and materials are also limiting factors.

Table 2.3: Comparision between Lime-Soda and Zeolite Process

S.N.	Lime-Soda	Zeolite
1	Plant occupies more space	Plant occupies less space
2	Treated water contains lesser amount of sodium salt	Treated water contain larger amount of sodium salts
3	Operation expanses are higher	Cheaper than lime soda process.
4	It can be used for treating acidic water	It cannot be used for treating acidic water because zeolite bed undergoes disintegration
5	May be used for water containing suspended material	Cannot be used for softening water that contain suspended material because pores of zeolite may be blocked hence bed loses its exchange capacity
6	Treated water contains lesser amount of dissolved solids	Treated water contains more dissolved solids
7	It involves problem of settling, coagulation, filtration and removal of precipitates	It does not involve such problems
8	Water of generally 15 – 50 ppm residual hardness is obtained	Residual hardness is 10 – 15 ppm

SOLVED NUMERICAL BASED ON ZEOLITE PROCESS

Example 1. The hardness of 1000 L of water was completely removed by zeolite softener. The zeolite has required 30L of NaCl solution containing 1500mg/L of NaCl for regeneration. Calculate the hardness of water sample. [RTU 2007]

Ans.

$$\text{Hardness} = \frac{50 \times m \times V_2}{58.5 \times V_1}$$

where V_1 = total volume of hard water to be softened

V_2 = total volume of NaCl containing *m* NaCl used for regeneration

m = 1500 mg/L

$$\text{Hence, Hardness} = \frac{50 \times 1500 \times 30}{58.5 \times 100} \frac{mg}{L}$$

Hardness = 38.46 ppm

Example 2. 10000 L hard water was made soft with zeolite. The exhausted zeolite required a total amount of 8L of NaCl solution containing 150 g/L for regeneration. Calculate the hardness of water.

Ans.

$$\text{Hardness} = \frac{50 \times m \times V_2}{58.5 \times V_1}$$

Where V_1 = total volume of hard water to be softened

V_2 = total volume of NaCl containing *m* NaCl used for regeneration

m = 1500 mg/L

$$\text{Hence, Hardness} = \frac{50 \times 150 \times 8}{58.5 \times 10000} \frac{g}{L}$$

$$= \frac{50 \times 150 \times 8 \times 10^3}{58.5 \times 10000} \frac{mg}{L}$$

Hardness = 102.6 ppm

Example 3. A zeolite softener was completely exhausted and then regenerated by passing 200 L of NaCl solution containing 100 g/L of NaCl. How many litres of water of hardness 500 ppm can be softened by the zeolite softener?

Ans. Hardness = $\dfrac{50 \times m \times V_2}{58.5 \times V_1}$

Where V_1 = Total volume of hard water to be softened

V_2 = Total volume of NaCl containing *m* NaCl used for regeneration

m = 1500 mg/L

Hence, $V_1 = \dfrac{50 \times m \times V_2}{58.5 \times hardness}$

$$V_1 = \frac{50 \times 100 \times 200}{58.5 \times 500} \frac{g \times L}{mg}$$

$$V_1 = \frac{50 \times 100 \times 200 \times 10^3}{58.5 \times 500} L$$

V_1 **= Total volume of hard water to be softened = 34188 L**

Example 4 : A zeolite softness was used to remove hardness of 80,000 litres of hard water completely the softwner required 450 litre of NaCl solution containing 16 g/L of NaCl for regneration. Calculate the hardness of hard water in ppm

Sol. Hardness (ppm) $= \dfrac{m \times V_2 \times 10^3 50}{V_1 \times 58.5}$

$$m = 16\,gm/L, V_2 = 450\,Lit, V_1 = 80{,}000\,litre$$

$$= \frac{16 \times 450 \times 10^3 \times 50}{80{,}000 \times 58.5}$$

$= 76.92$ ppm

2.1.2 (c) Ion Exchange Process {Deionization or Demineralization Process}:

The substances capable of exchange of its ions with ions of an electrolyte solution are called as ion exchangers. Ion exchange is a process by which ions held on porous, essentially insoluble solids are exchanged for ions in solution that is brought in contact with it.

Ion exchange resins are insoluble, cross- linked, high molecular weight organic polymers with a porous structure, and the function groups attached to the chains are responsible for the ion-exchange properties. They are classified as follows.

(1) Cation Exchange Resins: These type of exchangers exchange their cations (+ ions) with cations of electrolyte solution (in present case it is hard water containing Ca^{+2} and Mg^{+2} ions).

These are generally copolymers of styrene and divinyl benzene, which on sulphonation or carboxylation, become capable to exchange their hydrogen ions with the cations preaent in hard water. Such resins have acidic functional groups for exchanging their hydrogen ions with the cationic portion of hard water and hence they are termed as cation exchangers. These can be represented as R^-H^+ where R^- represents the insoluble polymer matrix.

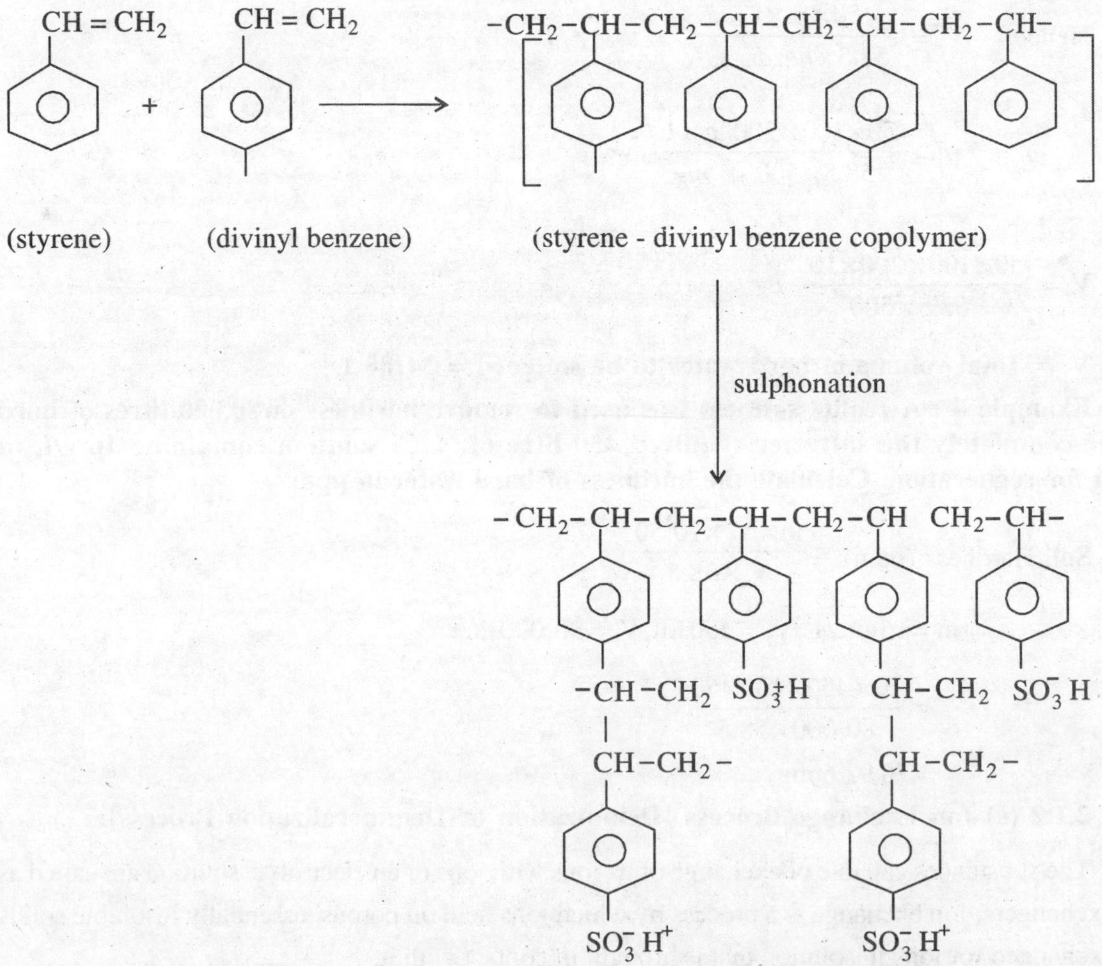

(cation exchanger)

(2) Anion Exchange Resins: These type of exchangers exchange their anions (– ions) with anions of electrolyte solution (in present case it is hard water containing Cl^-, SO_4^- and NO_3^- ions etc.).These type of copolymers contain basic functional groups such as amino or quaternary ammounium or quaternary phosphonium or tertiary sulphonium groups as an integral part of resin matrix. These, after treatment with dil. NaOH solution, become capable to exchange their OH^- ions with anions in water and therefore they are known as anion exchangers. These can be represented as R^+OH^- where R^+ represents the insoluble polymer matrix.

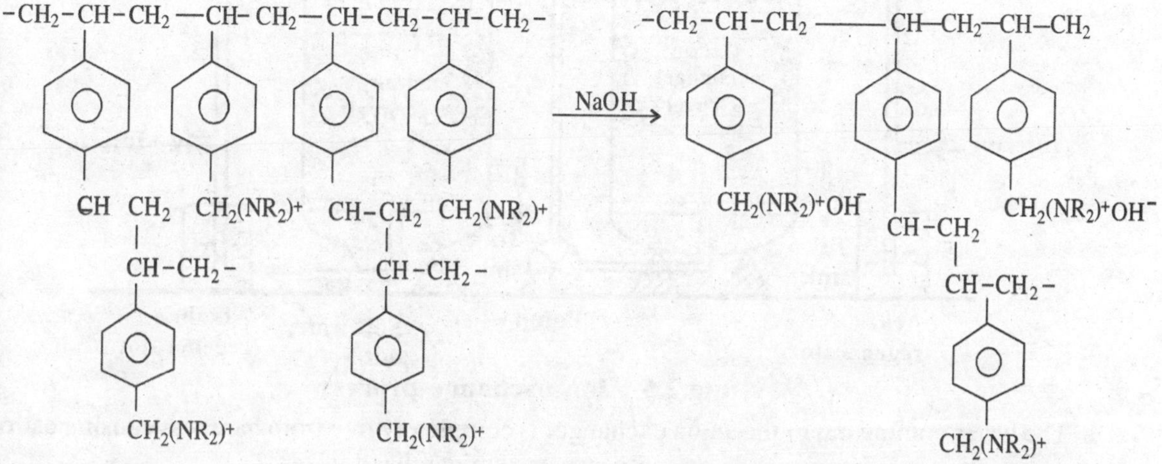

Process: In this method, hard water is passed through a tank having cation exchanger which absorbs all the cations (like Ca^{+2} and Mg^{+2} ions) present in water.

$$\underset{\text{Cation exchanger}}{2\,R^-H^+} + Ca^{+2} \rightarrow R^2Ca + 2H^+$$

$$\underset{\text{Cation exchanger}}{2\,R^-H^+} + Mg^{+2} \rightarrow R^2Mg + 2H^+$$

The cation free water is now passed through another tank having anion exchanger which absorbs all the anions (like Cl^-, SO_4^- and NO_3^- ions) present in the water.

$$\underset{\text{Anion Exchanger}}{R^+OH^-} + Cl^- \rightarrow RCl + OH^-$$

$$\underset{\text{Anion Exchanger}}{2R^+OH^-} + SO_4^{-2} \rightarrow R_2SO_4 + 2OH^-$$

$$\underset{\text{Anion Exchanger}}{R^+OH^-} + HCO_3^- \rightarrow RHCO_3 + OH^-$$

$$R^+OH^- + NO_3^- \rightarrow RNO_3 + OH^-$$

Anion Exchanger

H^+ and OH^- ions, released from both exchangers get combined to form water molecule.

$$H^+ \text{ and } OH^- \rightarrow H_2O$$

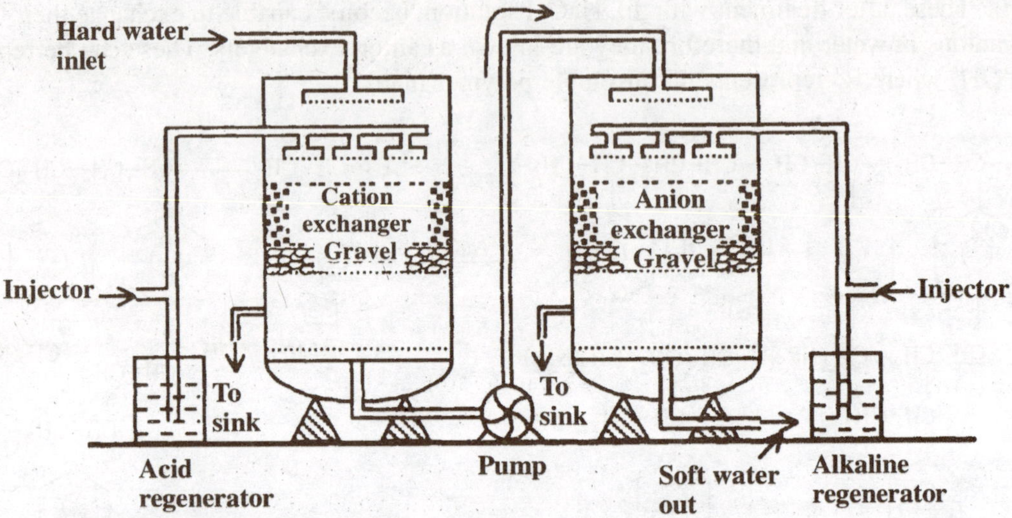

Fig.2.5 : Ion exchange process.

The water coming out of the anion exchanger is completely free from hardness causing cation and anions. Thus, it is known as deionised water or demineralized water.

Regeneration of Resins: Exhausted cation exchange resins are regenerated by passing i through a dilute solution of hydrochloric acid.

$$R^2Ca + 2H^+ \rightarrow 2\ R^-H^+ + Ca^{+2}$$

Exhausted Cation exchanger   Regenerated resin

Similarly, the exhausted anion exchange resins are regenerated by passing it through a dilut solution of sodium hydroxide.

$$RCl + OH^- \rightarrow R^+OH^- + Cl^-$$

Exhausted Anion Exchanger   Regenerated resin

Advantages of Ion Exchange Process:

- Highly acidic or alkaline water can be treated by this process.
- This produces water of very low hardness (nearly 2 ppm)

Disadvantages of Ion Exchange Process:

- The equipment is costly and more expensive chemicals are required.
- If water contains turbidity, then the output of the process is reduced.

Mixed bed Deioniser:

This consists of single cylinder containing an intimate mixture of strongly acidic cation exchang and strongly basic anionic exchanger. Originally, the cation exchanger is in the H^+ form. When har water containing say $CaCl_2$ is poured into the mixed resin bed from the top, pure water flows out at the bottom. Each Ca^{+2} ion displaces two H^+ ions and each Cl^- displaces one OH^- ions. Exactly equal numbers of H^+ and OH^- ions are produced which combine to from water.

To regenerate a mixed bed deionizer, it is first necessary to separate the two resins. Cation exchanger and anoin exchanger are then regenerated separately by washing with H_2SO_4 and NaOH respectively.

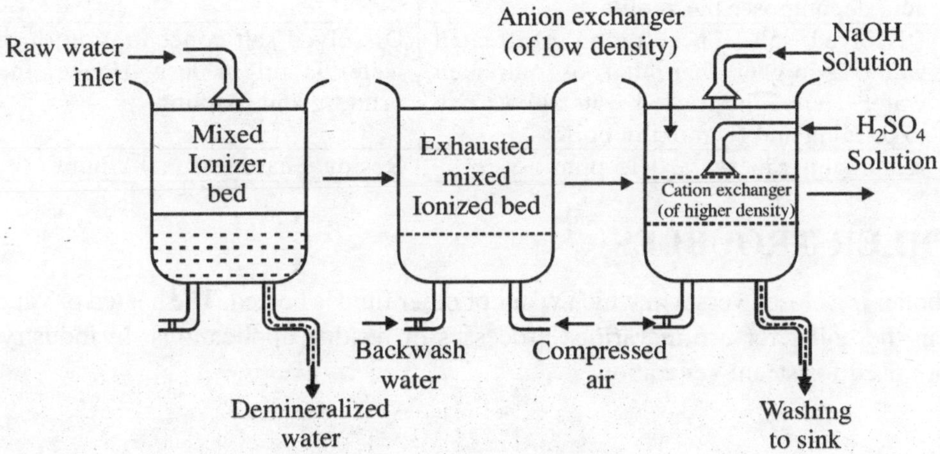

Fig. Regeneratin of mixed bed ion exchanger

Mixed bed deionizers are comparatively more convenient to use and are more efficient. But they are more costly too. It is widely used for purifying water used in chemical laboratories.

Table 2.4: Comparison between lime-Soda and Ion exchange process

S.N.	Lime-Soda Process	Ion exchange Process
1	It involves problem of settling, coagulation, filtration and removal of precipitates	It does not involve such problems
2	Capital cost is low	Capital cost is high
3	Automation is not possible	Automation is possible
4	Hardness causing salts are removed.	All salts are removed.
5	Turbid water can also be treated.	Turbidity clogs the pores of the ion exchange resins. Hence, such water cannot be treated.
6	Iron containing water can be treated.	Iron containing water cannot be treated because iron is irreversibly exchanged.
7	Lime and soda are required.	Cation and anion exchange resins are required
8	Residual hardness is 15-50 ppm	Residual hardness is 0-2 ppm

Table 2.5: Comparison between Zeolite and Ion exchange Process

S.N.	Zeolite Process	Ion exchange Process
1.	Operating expenses are low	Operating expenses are high
2	Plant occupies less space	Plant occupies large space
3	Exchanged only cation.	Exchanges cations as well as anions.
4	Acidic water cannot be treated because acid decomposes the zeolite.	Acidic water can be treated.
5	Dissolved salt concentration of treated water is higher than that of untreated water. Hence the treated water gives rise to priming and foaming in boilers.	Dissolved salt concentration of the treated water is nil or less. Hence, there is no priming and foaming.
6	Residual hardness is 10-15 ppm	Residual hardness is 0-2 ppm

2.2 BOILER TROUBLES

A boiler is a closed vessel in which water or other fluid is heated. The heated or vaporized fluid exits from the boiler for use in various processes or heating applications. In industry, generally boilers are used for steam generation.

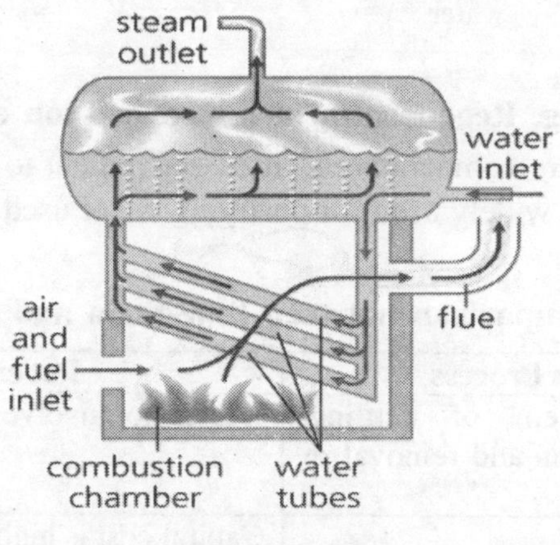

Fig. 2.7: Boiler

Boiler feed water should be of very good quality because it is directly related to safety, efficiency and economy of boiler. Various types of problems occur when water used in boiler for steam generation has hardness producing substances. These problems are called as boiler troubles. These are classified into following categories:

a. Sludge and scales

b. Caustic embrittlement

c. Boiler corrosion

d. Priming and foaming

2.2.1 Sludge and Scale Formation

Boilers are used for steam generation. When hard water is used in boiler, concentration of dissolved salts increases on continuous evaporation. When concentration of these salts reaches on saturation point they start precipitating. Two types of precipitates are formed during this process.

(i) Sludge: If the precipitates are soft, loose and slimy in nature, they are known as sludge. It is formed due to presence of hardness producing substances like $MgCl_2$, $MgCO_3$, $MgSO_4$ and $CaCl_2$. It is formed at competitively colder portions of the boiler and collects in the areas where flow rate of water is competitively slow (bends, plug openings, pipe connections etc.). It can be removed easily by scrapping off with brush.

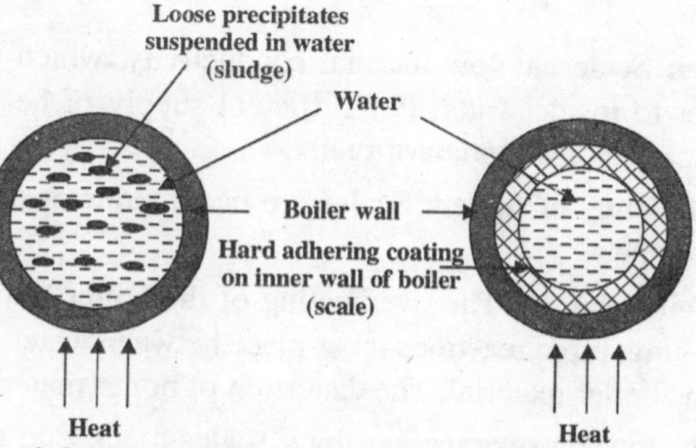

Fig. 2.8 (a) Sludge in Boiler (b) Scale in Boiler

Disadvantages:

- Sludge are poor conductor of heat, so they waste a large portion of generated heat.
- If sludge are formed along with scales, then sludge are entrapped in scales and get deposited as scales which are very difficult to remove.
- Excessive sludge formation settle in low flow rate water circulation regions such as pipe connections, plug openings etc. thus causing choking of pipes.

Preventions:

- Sludge formation can be avoided by using soft water in boiler for steam generation.
- Formed sludge can be removed by blow-down operation.

Blow-Down Operation: It is removal of concentrated portion of water, and replacement of it by fresh water. The fresh water which is added to make up the volume is known as make up water.

(i) Scale: These are hard and sticky precipitates formed during steam generation in boiler, which adhere firmly to the inner surfaces of the boiler. It cannot be easily removed by scrapping off with brush or with help of hammer and chisel. These may be formed due to the following reactions inside the boiler:

- **Decomposition of calcium carbonate:** When water containing bicarbonates is heated in boiler, the bicarbonates are converted into insoluble carbonates.

$$Ca(HCO_3)_2 \rightarrow \underset{\text{Scale}}{CaCO_3 \downarrow} + H_2O + CO_2 \uparrow$$

- **Hydrolysis of magnesium salts:** Dissolved magnesium salts unergo hydrolysis forming precipitates of $Mg(OH)_2$.

$$MgCl_2 + 2H_2O \rightarrow \underset{\text{Scale}}{Mg(OH)_2\downarrow} + 2HCl\uparrow$$

- **Deposition of calcium sulphate:** The solubility of calcium sulphate in water decreases with rise in temperature. In other words, $CaSO_4$ is soluble in cold water, but almost insoluble in very hot water. Thus, $CaSO_4$ gets precipitated as hard scale on the hot regions of the boiler.
- **Presence of Silica:** (SiO_2) even present in small quantity, deposits as silicates of calcium ($CaSiO_3$) or magnesium ($MgSiO_3$) and sticks firmly with the inner surface of boiler.

Disadvantage:

- **Wastage of fuel:** Scale has low thermal conductivity, which results in decreased rate of heat transfer from boiler to inside water. For sufficient supply of heat to the water excessive or overheating is done i.e. more consumption of fuel.
- **Decrease in efficiency of boiler:** Scales are bad conductor of heat, so they waste a very large portion of generated heat.
- **Lowering of boiler safety:** The overheating of the boiler leads to distortion of the boiler material. Due to overheating, rapid reactions takes place between water and iron at high temperature causing weakening of the boiler material. The distortion of boiler material is known as bagging.
- Danger of explosion: on overheating thick scales crack due to uneven expansion. Water comes suddenly in contact with overheated metal and large quantity of steam is formed instantaneously. This leads to development of very high pressure which may cause explosion of boiler.

Removal of scales:

- With the help of scraper or wire brush if scales are soft.
- By giving thermal shocks (i.e. heating the boiler and then suddenly cooling with cold water), if scales are brittle.
- By dissolving them with addition of chemicals, if they are adherent and hard. Thus, calcium carbonate scales can be dissolved by adding 5-10% HCl. Calcium sulphate scale can be dissolved by adding EDTA, with which they form soluble complexes.
- By frequent blow-down operation, if the scales are loosely adherent.

Prevention of scale formation: There are two methods for prevention of scale formation:

(a) Internal treatment: The internal treatment of boiler feed water refers to the treatment of water in the boiler itself. It involves addition of certain chemicals directly to the water to remove the scale forming salts, either by precipitation of these salts which can be removed by blow down operation or by converting these salts into soluble substances which will stay in dissolved form in water and thus do not cause any harm. The methods used for internal treatment of water are as follows:

(i) Colloidal Conditioning: Scale formation can be reduced by introducing colloidal substances like kerosene, tannin, agar-agar etc. to the boiler water. These substances act as protective coatings over the scale forming particles and thus produces non-sticky, loose precipitates which can easily be removed by blow-down operation..

(ii) Carbonate Conditioning: Scale formation can be avoided in boilers by adding sodium carbonate to boiler water. The scale forming salt (like calcium) is converted into calcium carbonate which can be removed easily.

$$CaSO_4 + Na_2CO_3 \rightarrow CaCO_3 + Na_2SO_4$$

(iii) Phosphate Conditioning: In boiler, scale formation can be avoided by adding sodium phosphate. It reacts with calcium and magnesium salts in the boiler water, forming easily removal soft sludge of calcium salts in the boiler water forming easily removal soft sludges of calcium and magnesium phosphates. The trisodium phosphate (Na_3PO_4), disodium hydrogen phosphate (Na_2HPO_4) and sodium dihydrogen phosphate (NaH_2PO_4) are generally used for this purpose.

$$3CaSO_4 + 2Na_3PO_4 \rightarrow Ca_3(PO_4)_2 + 3Na_2SO_4$$

(iv) Calgon Conditioning: This involves the addition of calgon or sodium hexametaphosphate $\{Na_2[Na_4(PO_3)_6]\}$ to boiler water. It interacts with calcium sulphate and prevents the scale and sludge formation by forming a highly soluble complex.

$$2CaSO_4 + Na_2[Na_4(PO_3)_6] \rightarrow \underset{\text{soluble complex}}{Na_2[Ca_2(PO_3)_6]} + 2Na_2SO_4$$

(v) Treatment with Sodium Aluminate : When sodium aluminate ($NaAlO_2$) is treated with boiler water, it gets hydrolysed to give sodium hydroxide and precipitate of aluminum hydroxide.

$$NaAlO_2 + H_2O \rightarrow NaOH + Al(OH)_3$$

The formed NaOH reacts with magnesium salts.

$$2NaOH + MgCl_2 \rightarrow 2NaCl + Mg(OH)_2$$

The flocculent precipitates of $Mg(OH)_2$ and $Al(OH)_3$ are adsorbed on finely suspended and colloidal impurities like sand and oil drops and can be removed by blow-down operation.

(b) External Treatment: The external treatment of water is performed outside the boiler. It can be done by following methods.

- o Lime soda process
- o Zeolite process
- o Ion-exchange process

We have already learned these methods in previous section.

Table 2.6: Differences between slude and scale

S.N.	Sludge	Scale
1	They are soft, loose and slimy precipitate floating in boiler water.	They are hard deposits adhering to the inner walls of boiler.
2	They can be removed easily.	They are very difficult to remove.
3	Sludge are formed by substances like $CaCl_2$, $MgSO_4$, $MgCl_2$, $MgCO_3$ etc.	These are formed by substances like $CaSO_4$, $Mg(OH)_2$ etc.
4	They decrease the efficiency of boiler but are less dangerous.	They decrease the efficiency of the boiler and there is chance of explosion also.
5	These are generally formed at comparatively colder regions of boiler.	These are formed at heated portion of the boiler.

Though, formation of sludge and scale both is undesirable but the formation of scale is far more dangerous than sludge as the sludge can be removed easily compare to scale.

2.2.2 Caustic embrittlement:

Caustic embrittlement is a type of boiler corrosion due to which boiler material becomes brittle in presence of high concentration of caustic and static stress. It is characterized by the formation of intergranular cracks on the boiler metal particularly at places of high stress like bends, joints etc. During softening by lime-soda process, residual sodium carbonate is usually present in softened water. Under the condition of high pressure in boiler sodium carbonate decomposes to form sodium hydroxide and CO_2.

$$Na_2CO_3 + H_2O \rightarrow 2NaOH + CO_2$$

Sodium hydroxide thus produced makes the water more alkaline or caustic. The caustic water flows into the hair line cracks present in the inner walls of the boiler by capillary action. On progressive heating and hence evaporation, the concentration of dissolved sodium hydroxide increases which attacks the iron in boiler material and converts it into sodium ferrate. Hence, embrittlement of stressed boiler takes place causing even failure of boiler. This is known as caustic embrittlement.

Caustic embrittlement arises due to setting up of concentration cell. The stressed iron part surrounded by conc. NaOH acts as anode while iron surrounded by dilute NaOH acts as cathode. The stressed part which acts as anode undergoes corrosion.

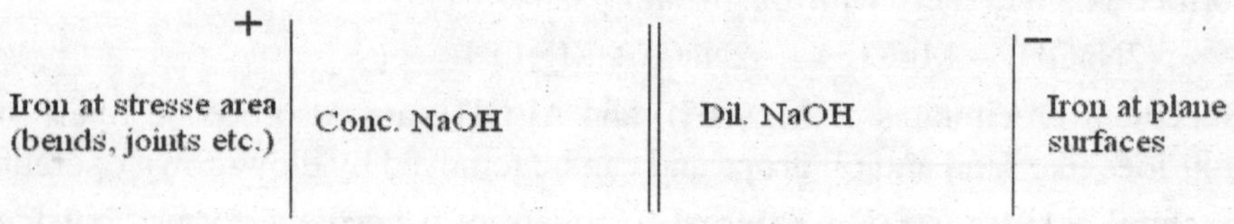

Prevention: Caustic embrittlement can be prevented by:

- Using sodium phosphate as softening agent instead of sodium carbonate in external treatment.
- Adding sodium sulphate to boiler water which clogs the hair cracks , reducing the chance of caustic embrittlement.
- Addition of tannin or lignin to boiler water blocks the hair cracks thus preventing the infiltration of caustic soda.

2.2.3 Boiler corrosion

"Loss of boiler body material or its useful properties by chemical or electrochemical interactions with its environment is known as boiler corrosion."

Corrosion in boiler may be due to the following reasons:

(i)Dissolved carbon dioxide: CO2 gas dissolved in water forms carbonic acid which has a corrosive effect on boiler material like any other acid. CO2 is also produced in water by decomposition of bicarbonates.

$$Mg(HCO_3)_2 \rightarrow \underset{\text{ppt.}}{Mg(OH)_2} + CO_2 + H_2O$$

$$Ca(HCO_3)_2 \rightarrow \underset{\text{ppt.}}{CaCO_3} \downarrow + CO_2 \uparrow + H_2O$$

$$CO_2 + H_2O \rightarrow \underset{\text{Carbonic acid}}{H_2CO_3}$$

Removal:

- Mechanical deaeration with O_2.
- By addition of calculated amount of ammonium hydroxide (NH_4OH).

$$CO_2 + 2NH_4OH \rightarrow (NH_4)_2CO_3 + H_2O$$

(ii) Dissolved oxygen: Dissolved oxygen is the most important factor causing boiler corrosion. Water contains approximately 8 *ppm* of dissolved oxygen at room temperature. Dissolved oxygen present in water attacks the boiler material according to the following reactions:

$$2Fe + O_2 + 2H_2O \rightarrow 2Fe(OH)_2$$

$$2Fe(OH)_2 + O_2 + 2H_2O \rightarrow 4Fe(OH)_3 \rightarrow \underset{\text{Rust}}{[Fe_2O_3 . xH_2O]}$$

Removal:

- O_2 is removed by adding oxygen scavengers like sodium sulphite (Na_2SO_3), sodium sulphide (Na_2S), hydrazine (N_2H_4) etc.

$$2Na_2SO_3 + O_2 \rightarrow 2Na_2SO_4$$

$$Na_2S + 2O_2 \rightarrow Na_2SO_4$$

$$N_2H_4 + O_2 \rightarrow N_2 + 2H_2O$$

Nitrogen is harmless, consequently hydrazine removes oxygen without increasing the concentration of dissolved salts/solids.

- It is also removed by mechanical de-aeration.

(iii) By acids from dissolved salts: $MgCl_2$ on hydrolysis forms HCl. The librated acid corrodes the boiler material as follows:

$$MgCl_2 + 2H_2O \rightarrow Mg(OH)_2 + 2HCl$$

$$Fe + 2HCl \rightarrow FeCl_2 + H_2$$

$$FeCl_2 + 2H_2O \rightarrow Fe(OH)_2 + 2HCl$$

HCl is produced in chain like manner and cause extensive corrosion.

Removal: This type of corrosion can be prevented by adding alkali to neutralize the acid formed.

2.2.4 Priming and foaming

When production of steam in boiler is rapid, then some droplets of liquid water are carried alongwith the steam. The process of formation of wet steam is called as priming.

Priming is caused by:

- The presence of large amount of dissolved solids
- High steam velocity
- Sudden boiling
- Improper boiler design and
- Sudden increase in steam production rate

Priming can be minimized by

- Proper designing
- Maintaining low water level
- Controlled rate of steam velocity
- Efficient softening

Formation : The formation of persistent bubbles in boiler water which do not break easily is known as foaming. Foaming is generally caused by the presence of oils and alkalis in water (which reduce the surface tension of water).foaming can be avoided by:

- o Addition of antifoaming agents like castor oil.
- o Removal of foaming agents (oil/alkali) from water.

Priming and foaming usually occur together. These create problems because:

(1) Dissolved salts in boiler water are carried by the wet steam to super heater and turbine blades, where they get deposited as water evaporates.

(2) Dissolved salts may enter to the other machinery parts, where steam is being used, thereby decreasing the life of machinery.

(3) The maintenance of the boiler pressure becomes difficult because of improper judgment of actual height of water column.

Review Questions

1. State the zeolite process for the removal of hardness of water. Discuss its merits over lime-soda process. **[RTU 2010]**
2. What are boiler troubles? Discuss their consequences. **[RTU 2010]**
3. Write short notes on:
   (i) Demineralization process of water softening
   (ii) Caustic embrittlement
   (iii) Carry over in steam boiler **[RTU 2010]**
4. What is softening of water? Describe deionization method of water softening with diagram.
5. Describe Lime-soda method for softening hard water. Discuss the advantages of the process and chemistry involved in it. **[RTU 2008]**
6. How is true exhausted zeolite bet regenerated? Give the merits and demerits of zeolite process.

7. Explain the zeolite method of water softening in detail. Give also the comparison of zeolite method with lime soda process. **[RTU 2009]**
8. Explain scale formation and sludge formation in boiler. How are they removed?
9. Write short notes on formation of scale and sludge formation. **[RTU 2008]**
10. Explain caustic embrittlement in boiler and how it can be avoided.
11. Discuss the disadvantage of using hard water in Boiler. Explain various internal treatment methods by which hardness of water can be minimized. **[RTU 2007]**
12. Compare lime-soda, zeolite and ion-exchange methods for softening of hard water.

Numerical Problems

1. A sample of water contains following impurities:
   $Mg(HCO_3)_2$ = 73 mg/L
   $CaCl_2$ = 222 mg/L
   $MgSO_4$ = 120 mg/L
   $Ca(NO_3)_2$ = 164 mg/L
   Calculate the quantity of lime (74% pure) and soda (90% pure) needed for softening 5,000 L of water. **[Ans.** L = 1Kg; S = 2.356 Kg**]**
2. Calculate the amount of lime and Soda needed for the treatment of 60,000 litres of water containing:
   CO_2 = 20 mg/L
   $Ca(HCO_3)_2$ = 20 mg/L
   $Mg(HCO_3)_2$ = 25 mg/L
   $Al_2(SO_4)_3$ = 40 mg/L
   $MgCl_2$ = 12 mg/L
   HCl = 8.4 mg/L.
   [Ans. L = 6.716 Kg; S = 33.6 Kg**]**
3. Calculate the amount of lime (88.3% pure) and Soda (99.2% pure) needed to soften of 24,000 litres of water per day for a year containing the following:
   $MgCO_3$ = 0.42 mg/L
   $MgCl_2$ = 0.76 mg/L
   $MgSO_4$ = 0.90 mg/L
   $CaCO_3$ = 1.85 mg/L
   $CaSO_4$ = 0.34 mg/L
   NaCl = 2.34 mg/L
   SiO_2 = 2.32 mg/L. **[Ans.** L = 32.3 Kg; S = 16.55 Kg**]**
4. Calculate the amount of lime and Soda required for the treatment of 10,000 litres of water containing: Ca^{2+} = 16 ppm; Mg^{2+} = 4.8 ppm; HCO_3^- = 73.2 ppm.
   [Ans. L = 592 g; S = Nil**]**
5. Calculate the amount of lime and soda required for softening of 15,000 litres of water, which analyzed as follows: temporary hardness = 20 ppm; permanent hardness = 15 ppm; permanent Mg hardness = 10 ppm. **[Ans.** L = 330 g; S = 238.5 g**]**

6. Calculate the amount of lime and soda required per litres for the chemical treatment of water containing: : Ca^{2+} = 80 ppm; Mg^{2+} = 36 ppm; HCO_3^- = 244 ppm; K^+ = 39 ppm; $FeSO_4.7H_2O$ added as coagulant = 69.5 ppm. **[Ans.** L = 277.5 mg; S = 185.5 mg]

7. Calculate the amount of lime and soda required for softening 20,000 litres of hard water, which analysed as follows:

   Analysis of raw water: Ca^{+2} = 380 ppm; Mg^{+2} = 144 ppm; HCO_3^- = 1586 ppm; Dissolved CO_2 = 110 ppm; $Fe_2SO_4.7H_2O$ = 278 ppm; NaCl = 58.5 ppm; Fe_2O_3 = 160 ppm.

   Analysis of treated water: OH^- = 34 ppm; CO_3^{-2} =30 ppm.

   [Ans. L = 34.48 kg; S = 10.6 kg]

8. A sample of water contains following impurities: $MgCO_3$ = 42 mg/L; HCO_3^- = 122 mg/L; $MgSO_4$ = 120 mg/L; $CaCl_2$ = 111 mg/L; $Al_2(SO_4)_3$ = 228 mg/L and NaCl = 35 mg/L. Calculate the quantity of lime and soda required for complete softening of 5000 litres water.

   [Ans. L = 2.25 kg; S = 1.59 kg]

9. A zeolite softener was used to remove the hardness of 90,000 litres of hard water completely. The softener required 450 litres of NaCl solution containing 16 g/L of NaCl for regeneration. Calculate the hardness of hard water in ppm. **[Ans.** 68.3 ppm]

10. An exhausted zeolite softener was regenerated by 300 litres of NaCl solution containing 55 g/L of NaCl. How many litres of hard water of hardness 220 mg/L can be softened by zeolite softener. **[Ans.** 64102 L]

❑❑❑

Unit - 3
POLYMER

3.1 INTRODUCTION

The term 'Polymer' is made up of two Greek words - 'Poly' means many and 'meros' means parts or units.Thus, polymers are macromolecules consisting of large number of simple repeating units. These repeating units are known as 'monomers' (mono means single) and the process of formation of polymers by combination of monomeric units are known as 'Polymerisation'. For e.g. Polythene is a polymer, which is formed by linking together of large number of monomeric units of ethene.

$$n\ \underset{Ethene}{CH_2=CH_2} \xrightarrow{Polymerisation} \underset{Polythene}{-\!\!\left[CH_2-CH_2\right]_n\!\!-}$$

Polymers are essential part of our life. Various products we are using in our daily life are polymers. Examples : Food (carbohydrate, proteins), rubber, plastics, clothes (Nylone, terylene), polythene, PVC, paper (celllose) etc.

3.1.1 Degree of Polymerisation

"The number of monomers combined to form polymer is known as degree of polymerisation." It is denoted by n :

$$n\ \underset{Ethene}{CH_2=CH_2} \xrightarrow{Polymerisation} \underset{Polythene}{-\!\!\left[CH_2-CH_2\right]_n\!\!-}$$

In this example, n monomeric units are combining to form polymer. Hence, the degree of polymerisation is n.

3.1.2 Functionality

The number of bonding sites present in a monomer is known as its functionality.

For e.g. Ethene $(CH_2=CH_2)$, when double bond breaks, there are two active sites at which another ethene molecule may combine. Hence, functionality of ethene monomer is two or in other words ethene is a bifunctional monomer.

$$CH_2=CH_2 \longrightarrow -CH_2-CH_2-$$

bonding sites

If a molecule is monofunctional (i.e. it has only one bonding site), it forms dimer not polymer.

$$M - + - M \longrightarrow \underset{Dimer}{M - M}$$

Thus, for a molecule to act as a monomeric unit, it must be bifunctional in nature, i.e. it must have at least two bonding sites.

The structure of a polymer is depend upon the functionality of monomeric units which are joining together. If bifunctional monomers combine together linear polymer is formed. When trifunctional monomer is mixed with bifunctional monomers branched chain polymer is formed. Combination of trifunctional monomer forms cross linked polymer. If B and T are bifunctional and trifunctional monomers respectively, then :

$$n\,B \xrightarrow{Polymerisation} \underset{Linear\ polymer}{-B-B-B-B-}$$

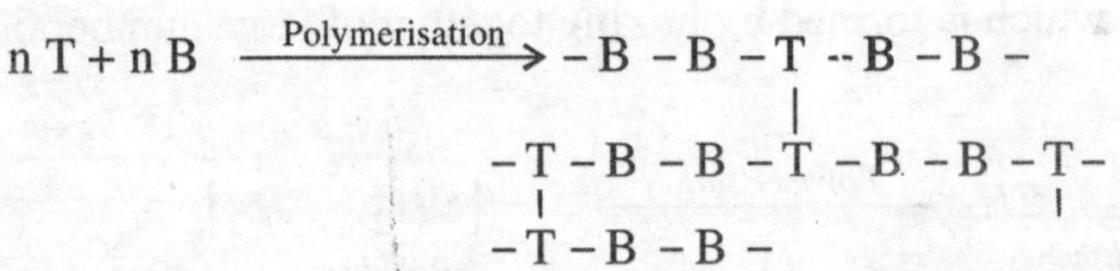

Branched Chain Polymer

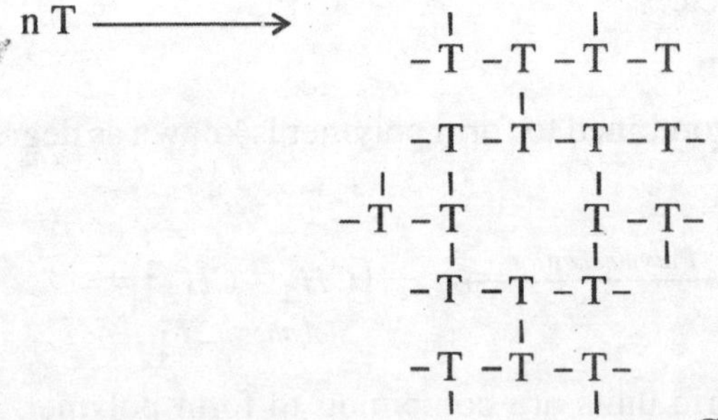

Cross linked Polymer

3.2 CLASSIFICATION OF POLYMERS

On various basis polymers may be classified as follow :

3.2.1 On the basis of origin

Polymers can be classified into two types on the basis of their origin : (i) Natural polymers (ii) Synthetic polymers

(i) Natural Polymers : Polymers which are obtained from the natural sources are called natural polymers.

e.g. Cellulose, starch, natural rubber etc.

(ii) Synthetic Polymers : Polymers which are prepared synthetically in laboratory are called synthetic polymers.

e.g. PVC, Nylon, polythene, bakelite etc.

3.2.2 On the basis of type of monomers

There are two types of Polymers :

(i) Homopolymers (ii) Copolymers

(i) Homopolymer : In these types of polymers all monomeric units are same. This type of polymers are formed by the polymerisation of one type of monomer.

$$nA \rightarrow [A]_n$$

$$nB \rightarrow [B]_n$$

e.g. Polythene, PVC etc.

(ii) Copolymer : In these type of polymers monomeric units are different. This type of polymers are formed by polymerisation of more than one type of monomer.

$$nA + nB \rightarrow [A-B]_n$$

e.g. Nylon, Terylene

Depending upon the arrangement of monomer units A and B in the polymeric chain, co-polymer may be classified into following categories :

(a) Alternating copolymers : Monomers are arranged alternatively in the polymeric chain.

$$-A-B-A-B-A-B-A-B-$$

e.g. Polyester, Polyamide.

(b) Random copolymers : Monomers are arranged randomly.

$$-A-A-B-A-B-B-A-B-A-B-$$

(c) Block copolymer : A block of one type of monomer is followed by the block of other type of monomer which is further followed by first type of monomer.

$$\underbrace{-A-A-A-}_{Ist\ block}\ \underbrace{B-B}_{IInd\ Block}\ \underbrace{-A-A-A}_{Ist\ Block}-B-B-A-A-A-$$

(d) Graft copolymers : One type of monomer segment is grafted on the main chain of another type of monomer segment.

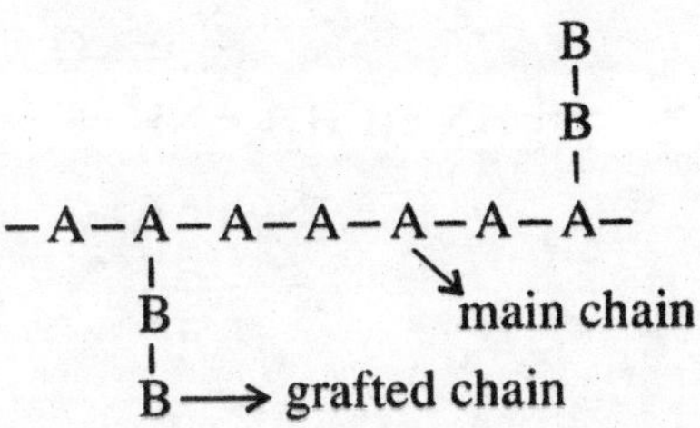

3.2.3 On the basis of mode of synthesis

There are two types of polymers in this category :

(1) Addition Polymers

(2) Condensation Polymers

(1) Addition Polymers : Polymers which are formed by the polymerisation of monomers without elimination of atoms or groups are known addition polymers.

e.g. Polythene :

$$n\,CH_2=CH_2 \xrightarrow{\text{Polymerisation}} \underset{\text{Polythene}}{\left[CH_2-CH_2 \right]}$$

$$nCH_2=\underset{\displaystyle CH_3}{\underset{|}{CH}} \xrightarrow{\text{Polymerisation}} \left[CH_2=\underset{\displaystyle CH_3}{\underset{|}{CH}} \right]_n$$

Plystyrene :

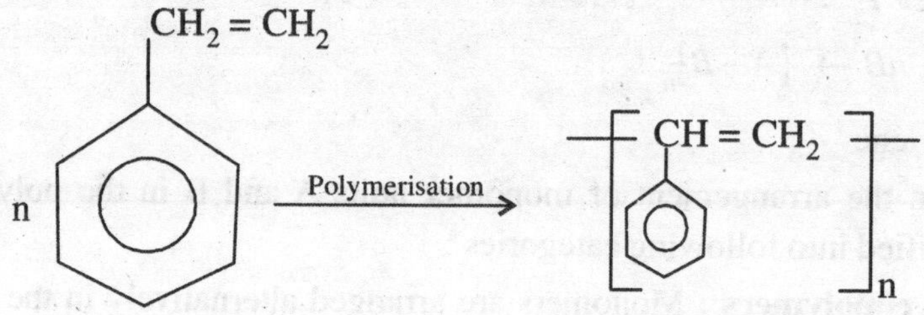

styrene polystrene

(2) Condensation Polymers : Polymers which are formed by the polymerisation of monomers with elimination of small molecules (like H_2O, NH_3, HCl etc.) are known as condensation polymers.

e.g. Polyamide

$$\underset{\text{Hexamethylene diamine}}{n\ H_2N-(CH)_6-NH_2} + \underset{\text{adipic acid}}{n\ HOOC-(CH_2)_4-COOH}$$

$$\downarrow \text{Polymerisation}, \ -2n\ H_2O$$

$$\underset{\text{Nylon 6 : 6}}{\left[HN-(CH_2)_6-NH-\overset{O}{\overset{\|}{C}}-(CH_2)_4-\overset{O}{\overset{\|}{C}} \right]_n}$$

Polyester :

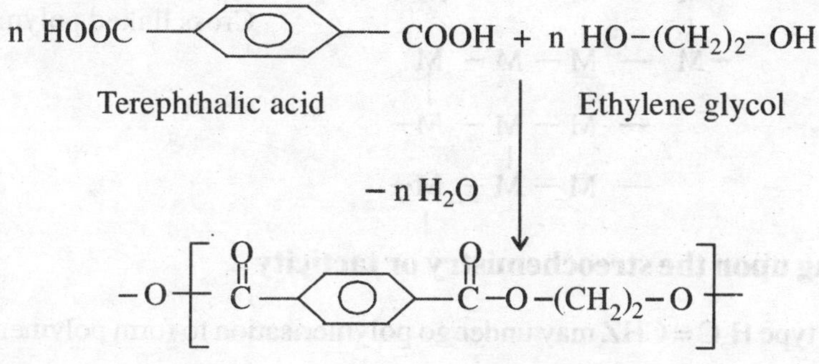

Terylene

3.2.4 On the basis of structure

Depending upon the structure of polymer, these are three types of polymers :

(i) Linear chain (ii) Branched chain (iii) Cross linked polymer

(i) Linear Chain : Linear chain polymers are those in which monomeric units are linked in chain. These types of polymers have high density, high tensile strength and high melting point.

e.g. Polythene, Nylons, Polyesters etc.

– M – M – M – M – M – Linear chain

where M is monomeric unit.

In these type of polymers, monomers are bifunctional.

(ii) Branched Chain Polymers : These type of polymers have side chains or branches in addition to their main chain. Branched chain polymers are formed when bifunctional and trifunctional monomers are joined together.

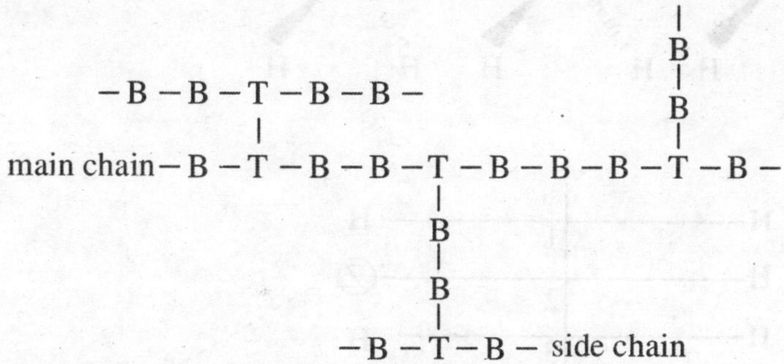

Where B is bifunctional monomer and T is trifunctional monomer.

e.g. Glycogen, starch etc.

(iii) Cross linked polymers : In these types of polymers, monometric units are cross linked to form a three dimensional network. When functionality of monomers are three or more then cross linked polymers are formed.

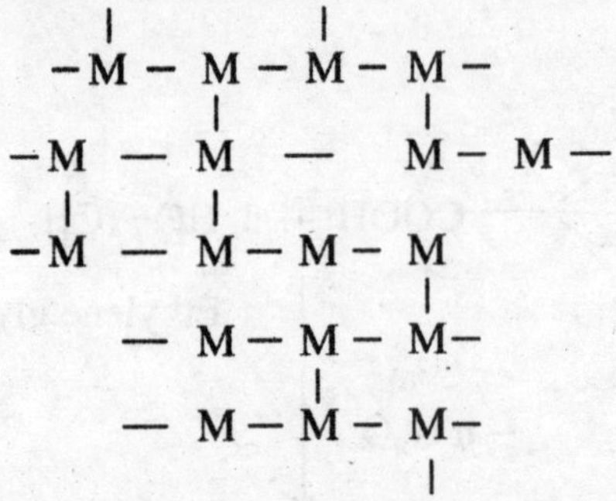

Cross linked polymer

3.2.5 Depending upon the streochemistry or tacticity

Alkenes of type $H_2C = CHZ$ may under go polymerisation to form polymers $(H_2C - CHZ)_n$ in which the functional group – Z are on the :

(a) same side of the main carbon chain or

(b) alternate side of the main carbon chain or

(c) randomly arranged along the main carbon chain.

polymers thus formed have different configuration or in other words orientation of monomeric units in polymeric chain may differ. This property is known as tacticity of polymer.

Depending upon tacticity, polymers are of three types :

(i) Isotactic (ii) Syndiotactic (iii) Atactic

(i) Isotactic : Polymers in which all the functional group Z, are on the same side of the main carbon chain are known as isotactic polymers. e.g. Cis-polyisoprene.

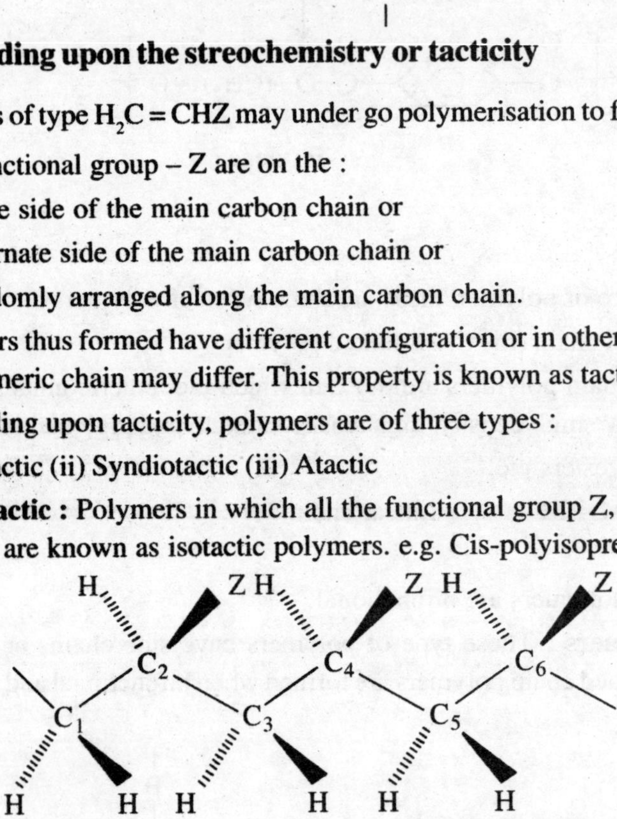

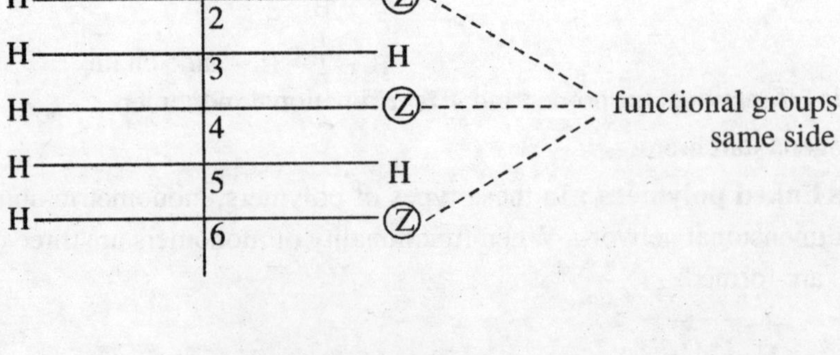

(ii) Sydiotactic : If the functional group 'Z' are on the alternate side of the main carbon chain the polymers are known as syndiotactic polymers.

e.g. trans-polyisoprene.

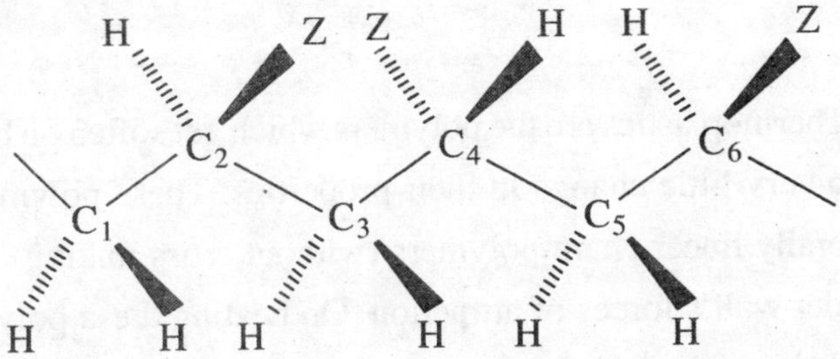

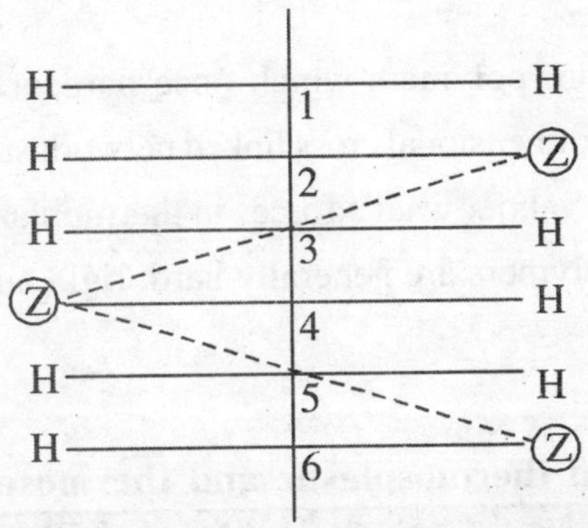

functional group Z on alternate side

(iii) Atactic : If the functional group 'Z' are arranged randomly along the main chain they are known as atactic polymers.

e.g. Polypropylene.

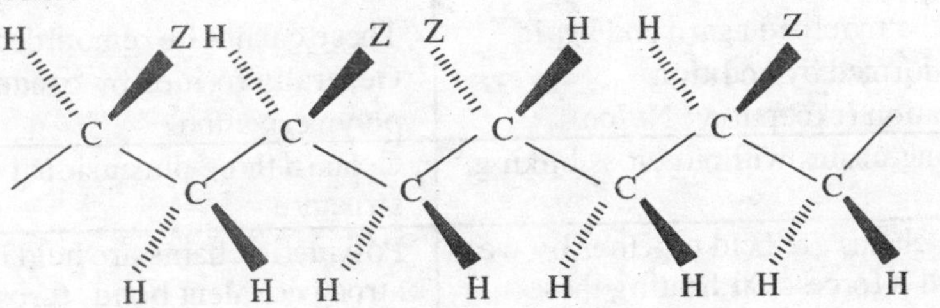

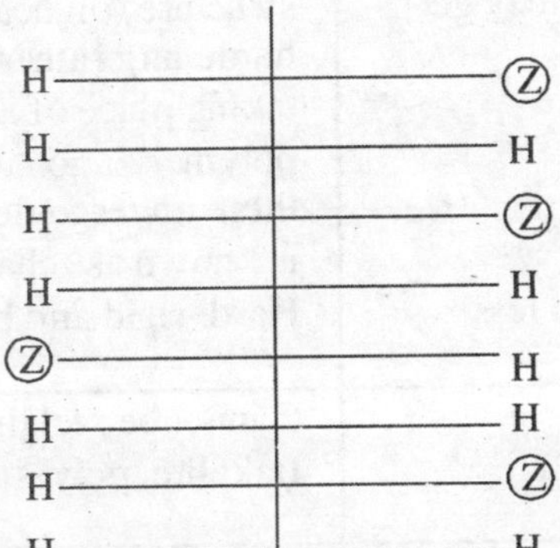

randomly arrangement of fundamental group

3.2.6 Based on the action of heat on Polymers :

There are two type of polymers :

(i) Thermoplastic

(ii) Thermosetting

(i) Thermoplastic : Thermoplastics are the polymers which get soften on heating and hardened on cooling without or with very little change in their properties. These polymers therefore can be remoulded. These are generally linear chain polymers (without cross linking) and different chains are held together with vander wall's forces of attraction. On heating these polymers melt and form a fluid which can be moulded into desired shape on cooling.

e.g. Polythene, PVC, Nylon 6 : 6 etc.

(ii) Thermosettings : Thermosets are polymers which once hardened cannot we softened again. These polymers generally have three dimensional cross linked network structure. The polymeric chains are linked with covalent bonds (like vander waal's forces in thermoplasts). Hence, on heating softening does not take place. So, these polymers are generally hard, rigid and brittle.

e.g. Bakelite, polysters.

Table 3.1. Difference between thermosplastic and thermosetting polymers.

S.No.	Thermoplast	Thermosetting
1.	Polymers which are softened on heating and hardened on cooling are known as thermoplasts.	Polymers which once hardened cannot be softened again are known as thermosets.
2.	These can be moulded again and again.	These cannot be remoulded.
3.	Generally formed by addition polymerization (exception : Nylon)	Generally formed by condensation polymerization.
4.	Contain long chains without cross linking.	Contain three dimensional cross linked structure.
5.	Polymeric chains are held together by weak vander wall's forces. On heating these secondary bonds break. Hence, they get softened.	Polymeric chains are held together by strong covalent bonds (cross linked structure) on heating these undergo hardening rather than softening because of taking place of any left over polymerization. On prolonged heating, these undergo degredation and the process is known as' charring'.
6.	These are usually soft, weak and less brittle.	Hard, rigid and brittle.
7.	Can be reclaimed from waste.	Cannot be reclaimed from waste.
8.	e.g. Polythene, PVC, Nylon.	Bakelite, polyesters.

3.2.7 On the basis of ultimate form

On this basis polymers can be classified in three categories :

(i) Elastomers (ii) Fibers (iii) Plastics

(i) Elastomers : The group of polymers having high degree of elasticity (reversible elongation 300% to 1000%), stretching at least twice of their original length under the action of tensile force and recover their original length after the removal of the applied force, are known as elastomers. e.g. Rubber.

These can be of two type

(a) Natural (b) Synthetic Rubber.

(ii) Fibers : Fibers are polymers having thread like structure with high aspect ratio.

$$\text{Aspect ratio} = \frac{\text{Length}}{\text{Diameter}} = \frac{l}{d}$$

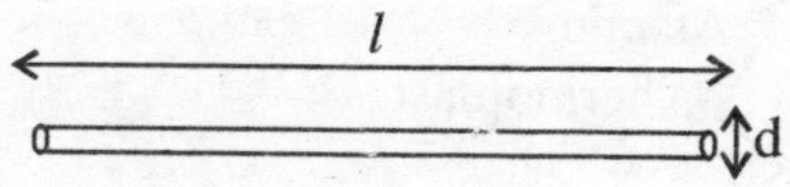

In case of fibers the minimum $l : d$ ratio is 100 : 1.

Fibers can be classified as:

(a) Natural : Example : Plant fibers (Cotton, Linen)

Animal fibers (Wool, silk)

(b) Synthetic : Example : Polyamides (Nylon)

Polyesters (Tarylene)

(iii) Plastics : The word 'plastic' has been derived from Greek word 'Plastikos' which means' fit for remoulding'.

Polymers which can be moulded into desired shapes by the application of heat and pressure are known as plastics.

These are of two types :

(a) Thermoplast : e.g. Polythene

(b) Thermosets : e.g. Bakelite.

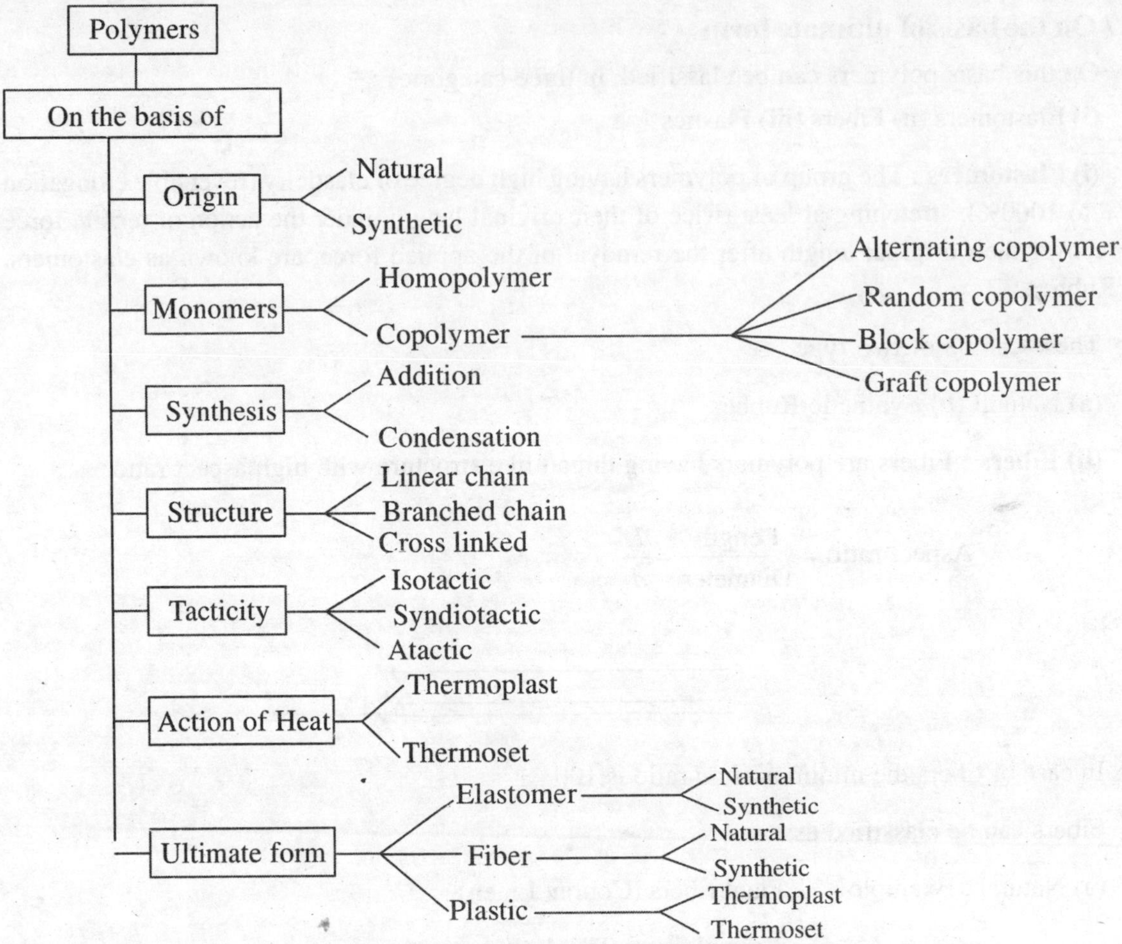

Fig. 3.1 : Classification of Polymers

3.3 TYPES OF POLYMERISATION

The polymerisation process is of two type :

(1) Addition Polymerisation (ii) Condensation Polymerisation

3.3.1 Addition Polymerisation

In this type of polymerisation polymer formed is an exact multiple of the manomeric units. In other words, we can say that the polymer is formed by simple addition of monomers, without elimination of any small molecule. Usually, monomers contains two or more double bonds. Hence, on addition do not eliminate any by product.

Mechanism of Addition Polymerisation : Addition polymerisation can be carried out by following four mechanisms :

(a) Free Radical Addition Polymerisation : The mechanism of free radical addition polymerisation involves following steps :

(I) Chain initiation : An organic peroxide is used as initiator. This peroxide undergo homolytic fission to form free radical. The free radical then attacks the monomer to initiate the chain reaction:

$$\underset{\text{Peroxide (Initiator)}}{R-\overset{O}{\overset{\|}{C}}-O \,\vdots\, O-\overset{O}{\overset{\|}{C}}-R} \xrightarrow{\text{Homolytic fission}} \underset{\text{(unstable)}}{2R-\overset{O}{\overset{\|}{C}}-O}$$

$$\downarrow$$

$$\underset{\text{Free radical}}{2R^{o} + 2CO_2}$$

(II) Chain propagation : Free radical formed in step I attacks another monomer to form new free radical, which then combine with other monomer molecule and the chain propagates.

$$R^{\bullet} + CH_2 = CH_2 \rightarrow R-CH_2-\dot{C}H_2$$

$$\underset{\text{Free radical}}{R-CH_2-\dot{C}H_2} + \underset{\text{ettrylene}}{CH_2=CH_2} \rightarrow \underset{\text{new free medical}}{R-CH_2-CH_2-CH_2-\dot{C}H_2}$$

$$R\,CH_2-CH_2-CH_2-\dot{C}H_2 + CH_2=CH_2 \rightarrow R(CH_2-CH_2)CH_2-\dot{C}H_2$$

i.e. in general

$$R-CH_2-\dot{C}H_2 + n\,CH_2=CH_2 \rightarrow R\,(CH_2-CH_2)_n\,CH_2-\dot{C}H_2$$

(III) Chain termination : Free medicals formed in step II undergo chain termination by following two modes :

(i) Combination :

$$\underset{\text{Free radical}}{R\,(CH_2-CH_2)_n-CH_2-\dot{C}H_2} + \underset{\text{Free radical}}{\dot{C}H_2-CH_2(CH_2-CH_2)_n R}$$

$$\Big\downarrow \text{ Combination}$$

$$R(CH_2-CH_2)_n-CH_2-CH_2-CH_2-CH_2(CH_2-CH_2)_n R$$

(ii) Disproportionation :

$$R(CH_2-CH_2)_n\ \underset{\displaystyle H}{\overset{\displaystyle H}{\overset{|}{\underset{|}{C}}}}-\dot{C}H_2+\dot{C}H_2-CH_2(CH_2-CH_2)_n R$$

$$\downarrow$$

$$R(CH_2-CH_2)_n\ CH=CH_2+CH_3-CH_2(CH_2-CH_2)_n R$$

In this step a hydrogen atom of one radical is transferred to another radical. Hence, two polymer molecules are formed, one is saturated and other is unsaturated.

(B) Catonic addition polymerisation : It involves formation of carbocations. Like free radical mechanism it also involves three steps :

(I) Chain initiation : Lewis acids like $AlCl_3$, BF_3, $SnCl_4$, $TiCl_4$ etc.are generally used as chain initiator in presence of water.

$$BF_3+H_2O \rightleftharpoons [BF_3OH]^{\ominus}+H^{\oplus}$$

The proton attacks the alkene molecule to form carbocation and chain reaction is initiated.

$$\underset{\text{Proton}}{H^{\oplus}}+\underset{\text{alkene monomer}}{CH_2=\underset{\displaystyle R}{\underset{|}{CH}}}\longrightarrow \underset{\text{carbocation}}{CH_3-\underset{\displaystyle R}{\underset{|}{\overset{\oplus}{C}H}}}$$

(II) Chain Propagation : Carbocation formed in step I attacks other alkene molecule to form new carbocation which then attacks the other molecule of alkene and the chain propagates.

$$CH_3-\underset{\displaystyle R}{\underset{|}{\overset{\oplus}{C}H}}+\underset{\text{monomer}}{CH_2=\underset{\displaystyle R}{\underset{|}{CH}}}\rightarrow \underset{\text{carbocation}}{CH_3-\underset{\displaystyle R}{\underset{|}{CH}}-CH_2-\underset{\displaystyle R}{\underset{|}{\overset{\oplus}{C}H}}}$$

$$CH_3-\underset{\displaystyle R}{\underset{|}{CH}}-\overset{\oplus}{C}H_2-\underset{\displaystyle R}{\underset{|}{CH}}+\underset{\text{Monomer}}{n\,CH_2=\underset{\displaystyle R}{\underset{|}{CH}}}\longrightarrow CH_3-\underset{\displaystyle R}{\underset{|}{CH}}\left[CH_2-\underset{\displaystyle R}{\underset{|}{CH}}\right]_n CH_2-\overset{\oplus}{C}H$$

(III) Chain termination : Carbocation formed in step II undergo chain termination either by

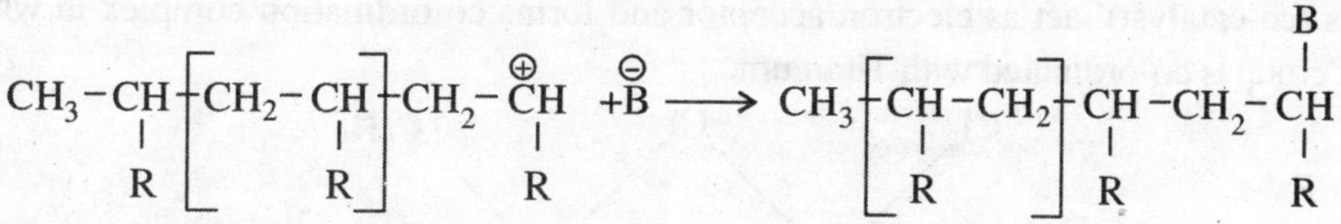

or (ii) by proton transfer

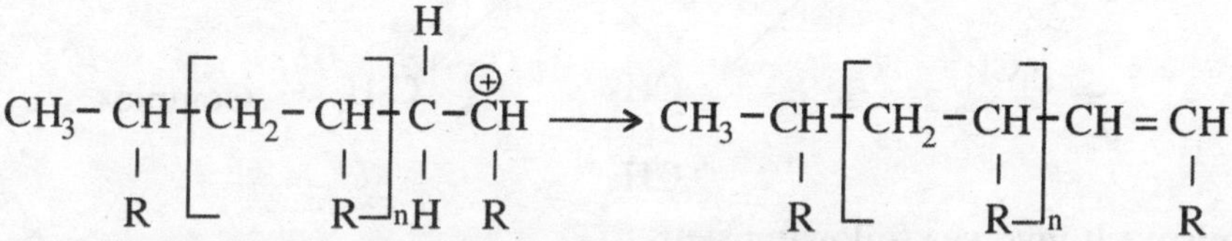

e.g. Isoprene, Isobutylene under go cationic polymerisation.

(C) Anionic Addition Polymerisation : Anionic addition polymerisation involves following steps :

(I) Chain Initiation : Bases like $LiNH_2$, KNH_2, nBuLi etc. are used as initiator.

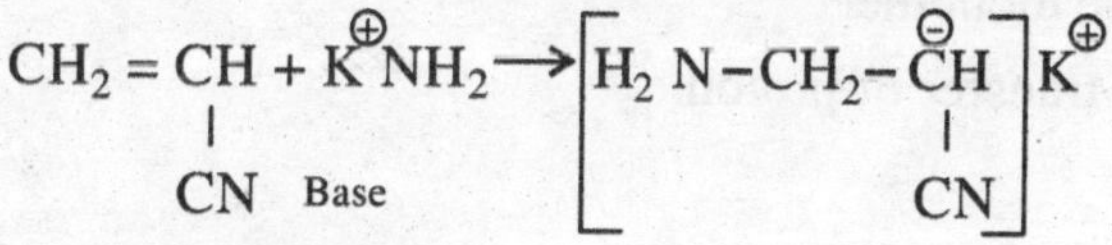

Acrylonitrile Monomer Carbanion

(II) Chain Propogation :

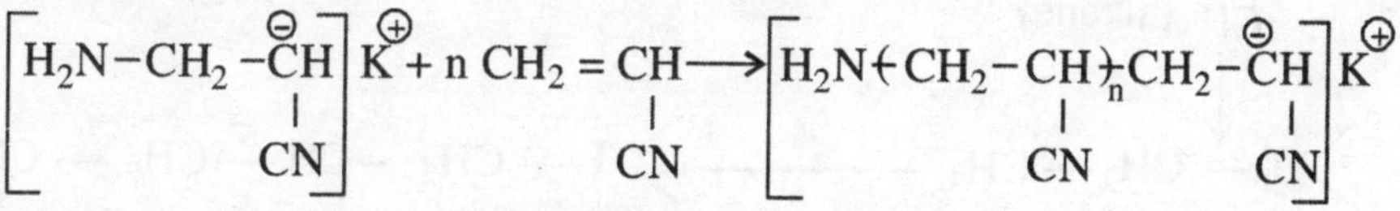

monomer

(III) Chain termination :

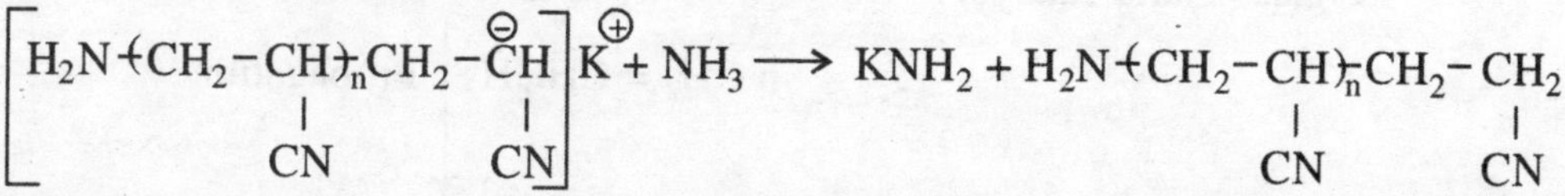

(D) Coordination Polymerisation or Zeigler - Natta Polymerisation : Coordination addition polymerisation is initiated by Zeigler - Natta catalyst, Zeigler - Natta catalyst comprises of two components :

(i) Halides of transition metals of group IV to VIII (Ti, Fr, Mo, V, Ni, Rh etc.). These are known as catalysts.

(ii) Organometallic compounds. e.g. hydrides, aryls or alkyls of group I to IV metals. These are know as co-catalyst.

Commonly used zeigler - Natta catalyst are :

	Catalyst		Co-catalyst
(a)	$TiCl_4$	+	$Al(C_2H_5)_3$
(b)	$TiCl_3$	+	$Al(C_2H_5)_3$
(c)	TiCl	+	$Al(C_2H_5)_2Cl$

In such combinations Titanium halides (catalyst) act as electron donor where as aluminimum alkyls (co-catalyst) act as electron acceptor and forms co-ordination complex in which carbon of alkyl group is co-ordinated with Titanium.

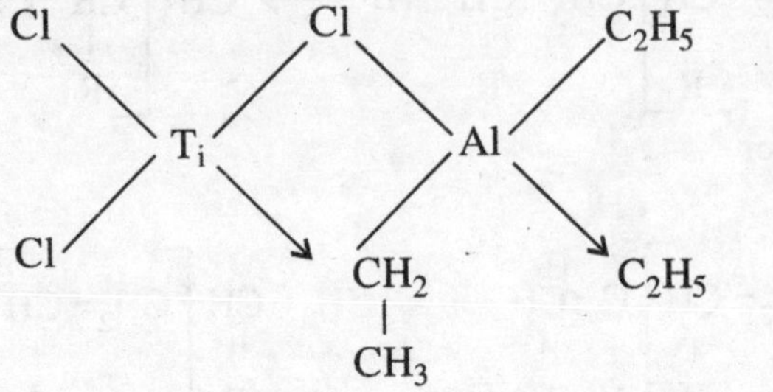

Complex

Mechanism : It involves following steps :

(1) In first step a complex is formed due to overlapping of π - cloud of alkene with the empty orbital of Ti.

(ii) Insertion of alkene between Ti-C bond.

(iii) Further addition of alkene monomer.

(iv) Termination of chain by transfer of proton.

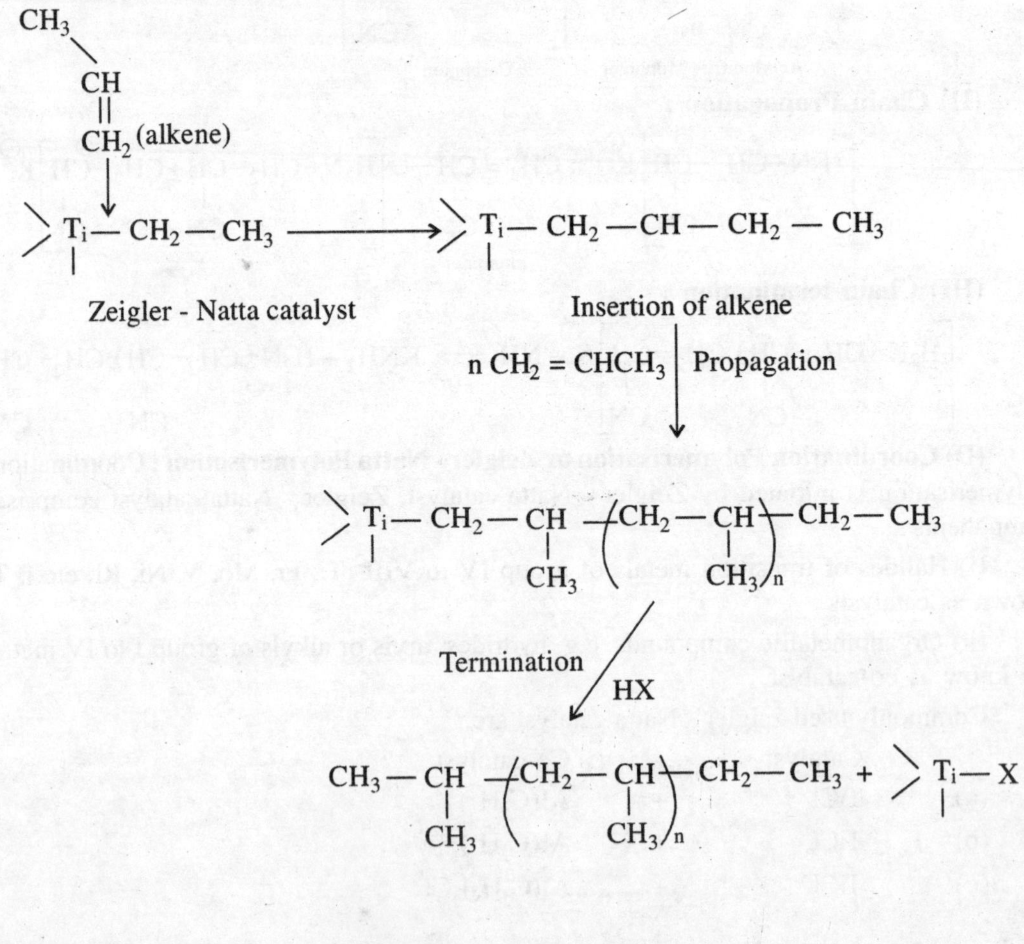

3.3.2 Condensation Polymerisation

This type of polymerisation occurs between monomers containing polar groups, with elimination of small molecules like H_2O, HCl, NH_3 etc.

Examples 1. : Nylon 6 : 6

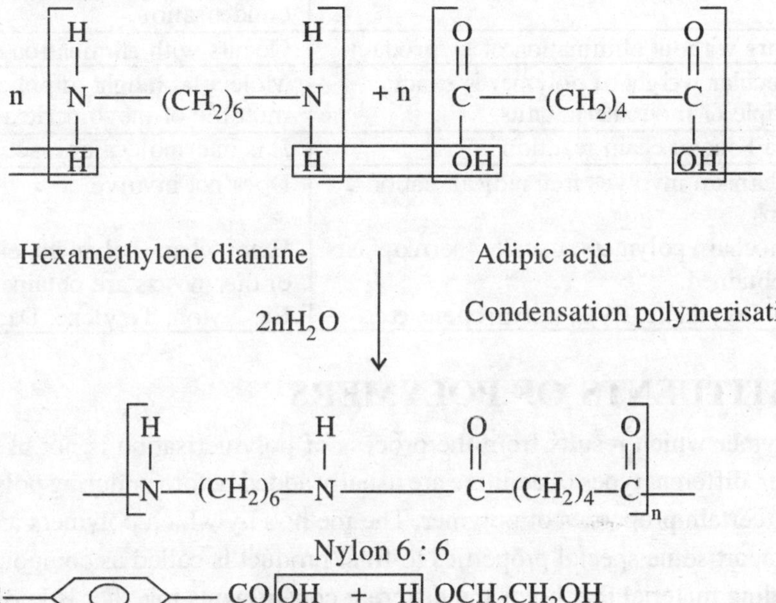

Nylon 6 : 6

Terylene :

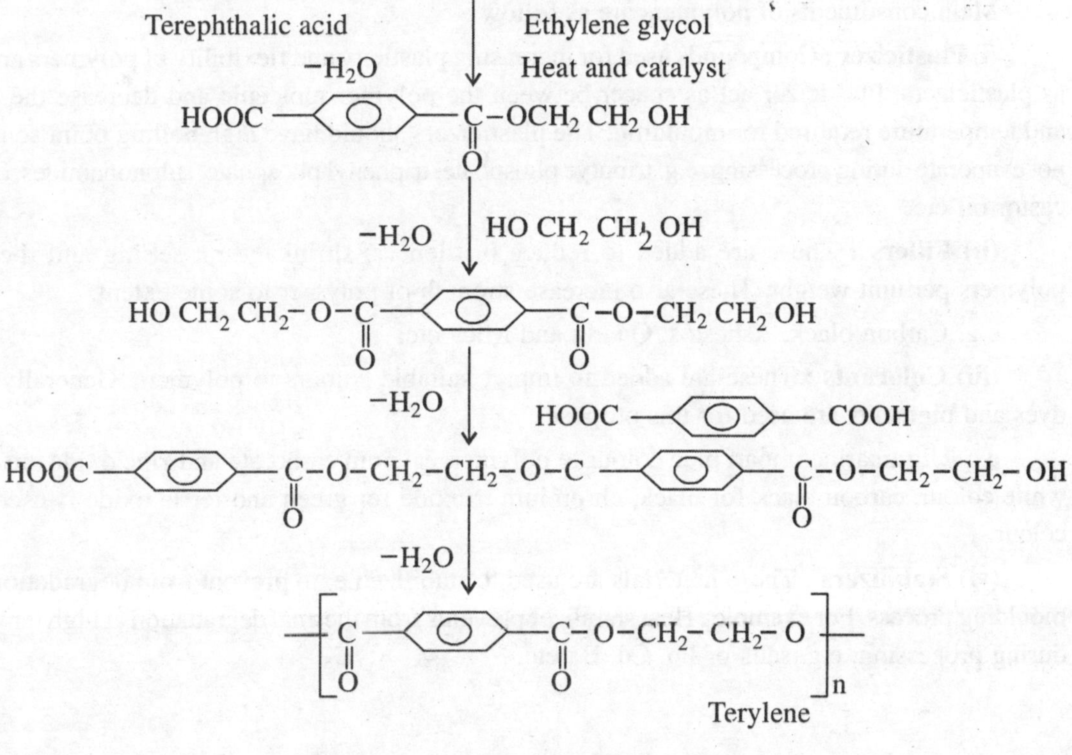

Terylene

Table 3.2 : Comparison between addition and condensation polymerisation

S.No.	Thermoplast	Thermosetting
1.	Monomer units contain at least one multiple bond (reactive site).	The monomer units contain atleast two similar or different functional groups which can react with each other to undergo condensation.
2.	Occurs without elimination of by product.	Occurs with elimination of by product.
3.	Molecular weight of polymer is exact multiple of monomeric units.	Molecular height of polymer is not exact multiple of monomeric units.
4.	It is a Kinetic chain reaction.	It is intermolecular reaction.
5.	Mechanism involves free radical, cations, anions.	Does not involve.
6.	Homochain polymers, usually thermoplasts are obtained. Ex. – Polythene, PVC, polypropene etc.	Heterochain polymers, either thermoplast or thermosets are obtained. Ex. Nylon, Terylene, Dacron, Bakelite etc.

3.4 CONSTITUENTS OF POLYMERS

The polymer which results from the process of polymerisation is not used as such on large scale. However, different types of additive are usually added before or during polymerisation process for improving certain properties of polymer. The method by which polymers are mixed with some additives to impart some special properties to final product is called as compounding of polymers. The basic binding material that holds the different constitments together is known as 'Resin'.

Main constituents of polymers are as follow :

(i) Plasticizer : Compounds used for increasing plasticity and flexibility of polymers are known as plasticizers. Plasticizer act as spacer between the polymer molecule and decrease the pressure and temperature required for moulding. The plasticizers should have high boiling point so that does not evaporate during processing. e.g. tributye phosphate, triphenyl phosphate, sulphonamides, camphor, castor oil etc.

(ii) Fillers : These are added to reduce brittleness, shrinkage on setting and the cost of polymers per unit weight. These also increase strength of polymer to some extent.

e.g. Carbon black, Asbestos, Quartz and Mica etc.

(iii) Colorants : These are added to impart suitable colours to polymers. Generally organic dyes and pigments are used for this purpose.

e.g. Ultramarine impart blue colour to polymer, calcium carborate and zinc oxide are used for white colour, carbon black for black, chromium trioxide for green and ferrie oxide is used for red colour.

(vi) Stabilizers : These materials are used to stabilize i.e. to prevent from degradation during moulding process. For example : Heat stabilizer prevents from thermal degradation at high temperature during processing. e.g. salts of Pb, Cd, Ba etc.

(v) Accelerators or Cross linking agents : These generally added to promote faster and more complete polymerisation.

e.g. H_2O_2, Cu, Ag, Pb, ZnO, etc.

(vi) Anti-oxidants : These are used to prevent polymers from oxidative degradation during processing.

e.g. phenyl - β - nephthylamine, di - t - butyl - p - cresol etc.

(vii) Lubricants : These are used to reduce friction and to improve flow characteristics. These also impart good finish to product and prevent polymeric material from stiking to the fabrication frame.

e.g. waxes, oils, soaps etc.

3.5 PREPARATION, PROPERTIES AND USES OF FEW IMPORTANT PLASTICS THERMOPLASTICS

3.5.1 Polythene

Polythene is homopolymer and one of the most important polymer which is thermoplastic in nature. These are of two types :

(A) Low density polythene (B) High density polythene

(A) Low Density Polythen (LDPE) :

Preparation : LDPE is prepared by the addition polymerisation of ethene monomers at high pressure (1000 – 1500 dtm), at a temperature of 250°C in presence of initiator O_2 (free radical mechanism).

$$\underset{\text{ethene}}{n\,CH_2=CH_2} \xrightarrow[\substack{250^\circ c \\ O_2}]{\text{high pressure}} \underset{\text{LDPE}}{(CH_2-CH_2)_n}$$

Properties :

(i) It has low density (around 0.910 - 0.925g/cm³).

(ii) These are highly branched. The branching occurs during the propagation step by inter/intra molecular chain transfer reactions.

(iii) LDPE is chemically inert and has good chemical resistance.

(iv) Its softening temperature is 115°C.

(v) It has low crystallinity (around 55%).

(vi) It is moisture resistant.

Uses :–

(i) It is used for making films, packing materials etc. due its flexibility and moisture resistance.

(ii) Used in squeese bottles and squeese tubes.

(iii) Ink tube for pens, moulded toys, mugs and other house wares.

(iii) For wire and cable insulations because of non - polar nature.

(B) High Density Polythene (HDPE) :

Preparation : HDPE is obtained by the addition polymerisation of ethene monomers in presence of Zeigler - Natta catalyst [$TiCl_4 + Al(C_2H_3)_3$] at low pressure and temperature.

$$\underset{\text{ethene}}{n\,CH_2 = CH_2} \xrightarrow[\substack{60\text{–}70^\circ c \\ \text{Zeiglar–Natta} \\ \text{catalysts}}]{6\text{–}7\text{ atm}} \underset{\text{HDPE}}{\left(CH_2 - CH_2\right)_n}$$

Properties :

(i) It has high density (around 0.941 - 0.965 g/cm^3).

(ii) The HDPE molecules are linear.

(iii) It has high crystallinity (80-90%).

(iv) Its softening temperature is 135°c.

(v) It has greater chemical resistance than LDPE.

(vi) It has low gas permeability.

(vii) It has greater tensile strength than LDPE.

Uses : (i) For manufacturing of domestic gas pipelines.

(ii) For manufacturing of over head tanks for water storage.

(iii) For manufacturing of buckets, bottle caps, toys, industrial containers (because it is more tough and stiffer than LDPE).

(iv) Containers for chemicals and drugs like syrups (due to its greater chemical inertness and grease proof nature).

3.5.2 Nylon

Nylons are example of polymides. Polymides are the polymer obtained by condensation polymerisation of acids (bifunctional) and amines (bifunctional) and they contain amide $\left(-\underset{\underset{O}{\|}}{C}-\underset{\underset{H}{|}}{N}-\right)$ groups.

$$\underset{\text{acid}}{-\overset{\overset{O}{\|}}{C}-OH} + \underset{\text{amine}}{H-\overset{\overset{H}{|}}{N}-} \xrightarrow[-H_2O]{} -\overset{\overset{O}{\|}}{C}-\overset{\overset{H}{|}}{N}-$$

Nylons are polyamides which are generally differentiated by numbering system. First numeral of the numbering system represents the number of carbon atoms in the amine monomer and second numeral represents the number of carbon atoms in acid monomer. Few examples of nylongs are as follow :

Preparation :

(A) Nylon 6 : 6 : Nylon 6 : 6 is obtained by the condensation polymerisation of hexamethylene diamine (6 carbon monomer) and adipic acid (6 carbon monomer).

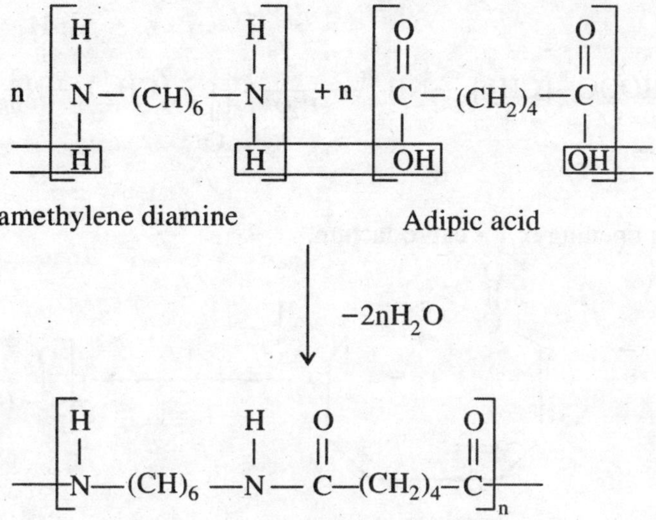

Nylon 6 : 6

(B) Nylond 6 : 10 : It is prepared by the condensation polymerization of hexamethylene diamine (6 carbon monomer) and sebacic acid (10 carbon monomer).

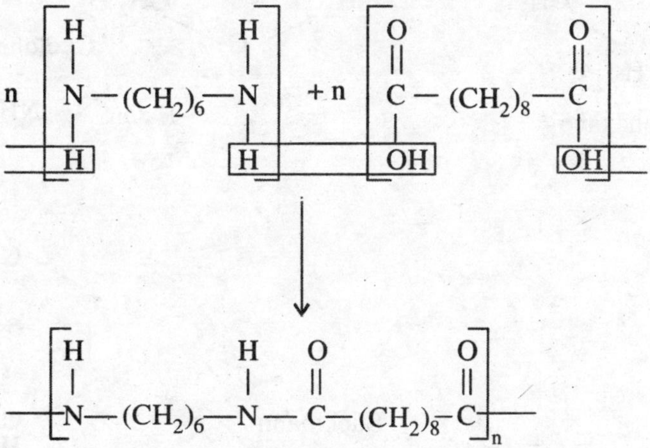

Nylon 6 : 10

(C) Nylon 6 : Nylon 6 is prepared by two methods :

(a) by self condensation ε - amino caproic acid (6 carbon monomer).

$$n\ HOOC-(CH_2)_5-NH_2 \xrightarrow{-H_2O} \left[\underset{\underset{O}{\|}}{C}-(CH_2)_5-\overset{\overset{H}{|}}{N} \right]_n$$

(b) by ring opening of ε - capro lactum.

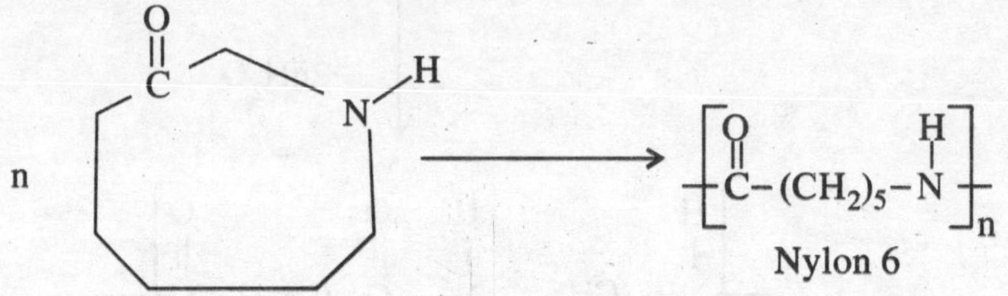

ε - Caprolactum

Monomer ε - caprolactum is obtained from cyclohexane by following reactions :

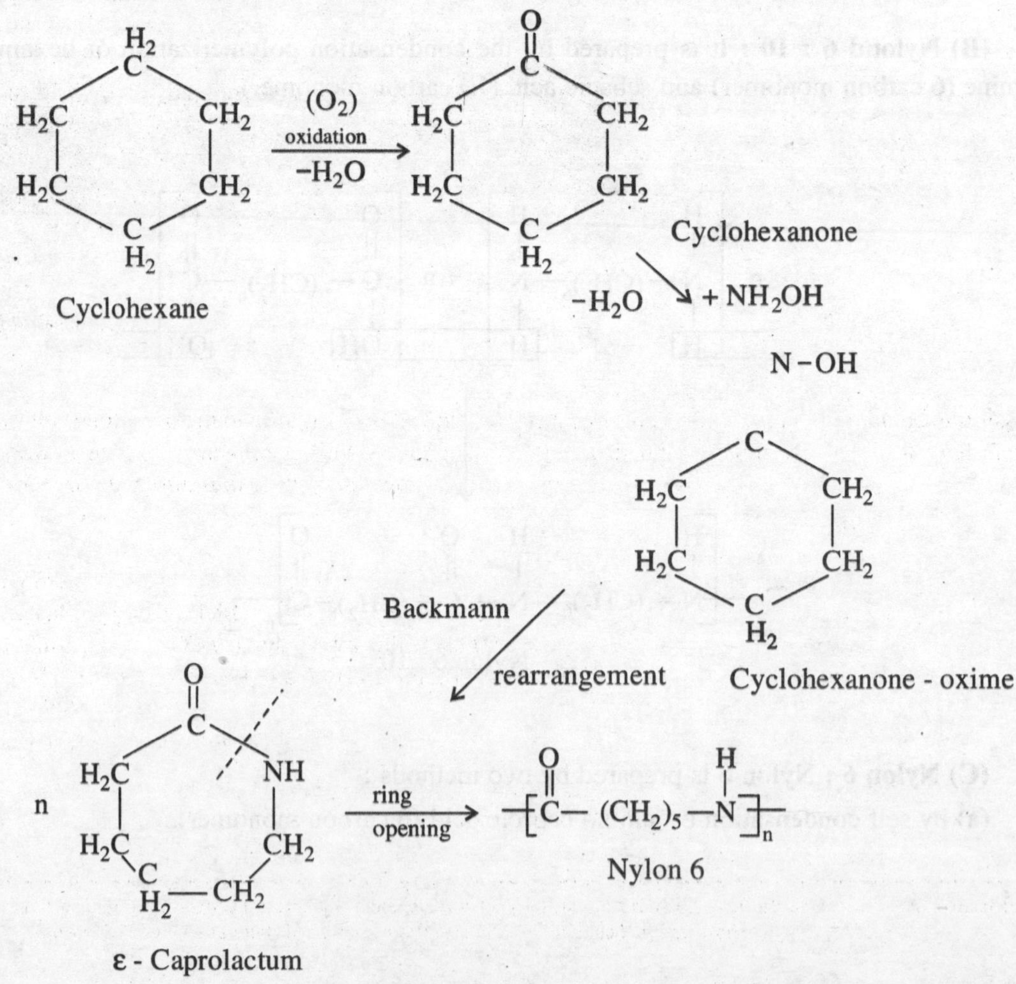

ε - Caprolactum

(D) Nylon 11 : Nylon 11 is prepared by self - condensation of ω - amino undecanoic acid (11 carbon monomer).

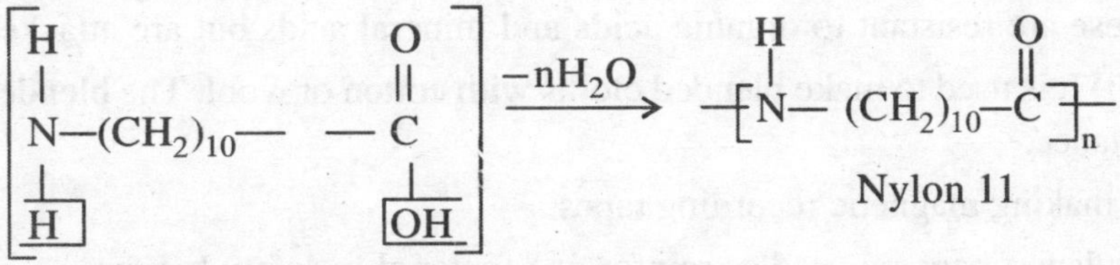

ω - amino undecanoic acid

Nylon 11

Properties :

(i) Nylons have high melting point and they posses high temperature stability.

(ii) They have good abrasion resistance.

(iii) They are resistant to chemicals.

(iv) These are soluble in phenol and formic acid while insoluble in benzene, acetone etc.

Uses :

(i) Nylon is used in fabrics (for making socks, carpet, ropes etc.).

(ii) It is also used in manufacture of bristles of brush tyre cords, gears, bearing etc.

THERMOSETTINGS

3.5.3 Terylene

Terylene is a type of polyseters. Polyesters are polymers obtained by the condensation polymerisation of acid (bifunctional) and alcohol (bifunctional) monomer and contain ester group

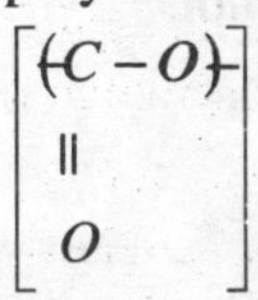.

Preparation : Terylene is prepared by heating excess of ethylene glycol with terephthalic acid. It is also known as 'Dacron'.

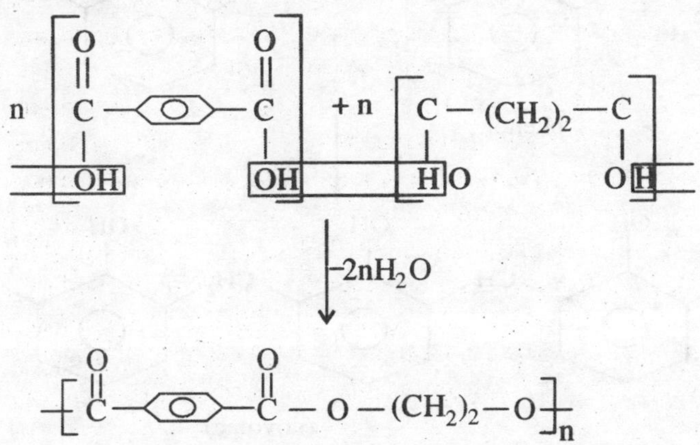

Telylene

Properties : (i) It has high crystallinity due to its symmetrical structure and presence of polar groups.

(ii) It can easily be spun into fibers and the fibers has high tensile strength and crease resistance.

(iii) These are resistant to organic acids and mineral acids but are attacked by bases.

Uses : (i) It is used to make blended cloths with cotton or wool. The blended cloths have good wrinkle resistance.

(ii) For making magnetic recording tapes.

(iii) Terylene fibers are used as reinforcing material in safety helmets.

3.5.4 Bakelite

It is also known as phenol-formaldehyde resin. It is a type of phenolic polymer.

Preparation : It is prepared by condensing phenol with formaldelyde in the presence of acid or alkaline catalysts.

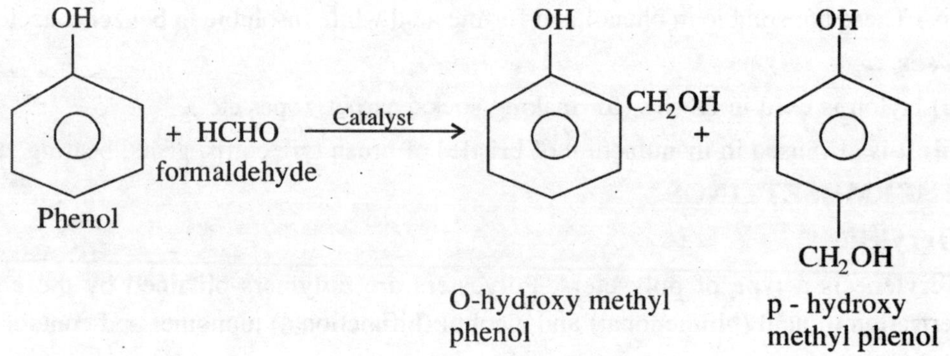

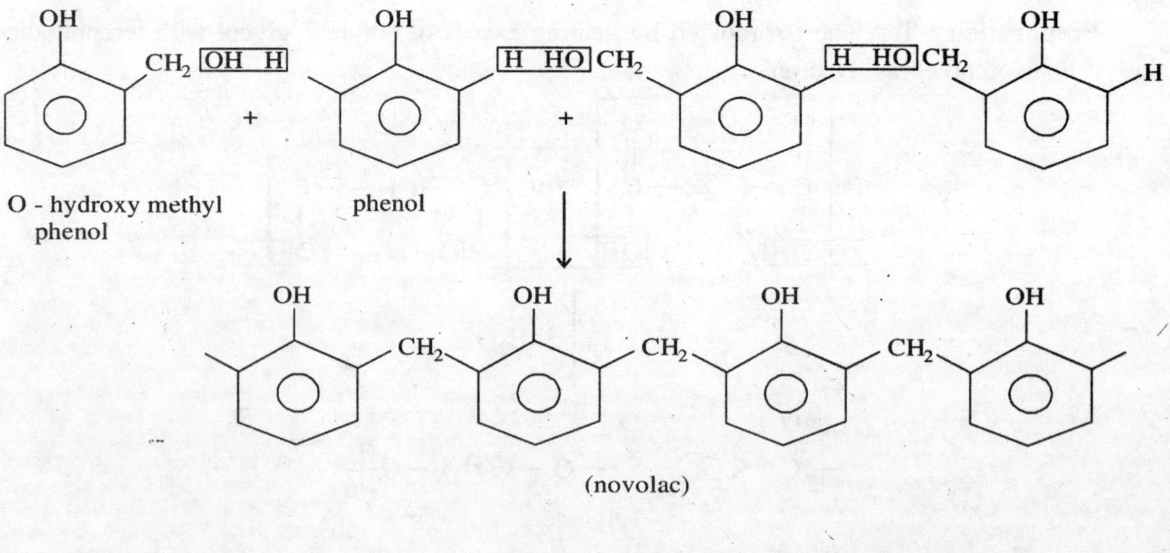

(novolac)

When novolac is heated with hexamethylene tetra amine $\left[(CH_2)_6 N_4\right]$ (which provides formaldehyde), it is converted into cross linked Bakelite.

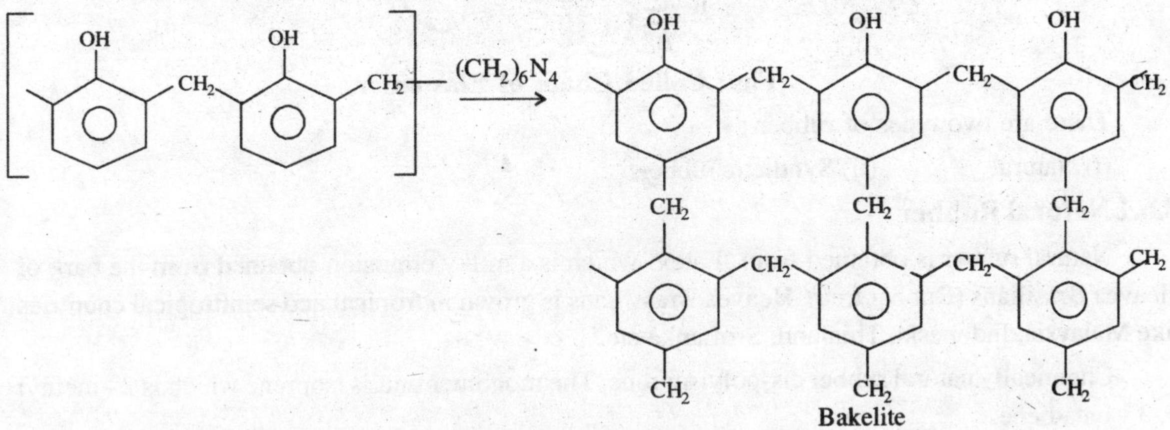

Properties : (i) Bakelite is hard, rigid, scratch proof and water resistant polymer.

(ii) It has resistance toward heat and chemicals.

(iii) It is dark pink coloured polymer.

(iv) It has large number of – OH groups in its structure hence, affected by alkalies.

(v) It has excellent electrical insulating property.

Uses : (i) For making domestic plugs and switches.

(ii) It is used in paper fabrics and wood industry.

(iii) Used in paints and varnishes.

(iv) For making handles of cooker and telephone parts etc.

3.6 ELASTOMERS

Elastomers are polymers which elasticity exhibit. Elastomers have long linear coiled chains and amorphons structure. The polymeric chains are held together by weak intermolecular forces. When such polymers are subjected to external force the coils opens up and get aligned in the direction of elongation. The aligned chains have a natural tendency to revert back in their original state as soon as the force is removed (for example rubber).

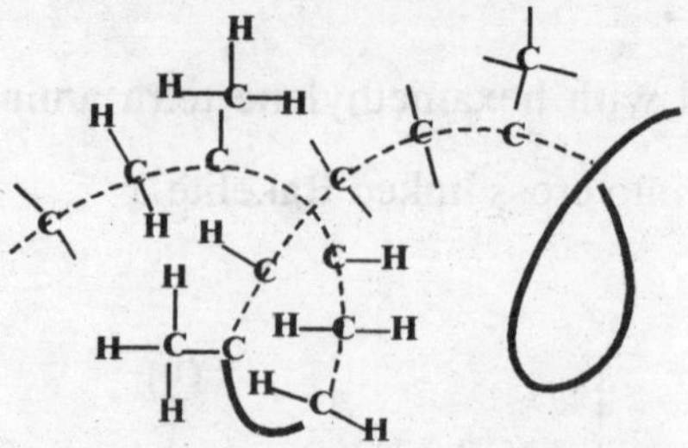

Fig.: Coiled Chain of Elastomer.

There are two types of rubber :

(i) Natural (ii) Synthetic rubber.

3.6.1 Natural Rubber

Natural rubber is obtained from 'Latex' which is a milky emulsion obtained from the bark of Heavea Brasilians (Rubber tree). Heavea Brassilians is grown in tropical and semitropical countries like Malaysia, Indonesia, Thialand, Sri Lanka etc.

Chemically natural rubber cis-polyisoprene. The monomer unit is isoprene which is 2 - methyl 1, 3 - butadiene.

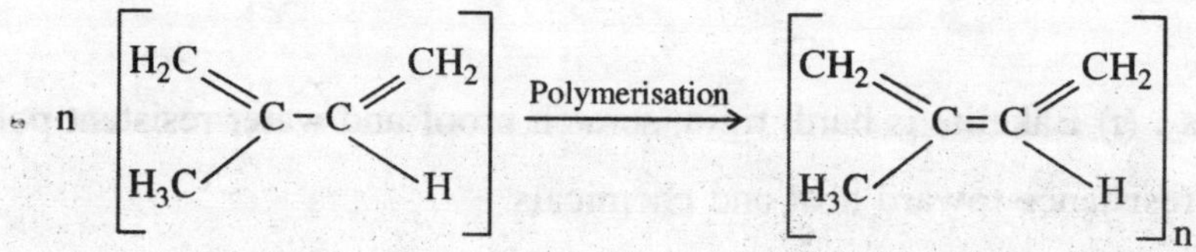

isoprene   Cis - poly isoprene (Natural rubber)

Processing of Natural Rubber

Rubber Tree
(Havea Brassilians)

↓

Latex
(contain 35% rubber in the form of milky emulsion)

↓

Diluted to contain 15 - 20% rubber and is filtered (to remove dirt)

↓ Added acetic acid (1 kg per 200 kg of rubber) for coagulation in large tank

Soft white mass

↓

Coagulated mass (coagulum) is washed and dried

↙ ↘

Crepe rubber	Smoked rubber
Coagulum is allowed to drain and is passed through creping machine consisting of rollers containing gloves on which water is sprayed. Sheet thus obtained has uneven surface appearance resembling to crepe rubber.	Coagulum is transformed into rubber slabes which is then passed through a rolling machine and ribbed rubber is obtained. Ribbed rubber is then hung in the smoke house for 4 days at 40-50°C. The rubber thus obtained is translucent.

Drawbacks of Natural Rubber :

(i) Raw rubber is weak due to its low tensile strength (200 kg/cm^2).

(ii) It has large water absorption capacity.

(iii) It is readily attacked by oxidising agents like conc. H_2SO_4, HNO_3 etc. It has less durability due to oxidation in air.

(iv) It become soft at high temperature and too brittle at low temperature. Therefore it can be used only in between the temperature range 10 - 62°C.

(v) It is non - resistant to non polar solvents like benzene, carbon tetra chloride etc. It swells in organise solvents and gradually disintegrates.

(vi) When two fresh surfaces of raw rubber are pressed together they coalesce to form a single piece. This process is known as 'tackiness'.

Vulcanisation : In order to improve the properties of rubber it is vulcanized by heating it with certain chemicals. Vulcanisation is the process by which rubber is converted from plastic condition to elastic condition by heating it with certain chemicals like sulphur, sulphur monochloride, hydrogen sulphide. However, sulphur is widely used chemical for vulcanisation.

Process : Raw rubber is heated with sulphur at 100 - 140°C. In this process, sulphur adds to the double bonds of different polymeric chains providing cross linking between them. Hence, it stiffen the raw rubber. The strenght of vulcanised rubber depends upon the amount of sulphur used. The greater the amount of sulphur used the more is the cross linking between rubber chains and hence the greater is the hardness. In extreme cases when all the double bonds are converted into cross links, the vulcanised rubber looses its elasticity completely.

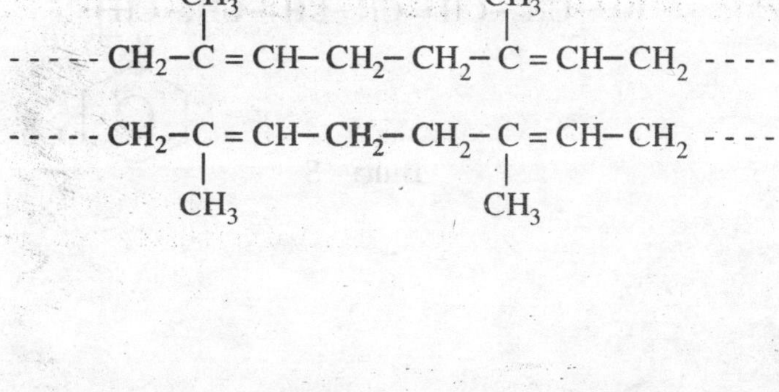

Chains of raw rubber

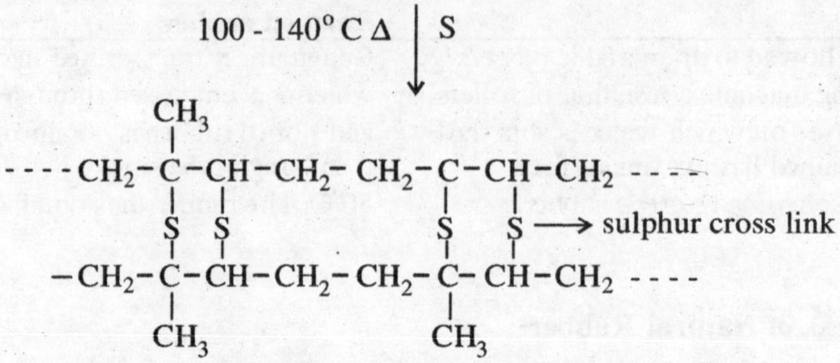

Vulcanised rubber

Advantages of Vulcanised rubber :

(i) Vulcanised rubber has good tensile strength (upto 2000 kg/cm^2).

(ii) Its working temperature range is wide (–40°c to 100°C) as compared to raw rubber (10°C to 60°C).

(iii) Its chemical resistance and oxidation resistance is greater than raw rubber.

(iv) It has low water absorption capacity.

3.6.2 Synthetic rubber

Synthetic rubber is group of high polymers which resembles natural rubber in their physical properties. They have improved physical and chemical properties as compared to natural rubber. The important synthetic rubber are :

(A) Buna - S : It is also known as GR - S or styrene - butadiene rubber (SBR). It is prepared by copolymerisation of 1, 3 - butadiene and styrene in the ratio of 3 : 1 (by weight) respectively.

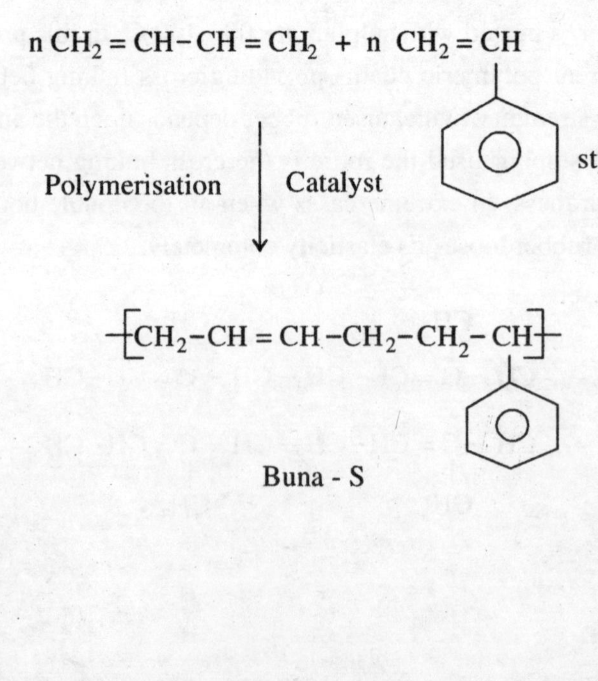

Buna - S

In Buna-S, words stand for :

Bu : Butadiene

Na : Sodium (used as catalyst)

S : Styrene

(GR-S : Government rubber - styrene)

Properties : (i) High abrasion resistance.

(ii) High load bearing capacity.

(iii) It has good insulating properties.

(iv) It can be vulcanised.

Uses : (i) It is used for wire and cable insulation

(ii) In shoe soles and footwear component.

(iii) For the manufacture of motor tyres.

(iv) For manufacture of floor tiles, adhesives. It is also used in tank - lining.

(B) Buna - N : It also known as GR-A, and nitrile - butadiene rubber (NBR). It is prepared by polymerisation of 1,3 - butadiene and acrylonitrile.

$$\underset{\text{1,3 - butadiene}}{n\ CH_2 = CH\ \ CH = CH_2} + \underset{\text{acrylonitrile}}{n\ CH_2 = \underset{\substack{|\\ CN}}{CH}}$$

$$\downarrow \text{Polymerisation}$$

$$\underset{\text{Buna - N}}{\left[CH_2 - CH = CH - CH_2 - CH_2 - \underset{\substack{|\\ CN}}{CH} \right]_n}$$

Properties : (i) NBR is resistant towards heat, sunlight, abrasion, oils, acids etc.

(ii) Due to presence of - CN group it is less resistant towards alkalies than natural rubber.

(iii) It can be vulcanised.

Uses : It is used in :

(i) Oil ressitant foams (ii) automobile parts

(iii) printing rollers (iv) adhesives

[C] Butyl Rubber or GR-I : It is obtained by copolymerisation of isobutene with small amount of isoprene (1-5%).

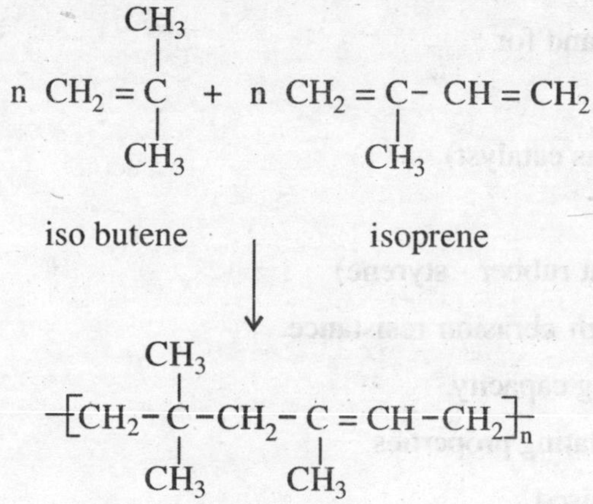

butyl rubber

Properties : (i) It has good insulating properties.

(ii) It has excellent heat, abrasion, and chemical resistance.

(iii) It is less permeability to air and other gases.

(iv) It has resistance to oxidation due to low degree of unsaturation.

Uses : (i) For manufacture of cycle tubes and car tyres due to its less gas permeability.

(ii) In the insulation of high voltage wires and cables.

(iii) For tank lining.

(iv) In making conveyer belts.

(D) Neoprene : It is homopolymer which prepared by polymerisationof **chloroprene** (2 - chloro 1, 3 – butadiene).

Neoprene is trans 1, 4 - polychloroprene.

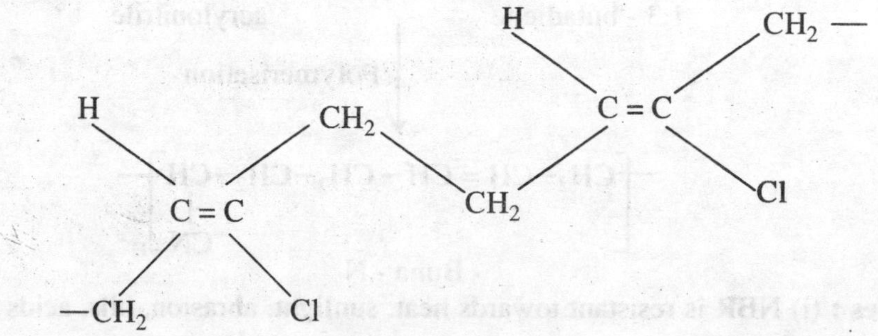

(Neoprene)

Properties : (i) The structure of neoprene is closely related to natural rubber. From the structure it is evident that in neoprene one H - atom is replaced by one Cl - atom. This substitution gives superior resistance towards vegilable and mineral oils.

(ii) It is resistant to oxidative degradation.

Uses : (i) Neoprene is used for making gas kets, sponges etc.

(ii) Lining of reaction vessels.

(iii) Damping vibrations in aircrafts.

Review Questions

1. Define the following terms :
   (i) Polymer (ii) Monomer (iii) Polymerisation (iv) functionality (v) Degree of polymerisation (vi) Tacticity.
2. What are polymers? Discuss their classification on different basis. *[RTU 2010]*
3. Differentiate between addition and condensation polymerisation with suitable examples.
4. Define functionality. What is the minimum functionality required for a compound to act as monomer? How does functionality affect the structure of a polymer?
5. Differentiate the thermoplasts and thermosets. *[RTU 2010]*
6. Explain mechanism of addition polymerisation.
   (i) Free Radical Polymerisation
   (ii) Cationic Polymerisation
   (iii) Anionic Polymerisation *[RTU 2010]*
7. What is Zeigler - Natta Catalyst? Discuss the mechanism of Zeigler - Natta polymerisation.
8. Write a note on constituents of polymer.
9. Describe preparation, properties and important applications of the following :
   (i) polythene
   (ii) Nylon
   (iii) Bakelite
   (iv) Terelene
10. What are elastomers? Discuss the following :
    (i) Natural Rubber and its Vulcanisation. *[RTU 2008, 2009]*
    (ii) Buna - N *[RTU 2008]*
    (iii) Buna - S
    (iv) Butyl rubber
    (v) Neoprene *[RTU 2010]*
11. Wrtie short notes on the followings :
    (i) Bakelite *[RTU 2008]*
    (ii) Nylon 6 : 6 *[RTU 2008, 2009]*
    (iii) BUNA Rubber
    (iv) Neoplene
    (v) Natural Rubber

(vi) Terylene

(vii) Polythene *[RTU 2008]*

(viii) Butyl Rubber

12. Explain the reactions involved in vulcanisation. *[R.T.U. 2010]*

13. Explain thermoplastic theromosetting polymers. *[[R.T.U. 2008, 2009]*

14. Name the row materials used for preparation of :

(i) Nylon 6 : 6 (ii) Terylene

(iii) Polypropylene (iv) Neoprene

(v) Bakelite (vi) Butyle rubber

❑❑❑

Unit - 4
CEMENT

4.1 INTRODUCTION

Cement in a general term is a powdered material, which initially has a plastic flow, when mixed with water it has tendency to form a hard solid in some hours. In other words, "the material having adhesive property and capable of binding material is called cement". Some examples of cementing material are gypsum, plaster of paris, lime etc. but most commonly term cement is used to indicate a fine grey powder which has a very desirable adhering property and is used in construction.

Definition : Cement is broadly defined as "any substance which have adhesive and cohesive properties and capable of bonding materials like bricks, stones, building block etc." The main constituents of cement are of various aluminates and silicates of calcium.

4.2 CLASSIFICATION OF CEMENT

Broadly, cement can be classified into two types :

(1) Hydraulic Cement : Which when treated with water undergo setting and hardening in hours. eg. Portland cement,

(2) Non - hydraulic cement : Which does not requires water and undergo setting and hardening when brought in contact with air. eg.

Other common types of cement are :

(1) Natural cement
(2) Pozzolana cement
(3) Portland cement
  (i) Oridinary portland cement
  (ii) Rapid hardening portland cement
  (iii) Extra rapid hardening portland cement
  (iv) Portland hast furnace cement
  (v) Low heat portland cement
  (vi) Sulphate resisting portland cement
  (vii) White portland cement
  (viii) Coloured portland cement
(4) High aluminia cement

(5) Super sulphate cement

(6) Special cement

(i) Quick setting cement

(ii) Expanding cement.

4.3 BASIC CONSTITUENTS AND THEIR SIGNIFICANCE

The cement has varying strength and bonding properties depending on the constituents present in it. Various types of cement have different composition and constituents but average range of composition with their constituents and significance are given in table 1.

Table 1 : Basic Constituents of Cement

S.No.	Components	% range (by mass)	Significance (Role)
1.	Lime (CaO)	60-68%	Affect the strength of cement. Both more or lesser a of lime reduce the strength as it makes the cement to expand and disintegrate.
2.	Silica (SiO_2)	17-25%	Affect strength of cement and prolongs the setting time.
3.	Aluminia (Al_2O_3)	3-8%	It is responsible for quick setting.
4.	Iron oxide (Fe_2O_3)	2-4%	It imparts grey color, strength and hardness to the cement.
5.	Magnesium oxide (MgO)	1-5%	It provides strength and hardness to cement.
6.	Sulphur trioxide (SO_3)	1-3%	It imparts soundness to cement.
7.	Alkali oxides ($Na_2O + K_2O$)	0.3-1.5%	It makes the cement efflorescent.

4.4 PORTLAND CEMENT

Introduction : The Portland cement was discovered in 1824 by Josphe Aspidin. He produced an improved cement by heating a mixture of lime stone and clay and crushing the resulting the product to a fine powder. This powder, on mixing with set to give a hard stone like mass which resembled in colour and hardness to stone taken out from mines in Portland Island, England. So,

Aspidin named it Portland Cement.

Manufacture of Portland Cement :

(1) Raw Material : The principle raw materials for manufacture of cement are :

(a) Calcrious materials : These are calcium carbonate containing materials such as lime stone, chalk, marble, etc.

(b) Argillaceous materials : These are main source of silicon and alumina. The argillaceous material used are clay, sand, slate and hast furnace slag etc.

(c) Ferriferous materials : These are main source of iron oxide such as clay, iron ore etc.

(d) Gypsum ($CaSO_4.2H_2O$).

(e) Powdered coal or fuel oil.

(2) Manufacturing Process : (Rotary Kiln Method) : Manufacture of cement by Rotaly Kiln technology involves following steps :

(a) Crushing and mixing

(b) Burning

(c) Grinding

(d) Packing.

(a) Crushing and mixing of raw material : The calcarious materials are crushed by crushers which reduces the size of raw materials to an approximately 3/4 inches and then stored for mixing.

Mixing of raw material can be done by two process; dry and wet process.

(i) Dry process : This process is employed with each when raw material used are quite hard. The crushed raw material is mixed in proper proportion other and then powdered in absence of water. This process is slow costly and produce inferior quality of cement.

(ii) Wet process : This process is applied when raw material is comparitively soft. Small amount of water is added during grinding the crushed material to convert it into paste like mass called slurry. The slurry contains about 40% of water. This process is faster and cheaper than dry process and it produce superior quality of cement. Fuel consumption and production cost is higher during this process.

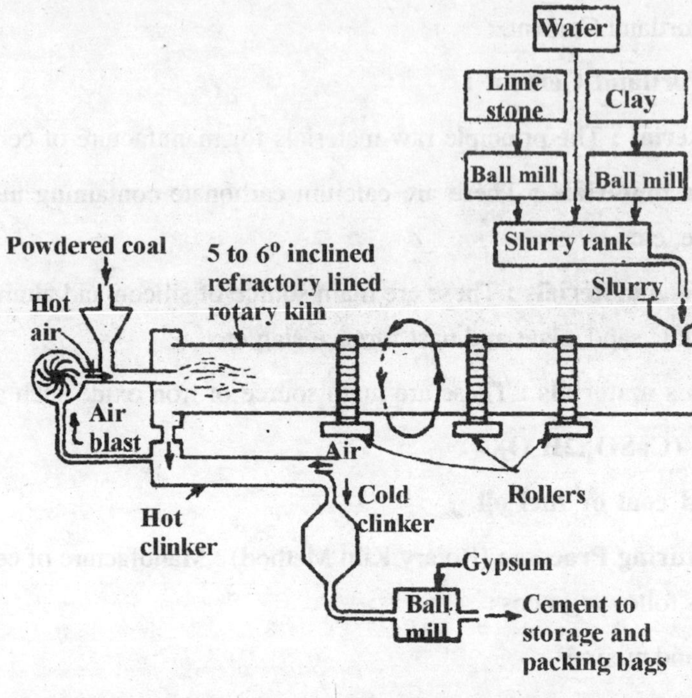

Fig. 4.1 : Rotary Kiln Technology

After this the properly mixed and crushed powdered material or slurry is sent to a "correction basis" where its chemical composition is analyzed and corrected, if necessary by adding the deficient raw material. The mixture is then stored in the storage tanks which are kept ready for feeding to a rotary kiln.

(b) Burning : The dry powder or wet sturry is transferred to rotary kiln where burning of raw material as well as actual chemical changes takes place. The mixture is fed from the upper end of rotary kiln while fuel is supplied from the lower end of the kiln.

Rotary kiln is a long steel cylinder and lined inside with refractory material. The length of Kiln is 30-160 m and diameter is 2-4 m. The kiln is slightly inclined downwards towards the exit end and fixed on rollers, which can be rotated with speed on revolution per minute. A rotary kiln may be divided into 3 major zones on the basis of the temperature and reactions taking place in that particular zone.

(i) Drying zone : It is the upper part of the kiln, where the temperature is around 400°C. Most of the water in slurry gets evaporated in this zone. Therefore it is called drying zone.

(ii) Calcination zone (Decarbonating zone) : Calcination zone is the central part of the kiln having temperature about 1000°C. In this zone, limestone of dry mixture or slurry decompose to form quick lime (CaO) and CO_2. The material gets converted into small lumps called nodules.

$$\underset{\text{(limestone)}}{CaCO_3} \rightarrow \underset{\text{(quick lime)}}{CaO + CO_2}$$

(iii) Clinkering zone : From calcination zone, material enters into the hottest zone where temperature reaches upto 1500 to 1700°C. This zone is also called burning zone. In this zone fusion of calcium oxide, silica, alumina takes place to form calcuium aluminates and silicates. Further these aluminates and silicates fuses together to from small (0.5 cm - 1 cm diameter) hard greyish stones called clinkers. These hot clinkers are then sent to small rotary kiln provided at the bottom of rotary kiln where cool air is supplied from opposite direction for cooling clinkers and hot air so produced is used for burning fuel. The reactions taking place during the process are as follows :

$$2CaO + SiO_2 \rightarrow \underset{\text{Dicalcium silicate}}{2CaO.SiO_2\ (C_2S)}$$

$$3CaO + SiO_2 \rightarrow \underset{\text{Tricalcium silicate}}{3CaO.SiO_2\ (C_3S)}$$

$$3CaO + Al_2O_3 \rightarrow \underset{\text{Tricalcium aluminate}}{3CaO.Al_2O_3\ (C_3A)}$$

$$4CaO + Al_2O_3 + Fe_2O_3 \rightarrow \underset{\text{Tetracalcium alumino ferrilt}}{4CaO.\ Al_2O_3.Fe_2O_3\ [C_4AF]}$$

(c) Grinding : After cooling, the clinkers are grounded to a fine powder in ball mills. Finely ground clinkers set very quickly by absorption of moisture from atmosphere. Therefore, 2-3% of gypsum is added to final powder to prevent quick setting of cement.

Role of gympsum : Gympsum works as retarding agent for early setting of cement i.e. it increases setting time of cement. Gypsum retards the dissolution of tricalcium aluminate (C_3A) by forming insuluble tricalcium sulphoaluminate $[3CaO.Al_2O_3.xCaSO_4.2H_2O]$.

$$\underset{(C_3A)}{3CaO.Al_2O_3} + \underset{\text{Gypsum}}{xCaSO_4.2H_2O} \rightarrow \underset{\text{Tricalcium sulphoaluminate (insoluble)}}{3CaO.Al_2O_3.xCaSO_4.\ 2H_2O}$$

Formation of insoluble product prevents too early reactions of setting and hardening.

This mixture of ground clinkers and gypsum is known as portland cement.

(d) Packing : The ground fine powder of cement is stored in silos from which it is packed by automatic machines in packates of desirable weight.

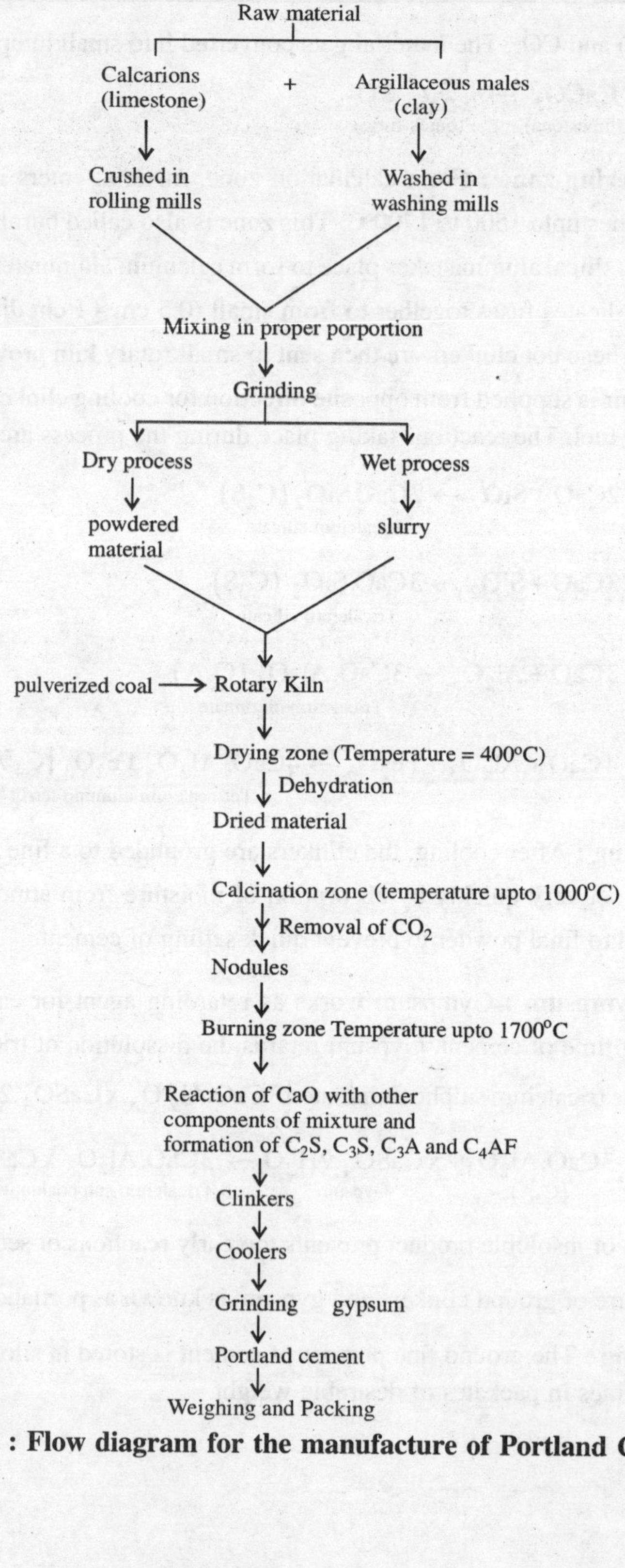

Fig. 4.2 : Flow diagram for the manufacture of Portland Cement

4.5 CHEMISTRY OF SETTING AND HARDENING

When cement is mixed with water, hydration and hydrolysis reaction of the compounds takes place. The process of solidification consists of three step, i.e. initial setting, final setting and hardening.

"Setting of cement" is defined as the stiffening of the original plastic mass due to initial gel formation of cement paste.

"Hardening of cement" is development of strength due to formation of crystalline products. The strength developed by cement paste depends upon the amount of gel formation and the extent of crystalization and amount of heat liberated.

Initial and final setting : Intial setting of cement is mainly due to the hydration of tricalcium aluminate and tetracalcium alumina ferrite constituents. Dicalcium silicate also contributes to initial setting by forming a tobermonite gel. [This gel has enormous surface area and very strong adhesive strength].

Chemical reactions involved in initial and final setting :

(i) Setting hydration of tricalcium aluminate :

$$\underset{\text{Tricalcium aluminate}}{3CaO.Al_2O_3} + CH_2O \rightarrow \underset{\text{Hydrated tricalcium duminate (crystals)}}{3CaO.Al_2O_3.6H_2O} + 880\ KJ/Kg$$

(ii) Hydration of tetracalcium aluminoferrite :

$$4CaO.Al_2O_3.Fe_2O_3 + 7H_2O \rightarrow \underset{\text{(crystal)}}{3CaO.Al_2O_3.6H_2O} + \underset{\text{(gel)}}{CaO.Fe_2O_3.H_2O} + 420\,KJ/Kg$$

(iii) Hydration of dicalcium silicate :

$$2[2CaO.SiO_2] + 4H_2O \rightarrow \underset{\text{Tabermonite gel}}{3\,CaO.\,2SiO_2.3H_2O} + \underset{\text{crystal}}{Ca(OH)_2} + 250\ KJ/Kg.$$

Role of gypsum : After the initial setting the paste becomes stiff. However, the gypsum is added to retard the dissolution of the tricalcium aluminate by forming insoluble calcium sulphoaluminate.

$$\underset{\text{Tricalcium aluminate}}{3CaO.Al_2O_3} + \underset{\text{gypsum}}{x\,CaSO_4.2H_2O} \rightarrow \underset{\text{Tricalcium sulphoaluminate}}{3CaO.Al_2O_3.x\,CaSO_4.2H_2O}$$

Hardening of Cement : Hardening of cement is mainly due to the formation of tobermonite gel $(C_3S_2.3H_2O)$ plus crystalization of $Ca(OH)_2$ and hydration of tricalcium aluminate (C_3A).

$$2[3CaO.SiO_2] + 6H_2O \rightarrow \underset{\text{Tobermonite gel}}{3CaO.2SiO_2.3H_2O} + 3Ca(Cn)_2 + 500\,KJ/Kg.$$

The hydration of cement is an exothermic crystal reaction and the volume of cement increases with hydration. The heat is evolved during the first seven days of hardening. The compounds responsible for the evolution of heat are tricalcium aluminate, tricalcium silicate, tetra calcium aluminoferrite and dicalcium silicate in the descending order $(C_3A > C_3S > C_4AF > C_2S)$. The heat evolved is used in the setting of cement.

The changes occuring in the setting and hardening of cement may be depicted as

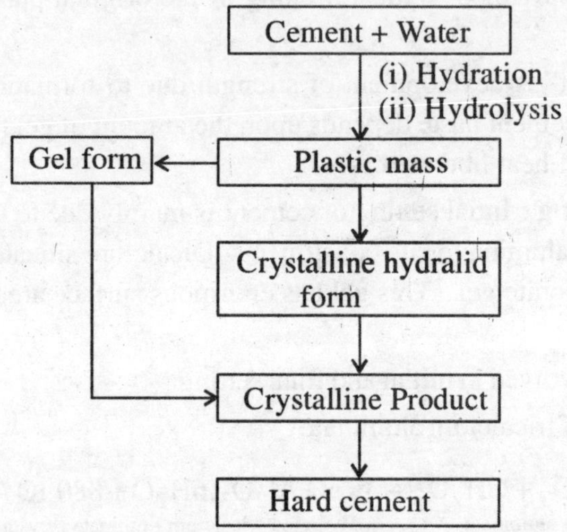

Fig. 4.3 : Setting and hardening of cement.

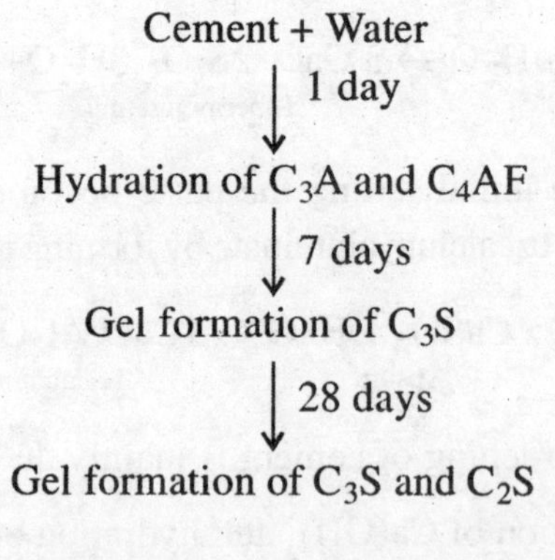

Fig. 4.4 : Changes during setting and hardening of cement.

Table 2 : Facts About Port Land Cement

Contents	Facts about Portland Cement					
	Abbreviations	Average %	Setting time in days	Heat of hydration (KJ/Kg)	Rate of hydration	Strength
$3CaO.SiO_2$	C_3S	45	7	880	Medium	High Ultimate strength
$2CaO.SiO_2$	C_2S	25	28/	420	Slow	Low early strength Ultimate strength
$3CaO.Al_2O_3$	C_3A	1	1	250	Slow	Poorest early strength
$4CaO.Al_2O_3.Fe_2O_3$	C_4AF	9	1	418	Slow	Medium early strength
CaO	-	2	-	-	-	-
MgO	-	4	-	-	-	-
$CaSO_4$	-	5	-	-	-	-

Review Questions

1. (a) Discuss the rotary kiln technoogy of manufacturing of cement.

   (b) Give chemical reactions involved in the formation of clinker during manufacturing of cement. *[R.T.U. June, 2008]*
2. Give the chemistry of setting and hardening of cement. *[R.T.U. Jan, 2008, 2009]*
3. Describe the wet process of manufacture of Portland Cement with the chemical reaction involved in it. Discuss the role of gypsum is portland cement. *[R.T.U. 2007, 2009]*
4. What are the disadvantages of using excess of lime during manufacture of cement?
5. Which constituents of cement causes its initial setting? Give chemical reactions.
6. Name the raw materials necessary for the preparation of Portland Cement.
7. Write the functions of ingradients of cement.
8. Discuss the chemical and physical change that occur during setting and hardening of cement.
9. Draw a labelled diagram of rotary kiln required. Write chemical reactions taking place in the various zones of rotary kiln. *[R.T.U. 2010]*
10. Describe the process of setting and hardening of cement concrete, giving the reactions involved in such process. What is the difference, if any, between 'setting' and 'hardening' *[R.T.U. 2010]*

❑❑❑

Unit - 5
GLASS

5.1 INTRODUCTION

Glasses are defined as amorphous, transparent, rigid, hard, brittle, supercooled liquid of high viscosity having no sharp melting point, definite formula or crystalline structure. Glass is obtained by fusing a mixture of a number of metallic silicates, most commonly of Na, K, Ca and Pb. In some glasses, SiO_2, may be replaced by Al_2O_3, B_2O_3, P_2O_5 etc. Glass may be represented as xR_2O. yMO, $6SiO_2$, where R is an atom of monovalent alkali metal like Ma, K etc; M is an atom of a bivalent metal like Ca, Pb, Zn etc. x and y are whole number. Approximate composition of soda lime glass is Na_2O. CaO. $6SiO_2$.

5.2 PROPERTIES OF GLASS

Physical properties

1. They are usually transparent amorphous solids.
2. Glass is completely vitrified product.
3. They are hard, rigid and have no definite melting poise.
4. They have sufficiently high viscosity (greater than 10^{13} paise).
5. They can incorporate colouring material, with retaining transparency.
6. Glass is bad conductor of electricity and heat and is often used as an insulator.

Chemical properties :

1. Glass is not attacked by air and oxidising agent.
2. Ordinary glass is readly attacked by alkalies. If NaOH solution is kept in a burette for some days, slopper will stick to the socket and cannot be opened.
3. Glass is very resistant to acids (HF is exception which dissolves the glass).

$$Na_2O.SiO_2 + 6HF \rightarrow 2NaF + SiF_4 + 3H_2O$$

$$CaO.SiO_2 + 6HF \rightarrow CaF_2 + SiF_4 + 3H_2O$$

5.3 MANUFACTURING OF GLASS

5.3.1 Raw Material

The raw material used for manufacture of various glasses are given below :

(i) Soda Ash (Na_2CO_3) : It is the source of Na_2O. Other sources of Na_2O are sodium nitrate ($NaNO_3$), sodium sulphate (Na_2SO_4).

(ii) Potash feld spar ($K_2O.\ Al_2O_3.\ 6H_2O$) : It is the source of K_2O to prepare hard and superior glass. Other source of K_2O are potassium carbonate (K_2CO_3) and potassium nitrate (KNO_3).

(iii) Lime stone ($CaCO_3$) : It is the source of CaO. Other source of CaO is burnt dolomite. MgO is used as substitute of lime.

(iv) Red lead (Pb_3Q_4) or Litharge (PbO) : It is the source of PbO.

(v) Silica (SiO_2) : The source of SiO_2 are quartz or white silica sand, which washed before use in order to make it free from iron oxide (since iron oxide acts as colouring agent).

(vi) Borex ($Na_2B_4O_7$ .10 H_2O) : It is the source of B_2O_3. Borex also decreases the coefficient of expansion of glass and due to this property it is used in modern heat resistant glass and increases its durability.

(vii) Zinc oxide (ZnO) : ZnO is used along with boric acid, which decreases the effect of suddent changes in temperature and also lowers the expansion coefficient.

(viii) Phosphoric acid (P_2O_5) : It gives brightness to glass.

(ix) Calcium phosphate [$Ca_3(PO_4)_2$] : It gives an opalescent appearance to finished glass. Other opaliging agent are fluoride, antimony and arsenic oxide etc.

(x) Refining agents : Sodium sulphate, sodium nitrate, sodium chloride, calcium fluoride, carbon are refining agents which mixed with raw materials to promote refining i.e. the removal of small gas buble from the glass.

(xi) Colouring agents : These are added to the motten mass during the manufacture of coloured glasses. Important colouring agents are :

S.No.	Colouring agent	Colour
1.	Chromic oxide (Cr_2O_3)	Green
2.	Ferrous oxide (FeO)	Green
3.	Ferric salt	Yellow
4.	Manganese dioxide (MnO_2)	Purple
5.	Cadmium sulphide	Yellow
6.	Cobalt oxide (CaO)	Blue
7.	Cuprous oxide (Cu_2O)	Red
8.	Selenium oxide	Red
9.	Cupric salt	Peacock blue
10.	Cryolite or calcium phosphate	Milky white

(xii) Cullet : It is crushed or broken glass from imperfect defective articles. It makes the melting easy and utilise waste glass.

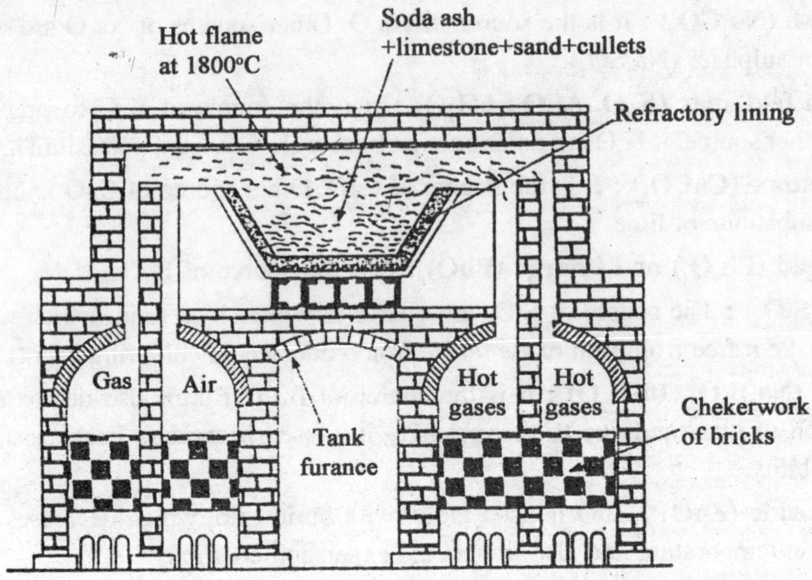

Fig.5.1. Manufacturing of Glass

Manufacturing Process : The manufacturing of glass is done in four steps.

(i) Melting (ii) Shaping (iii) Annealing (iv) Finishing.

(1) Melting : The raw materials are grounded and mixed with cullets and again ground to get finally powdered and intimate mixture called 'batch'. Melting of glass batch is done by heating either in pot or in tank furnaces. A common tank furnace consists of a large rectangular dry tank. It is heated by producer gas and work on the regenerative system of heat economy. Pot furnaces are employed mainly in the manufacture of optical glass, special glass or fine quality of glass.

The cullets are added to lower the melting point. The furnace is heated at about 1800°C. At this temperature the material melts and fused with hot gases. On continued heating, the entire amount of CO_2 escapes out and a transparent viscous fused mass is obtained which is called **'plain'**. Now stop the heating and allow the whole mass to cool down.

The chlorides and sulphates of Ca, Al and alkali metals which remained undecomposed seperates in the form glass ball and can be removed easily and then cooled to 800°C.

The melt is down from working pits for shaping.

Chemistry of melting : Melting of glass is a high temperature process which depends on the composition of raw materials and temperature of the mixture. Reactions involved in the preparation of soda glass (soft glass) are as follow :

(a) below 600°C (b) at 700 - 900°C

(c) at 900 - 960°C (d) 1010°C

(i) below 600°C moisture, chlorides of Na, K, Pb, Sn, sodium sulphate and small amount of oxides of As, Sb, Pb, B are evaporated.

(ii) Silica reacts with soda ash (Na_2CO_3) (SiO_2) to form sodium silicates and CO_2 escapes out.

$$Na_2CO_3 + SiO_2 \xrightarrow{700^\circ-900^\circ C} Na_2SiO_3 + CO_2 \uparrow$$

(iii) $CaCO_3$ decomposes to CaO and CO_2

$$CaCO_3 \xrightarrow{900-960^\circ C} CaO + CO_2 \uparrow$$

(iv) CaO reacts with SiO_2 to form calcium silicate

$$CaO + SiO_2 \xrightarrow{1010^\circ C} CaSiO_3$$

Sodium calcium silicate is produced when both Na_2CO_3 and $CaCO_3$ are present.

$$Na_2CO_3 + CaCO_3 + 6SiO_2 \rightarrow Na_2O.CaO.6SiO_2 + 2CO_2$$

Sodium corbonate may be replaced by salt cake (Na_2SO_4) and charcoal and reaction are as below :

$$2Na_2SO_4 + 2SiO_2 + C \rightarrow 2Na_2SiO_3 + CO_2 + 2SO_2 \uparrow$$

$$Na_2SiO_3 + CaCO_3 + 5SiO_2 \rightarrow Na_2O.CaO.6SiO_2 + CO_2 \uparrow$$

(ii) Shaping (forming) : Molten mass is shaped into desired articles by either blowing or moulding.

(iii) Annealing : After shaping the glass articles are allowed to cool gradually at room temperature by passing through a series of different chambers with descending temperature. Cooling of glass article in such a manner is called 'annealing'. If glass is allowed to cool rapidly glass being bad conductor of heat, the superficial layer cool down first leaving the interior portion in state of strain. Owing to this unequal expansion, the articles are likely to crack into pieces. The longer the annealing period, the better the quality of the glass.

(iv) Finishing : All glass articles, after annealing, are subjected to finishing process such as cleaning, grinding, cutting, polishing, sand blasting etc.

5.3.2 Devitrification

Glass has the characteristic of a transparent amorphous solid. A transparent viscous liquid is formed on heating the raw materials used during glass manufacturing. This liquid is assume to form a transparent amosphour solid. Formation of crystalline solid is avoided during whole process. Such a process is called vitrification and the opposite process of vitrification and the opposite process of vitrification which involves the crystallisation of glass is known as devitrification. Devitrification of glass is avoided since devitrified glass losses plasticity and hence, the ability to be shaped.

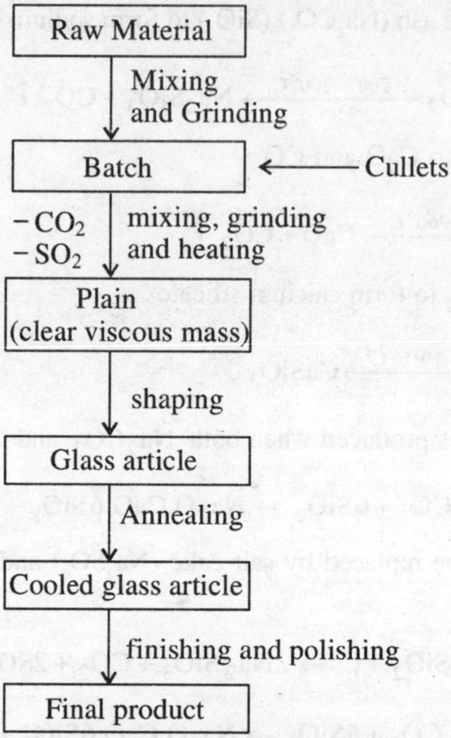

Fig. 5.2. Flow Chart.

5.4 TYPE OF GLASS

Different variety of glass can be produced by changing the composition of the batch.

5.4.1 Soda lime glass or soft glass

It is the ordinary glass, which is prepared by fusing the Na_2CO_3, $CaCO_3$ and SiO_2. Approximate composition is $Na_2O.CaO.6\ SiO_2$.

Properties :

(a) Low melting

(b) Low cost

(c) Resistance to devitrification

(d) Attacked by common reagents like acids

(e) Poor resistance towards high temperature.

Uses : It is widely used for

(a) Window glasses

(b) Cheaper tablewares like bottles, jars etc.

(c) Cheap laboratory glassware

(d) Electric bulb.

5.4.2 Potash Glass or Hard Glass

It is prepared by fusing $K_2CO_3, CaCO_3$ and SiO_2. Its average composition is $K_2O.CaO.6SiO_2$.

Properties :

(a) More costly

(b) Hard

(c) Fuse with difficulty

(d) More resistant to acids, alkalies and other solvents.

(e) Has high melting point and can withstand high temperature.

Uses : It is used for heating operations like chemical apparatus and combusion tubes.

5.4.3 Lead glass or Flint glass

Preparation : It is prepared by fusing K_2CO_3, red lead and SiO_2. The approximate composition is $K_2O.PbO.6SiO_2$. As 80% PbO is incorporated for dense optical glasses.

Properties :

(a) Bright and lustrons due to high refractive index.

(b) Specific gravity is high 3 to 3.3.

(c) Softening temperature is lower than soda glass thus it is much easier to shape and work it.

Uses : It is used for

(a) Making prisms, lenses and other optical devices.

(b) Making high quality table ware and art objects, because of high lusture.

(c) High lead content flint glass is used for making windows to protect from X - rays and γ - rays in atomic energy and medical field respectively.

5.4.4 Borosilicate glass/Proprexe glass/Jena glass

It contains boron trioxide (B_2O_3) and silica with small amount of alumina and alkali metal oxide. The percentage composition of different components are as follows :

80% silica (SiO_2), 13% B_2O_3, 3% Al_2O_3, 3% K_2O,0.5% Na_2O.

Properties :

(i) Low thermal coefficient of expansion

(ii) High chemical resistance power.

(iii) Excellent shock - resistance capacity.

(iv) High softening point.

Uses : It is used in

(a) Superior laboratory apparatus like flasks, beakers etc.

(b) Television tubes, electrical insulator etc.

(c) Industry for pipelines for corrosive liquids.

5.4.5 Aluminosilicate Glass

Aluminosilicate glass has higher percentage of Al_2O_3 and lower percentage of B_2O_3 than borosilicate glass. The % composition of different components are as below :

% SiO_2 = 55, Al_2O_3 = 23, B_2O_3 = 7, MgO = 9 % CaO = 5. $Na_2O + K_2O$ = 1.

Properties : It possesses exceptionally high softening temperature.

Uses : (a) Chemical combustion tubes.

(b) Certain domestic equipments etc.

(c) High pressure mercury discharge tubes.

5.4.6 Optical or Crook Glass

They contain phosphorous and lead silicate together with a small amount of cerium oxide.

Properties :

(a) Low viscosity so that it becomes free from bubbles in molten state.

(b) No devitrification even upon long annealing.

(c) Ability to take up the desired polish on grinding and polishing.

(d) Even on long exposure to the atmosphere, no spoilage of its ourface.

(e) Relatively soft.

(f) They have low melting point, low durability and low chemical resistance.

Optical glass contain cerium oxide which is capable of absorbing the UV light.

Uses : They have high refractive index and used for the manufacture of lenses.

5.4.7 Safety glass or laminated glass

Preparations : It is prepared by placing a thin layer of vinyl plastic between two sheets of glass. Then the plastic and glass sheets are pressed together under heat, so that the plastic thin layer is sandwiched in between the glass sheets. The edges of the combined sheet are sealed with some water resistant compound.

Properties :

(a) Safety glass and shatter proof.

(b) It is quite tough.

Uses :

(a) Three layer laminated glass is used as wind shields in automobile and aeroplane industries.

(b) Five layer laminated glass is used in building construction.

(c) Several layer laminated glass is bullet proof and used for making looking windows, automobile wind screens.

5.4.8 Toughned glass

Preparation : The hot articles are dipped in oil bath so that some cooling takes place. The outer layer of the articles shrink and compress, while inner layers are in state of tension.

Properties :

(a) It is more elastic.

(b) It is capable to withstand thermal and mechanical shocks.

(c) When it breaks, it is reduced to fine powder and the pieces do not fly away.

Uses : (a) It is used for making window shields of trucks, cars, aeroplanes and other fast moving vehicles.

(b) Window shields of furnaces.

(c) Automatic opening doors.

(d) Large show cases.

5.4.9 Glass wool

It is intermingled fine threads or filaments of glass.

Preparation : It is prepared by forcing motten mass of glass through small holes of average diameter of 0.05-0.07 mm continuously. These fibers are thrown over a rapidly revolving drum to get the material in wool like form.

Properties :

(a) Glass wool is non combustible, fire proof and heat proof.

(b) Resistant to moisture and chemicals.

(c) Its tensile strength is about eight times that of steel.

(d) Its density is quite low about 65 Kg/m^3.

Uses :

(a) It is used in domestic and industrial appliances like oven, insulation of metal pipelines, motors, vacum cleaners etc.

(b) It is used for filteration of acidic and other corrosive liquids.

(c) It is used for electrical and sound insulation.

(d) It is also used for making costumes of firemen.

5.4.10 Wired Glass

Preparation : Wiremesh is embedded at the centre of this glass during casting of glass sheet.

Properties :

(a) More fire resistant than ordinary glass.

(b) Shatter proof.

Uses : Used in making fire resisting doors, roofs, windows and sky lights.

5.4.11 Photochromatic Glass

It changes colour in the presence of high energy radiation usually UV radiation but reverts back to their original appearance in the absence of these radiation.

Preparation : Photochromatic glass is prepared by adding silver, copper nitrate and metal halide to basic composition of borosilicate glass and then heated at approximately 1200ºC. As the glass cools small crystals of AgCl form, along with a small portion of copper holide. The crystallites of approximate 10 mm diameter and 100 nm apart are too small to absorb visible light and thus the glass appears transparent in dark.

Table 1 : Different types of Glasses

S.No.	Types of glass	Constituents	Properties	Uses
1.	Sodalime glass or soft glass. $Na_2O.CaO.6SiO_2$	SiO_2, Al_2, O_3, CaO, MgO, Na_2O, Fe_2O_3	Viscous water resistant, low cost, low m.p., melts easily attacked by acids and resistant to devitrification.	Containers, flat glass, tumblers, wire, plates, cheaper table wares etc.
2.	Potash glass or hard glass. $K_2O.PbO.6SiO_2$	K_2O,CaO, SiO_2	Hard, high m.p. and resistant to acid and alkalis.	Heating apparatus, combustion tubes etc.
3.	Flint glass or lead glass. $K_2O.PbO.6SiO_2$	K_2O, PbO, SiO_2, B_2O_3	Insulation, low thermal conductance, chemically resistant, higher refractive index.	Electrical and optical instruments, prisms, lenses, neosign tube etc.
4.	Borosilicate	B_2O_3, K_2O, Al_2O_3, Na_2O, SiO_2, CaO	Low expansion coefficient, electrically resistant, resistant to shocks, chemically stable, high softening temperature.	For making dishes, laboratory glass ware pipelines for corrosive liquids insulators, T.V. tubes etc.
5.	Alumina silicate glass	Al_2O_3, SiO_2, CaO, MgO, Na_2O, K_2O, B_2O_3	High softening temperature.	High pressure HF discharge tubes, chemical combustion tubes, domestic equipments etc.

6.	Optical glass or crooks glass	Phosphorous, lead silicate, cerium oxide in little amt. to absorb U.V. radiation	Low durability, low viscosity, optical clarity no devitrification, high refractive index, relatively soft, low chemically resistant, low m.p.	Optical instruments like lenses, microscope, telescope etc.
7.	Safety glass	Thin glass sheet merged with non brittle plastic.	Has good strength.	Doors, windows, automobiles pipes, wind shields etc.
8.	Toughened glass	By dipping hot articles in oil bath.	More elastic mechanical and thermal shock proof, when breaks reduced to fine powder.	Window shields of fast moving vehicles, automatic opening doors, large show case etc.
9.	Glass wool	SiO_2, B_2O_3 (consists of fine threats)	Non combustible, fire proof, low electrical conductance, chemically resistant, low density, low thermal conductance, high tensile strength.	Used for insulation in ovens, metal pipelines, motors, walls, roofs and domestic appliances, infiltration of corrosive liquids etc.
10.	Wired glass	Embedded wiremesh in glass sheet	Fire resistant and shatter proof.	Fire resisting doors, roofs, windows and sky lights.
11.	Photo chromatic glass	AgX, SiO_2	Chemically resistant, high refractive index, become dark on exposure to U.V.	Photo chromic uses.
12.	Vitreosil or 95.5% silica glass	SiO_2, B_2O_3, borosilicate, alkali oxide.	Low thermal expansion, translucent, resistant to thermal shocks, resistant to acids and bases (except HF)	Chemical glass wares, insulating materials, electric heaters, furnace crucible. Pipe lines for hot cone, acids etc.
13.	Coloured glass	Cr_2O_3, SiO_2, Mn, Fe, CO, NiO, SeO_2	Insulator, chemically stable.	Decoration, traffic, lights, lantern, globes etc.

Review Questions

1. (a) Discuss the composition, uses and types of glasses.

   (b) Discuss the chemistry of preparation of oridinary glass. *[R.T.U., June 2008]*

2. (a) What is glass? How it is manufactured? Explain the importance of annealing of glass. *[R.T.U. 2007, 2006, 2005]*

3. Discuss the following in brief :

   (i) Laminated glass

   (ii) Borosilicate glass

   (iii) Optical glass

   (iv) Glass wool.

4. Write properties of glass.
5. Give briefly the constituents of various glass.
6. What are the main constituents and use of phochromic glass and safety glass?
7. Explain the properties and uses of at least four important types of glass.
8. Explain annealing and why it is necessary ?
9. Give the composition, properties and uses of borosilicate glass. *[RTU 2010]*
10. Discuss the manufacture of glass. *[RTU 2010]*
11. Write brief note on types of glass. *[RTU 2010]*
12. Discuss and account of soda lime glass and safety glass. *[RTU 2010]*

❑❑❑

Unit - 6
REFRACTORIES

6.1 INTRODUCTION

Refractories are those material, which can withstand extremly high temperature without any deformation in shape and size by virtue of their high melting point. They are able to retain their chemical and physical identity at the elevated temperature and are made up of high melting oxides like SiO_2, Al_2O_3, CaO, MgO etc.

Refractories are generally use to made inner wall of furnaces, for many other purpose where high temperature is required and libe crucible, ladles etc. Besides resistance to elevated temperature refractory material is required to resist other factors like heavy load, corrosive fluids (such as slag, gasesemitted during metallurgy) thermal shock, abrasion resitance etc.

6.2 CLASSIFICATION OF REFRACTORIES

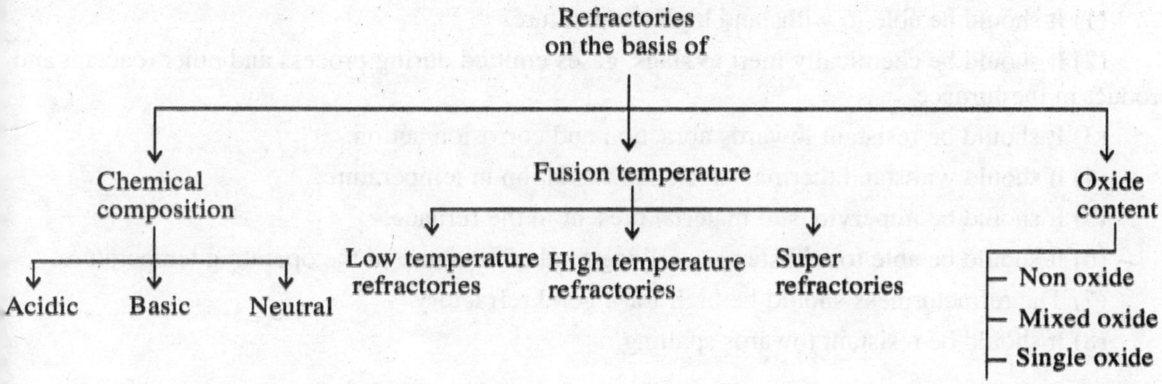

Refractories are classified into the following three categories :

(A) On the basis of chemical composition :

(a) Acid refractories : These are made up of acidic oxides like alumina (Al2O$_3$) and silica (SiO$_3$). Due to acidic nature these are resistance to acidic material but are easily attacked by basic substance. eg. - silica refractories, fire clay refractories etc.

(b) Basic refractories : Basic refractories are composed of basic material such as magnesia [MgO], dolomite etc. These are attacked by acidic material but are resistant towards basic material.

(c) Neutral refractories : These are the materials which are neither acidic nor basic in nature and hence applicable in both media. This group includes a wide range of material such as chromite, silicon carbide, zirconia etc.

(B) On the basis of fusion temperature range :

(a) Low refractory (1600°c – 1800°c)

eg. fire clay refactory

(b) High refractory (1800 - 2000°c)

eg. chromite refractory

(c) Super refractory (> 2000°c)

eg. Zircon refractory.

(C) On the basis of oxide content :

(a) Single oxide refractory :

eg. alumina, magnesia and zirconia refractories.

(b) Mixed oxide refractory

eg. Spinel, mullite refractories.

(c) Non oxide refractory :

eg. Borides,carbides and silicides refractories.

6.3 REQUISITES OF GOOD REFRACTORY

(1) It should be able to withstand high temperature.

(2) It should be chemically inert to slags, gases emitted during process and other reactant and product in the furnace.

(3) It should be resistant towards abraction and corrosion action.

(4) It should withstand thermal shock and ficulation in temperature.

(5) It should be impervious to material present in the furnace.

(6) It should be able to withstand overlying load of structure at the operating temperature.

(7) The refractoriness should be high for a good refractory.

(8) It should be resistant towards spalling.

6.4 PROPERTIES OF REFRACTORIES

Refractories are characterized by a set of properties. Each refractory is constituted by a mixture of materials and their composition is not well defined, therefore the physical and chemical properties of refractories are also not well defined like those of a compound. The important properties of refractories are :

(1) Refractoriness : Refractoriness indicates the capacity of a material to withstand heat without appreciable deformation or softening. It is therefore common practice to determine softening temperature or fusion temperature. Fusion temperature is that temperature at which the refractory starts to soften. It should be well above the operating temperature of the furnace.

Measurement of fusion temperature is done by pyrometric cone equivalent (PCE) test, also called as Seger Cone Test.

In this test, comparision is made for the effect of heat on sample refractory cone and with a series of standard seger cone. These cones are smal pyramid having triangular base of 19 mm and 38 mm height. Each standard cone is made of a particular refractory material of a definite softening temperature and each cone is assigned a specific no. to form a range of serieal number. No. is assigned to cone is increasing softening temperature. To determine the refractoriness sample cone is heated uniformily at 10°C/min.

Note : The temperature range at which the test cone starts to softens and touches tip at base is known as softening temperature. Now and compare it with softening temperature range of standard pyrometric cone. The sample cone is assigned the serial no. of that standard cone whose softening temperature watches to the softening temperature of sample cone. This no. is called pyrometric cone equivalent (PCE) of the test cone. For eg. the silica brick has a PCE of 33 with a softening temperature range of 1700 - 1750°C. It indicates that this refractory can be used in the furnace with operating temperature upto 1700°C. Refractoriness is the most important property, since the primary function of a refractory is to withstand high temperature.

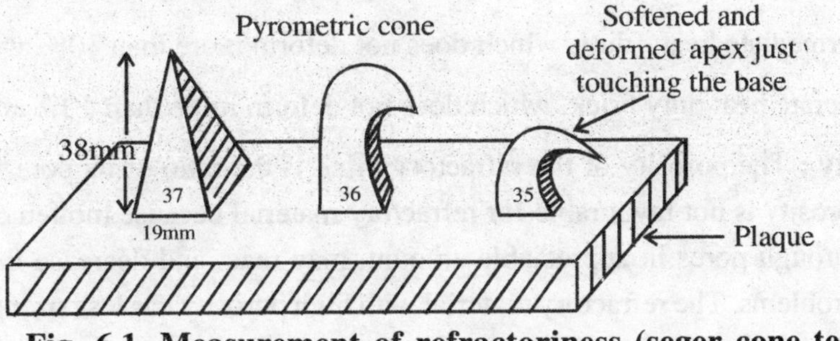

Fig. 6.1. Measurement of refractoriness (seger cone test)

Table 1 : Fusion Temperature of Refractories

S.No.	Type of Refractory	Refractory Material	Fusion Temperature (°C)
1	Acidic	Alumina (Al_2O_3)	2050
2.	Acidic	Silica bricks	1700
3	Acidic	Fire clay brick	1600-1750
4.	Acidic	High alumina clay bricks	1800-1850
5.	Basic	Magnesia brick	2200
6.	Basic	Dolomite brick	1700
7.	Neutral	Graphite (C)	3500
8.	Neutral	Zirconia (ZrO_2)	2710
9.	Neutral	Silicon carbide (SiC)	2700

(2) Refractoriness under load or strength (RUL) : This represents the resistance of refractory material to combined effects of heat and load. For eg. fire clay and high alumina refractories soften gradually over a range of temperature, but under load they collaps much below their softening temperature. For a good refractory it is necessary that refractory material should have high refractoriness under load.

Refractoriness under load can be determined in two ways (i) rising temperature test (ii) maintained temperature test.

In former way a constant load of 3.5 kg is applied over a sample refractory of size 5 $cm^2 \times 75$ cm high. The sample is then heated at the rate of 10°C/min. Then height of the sample is plotted against applied temperature. RUL is expressed as the temperature at which 10% deformation takes place. In the latter case (maintained temperature test), the amount of deformity is recorded at a given temperature in a given time, for measuring deformity, the sample is taken out, cooled and height is noted.

On the basis of RUL, refractory materials are classified into following three types :

(i) A high heat duty bricks, which does not deform more than 10% at 1350°c.

(ii) An intermediate heat - duty, which does not deform more than 10% at 1300°c.

(iii) A moderate heat duty brick, which does not deform more than 10% at 1100°c.

(3) Porosity : The porosity of the refractory brick is the ratio of its pore volume to the total volume. High porosity is not favourable for refractory material because molten charge, gases, slags etc. may enter through pores in appreciable amount, may react and decrease the life of refractery and may create problems. The refractory material with high porosity has less strength, poor resistance to abrasion and greater tendency of being corroded by slags etc. So a good refractory material should have lower porisity. High porosity also reduce the thermal conductivity of refractory as air in pores acts as thermal insulator.

Porosity can be estimated by measuring the volume of H_2O or liquid absorbed by the specimen. This will be apparent porosity, since it does not include the pore space of sealed pores also. Porosity can be calculated as :

$$\text{Porosity} = \frac{\text{Pore volume}}{\text{Bulk volume}}$$

$$\text{Porosity}(\text{p}) = \frac{W - D}{V} \times 100$$

$$= \frac{W - D}{W - S} \times 100$$

where, W = weight of saturated sample

D = weight of dry sample

S = weight of saturated sample submerged in H_2O.

Porosity in refractories can be controlled by the following :

(a) Control of texture

(b) Method of making

(c) Control of firing temperature.

(4) Chemical inertness : On the basis of chemical nature, refractories may be acidic, basic or neutral. A good refractory should be chemically inert. It is advisable to employ acid refractory for acidic product and basic refractory for basic product. Neutral refractory can be used for both acidic and baisc product.

(5) Thermal spalling : The breaking, cracking or peeling off of the refractory material is known as spalling. It results from the uneven expansion or contractions in the refractory due to thermal shock. Uneven thermal expansion and contraction leads to development of internal stresses and strains which finely results in cracking or breaking. This is called thermal spalling. A good refractory must show a good resistance to thermal spalling.

(6) Thermal conductivity : Refractory material should have low thermal conductivity to avoid loss of heat. High thermal conductivity is required in some cases (coke oven walls, muffle furnaces) where heating is done from outside.

(7) Permeability : It is the rate of diffusion of gases, liquids and molten solids through the pores of refractory material. For a good refractory the permeability should be low.

(8) Corrosion and erosion resistance : A good refractory should be resistant towards corrosion and erosion caused by emitted gases or molten mass which is in contact with refractory material.

(9) Heat capacity : It may be high or low, according to object. A dense and heavy fire clay bricks have higher heat capacity whereas for intermittently operated furnaces, low heat capacity or light weight refractory bricks are required to achieve the working temperature. Lesser amount of fuel is required to heat these refractory.

(B) Dimensional stability : It is resistance of a material to any change in volume when it is exposed to high temperature over a prolonged time, it is of two types :

(i) When a refractory is subjected to high temperature for long time the low fusible constituent melts away and form a liquid which fills the pores of the refractory causing contraction and vitrification eg. - fire clay bricks.

(ii) Permanent expansion : When a refractory is subjected to high temperature for long time. One crystalline form of refractory transform into another low density form leads to expansion of refractory. eg. - silica bricks.

6.5 MANUFACTURING OF REFRACTORIES

Manufacturing of refractories consists of the following steps :

1. Crushing : Raw materials are crushed to 25 mm in size.

2. Grinding : Crushed material are ground to 200 mesh in size.

3. Screening : Screening is done to purify the refractory material which is useful to remove the unwanted substances.

4. Storage : After screening the pure materials are stored in storage kilns.

5. Blending/mixing : Blending is done to ensure proper distribution of materials throughout the mass. This makes moulding easier.

6. Moulding : It may be done either by manually or mechanicaly by the application of high pressure.

7. Drying : It is done for removing the moisture content from refractories. It is carried out under controlled humidity and temperature.

8. Firing : The dried refractory is burn for vitrification and development of stable structure. Firing process of refractory involved the following changes :

(i) Removal of water hydration

(ii) Calcination of carbonates

(iii) Oxidation of Fe^{+2} to Fe^{+3}

(iv) Shrinkage in volume

(v) Vitrification.

These changes transform the raw materials into refractory.

6.6 SILICA REFRACTORIES

Silica refractories are manufactured from 95% pure silica (SiO_2) and about 2% lime.

Manufacturing :

Silicious raw material is crushed and ground with 2% lime. Now H_2O is added to it till a uniform paste is obtained. The thick paste then moulded into bricks either by hand or machine pressing. Moulded bricks are dried in air or in heated rooms. The dried bricks are burned into a kilns : the temperature of kiln is raised to about 1500°C and maintained nearly for 14 hours. During this operation quarzite is converted into crystobalite. After this cool it slowly. On cooling crystobalite changes to tridyamite. So, at least silica brick have a mix of crystobalite and tridymite.

95% Pure silica + 2% CaO (as binder)

↓ Crushing and Grinding

Powered raw materials

↓ $+H_2O$

Grinding of silica mass

↓

Paste formation

↓ Moulding

Wet bricks

↓ Drying (at 90-120ºc)

Dry bricks

↓

Rise the temperature slowly upto 1500ºC in 24 hrs.

↓

Allotropic conversion

quartizite $\xrightleftharpoons{1470^oC}$ crystobalite

↓

Slow cooling is done in 10-15 days.

↓

Crystobalite $\xrightleftharpoons{170^oC}$ tridymite

↓

Silica bricks

A mixture of crystobalite and tridymite

Fig. 6.2. Manufacturing of Silica Refractory

Properties :

1. Colour : Silica bricks are yellowish to brown in colour.

2. Composition : SiO_2 = 95%, Al_2O_3 = 0.80%, Fe_2O_3 = 0.5%, CaO = 2% and MgO = 0.05%.

3. Hardness : These are hard and abrasion resistant.

4. Porosity : 20 - 35% porosity which imparts low spalling and good thermal characteristics to silica bricks.

5. Refractoriness : The fusion temperature of silica refractory is about 1700°C, thus its refractoriness is high, therefore, it can be used at an operating temperature of 1695°C.

6. Chemical nature : Silica brick are acidic is nature.

7. Load bearing capacity : It is 5 Kg/cm^2 at 1600°c.

8. Texture : They have homogenous texture free from air voids and other moulding defects.

9. Thermal conductivity : It is higher than fire clay bricks.

10. Spalling resistance : Little or no spalling when subject to sudden temperature change.

Uses : The main use of silica refractories are in lining roof of open hearth furnaces, walls of coke ovens glass furnaces, gas reactor retarts, copper domes, etc.

6.7 FIRE CLAY REFRACTORIES

Fire clay refractories are the most widely used refractory materials. This is called alumino silicate refractory having the composition $Al_2O_3.2SiO_2.2H_2O$. Since these clay can withstand high temperature, these are called fire clay refractories.

Manufatur : There are prepared from finely ground raw material. The exact proportion of the constituents depends on the type of bricks to be designed. For example acidic fire clay contain 55% SiO_2 and 35% Al_2O_3 and neutral fire clay contains 40% SiO_2 and 55% Al_2O_3. [Hydrate aluminimumsilicate ($Al_2O_3.2SiO_2.2H_2O$) having 18 - 45% of Al_2O_3]

Properties :

1. Colour : The fire clay bricks are cream to light brown coloured.

2. Hardness : A well fired brick is as hard as steel. Hardness of it depends on firing temperature.

3. Porosity : It is between 8% to 24%.

4. Refractoriness : The fusion temperature for fire clay bricks is the range 1770 - 1790°C to 1580 - 1670°C.

5. Thermal conductivity : These bricks are poor conductors of heat.

6. Chemical nature : The fire clay refractory is acidic in nature.

7. Load bearing capacity : It is 50 Kg/cm^2 at 800°C.

8. Spalling : They have good spalling resistance. However, it varies with the porosity.

Uses : These are used for lining of open hearth blast furnaces, ovens, crucible brass and copper furnaces, ceramic pottery etc.

Raw Material
↓ Grinding
Fire powdered fire clay
↓ Water added
Moldable plastic clay
↓
Moulding
↓
Wet refractory bricks
↓ air drying
Dry refractory bricks
↓
Firing in Kiln at 1200-1400°c
↓
Dry hard fire day bricks

Fig. 6.3. Manufacturing of Fire Clay Refractory

Review Questions

1. (i) What are the requisites of a good refractory ?
   (ii) Discuss the seger's (Pyrometric) cone test.
   (iii) Write short notes on RUL test. ***[RTU 2010]***
2. What are refractories? Write briefly on Silica refractory. ***[RTU 2010]***
3. Discuss classification of refractories. ***[RTU Jan 2008]***
4. How can you measure the refractioness and refractoriness under load of a refractory material ? ***[RTU June 2008]***
5. What are refractories? Discuss essential properties of a good refractory material. ***[Raj. Univ. 2005]***
6. What do you understand by following terms in relation to refractories :
   (i) Dimensional stability
   (ii) Thermal spalling
   (iii) Porosity ***[RU 2001]***

❑❑❑

Unit - 7
LUBRICANTS

7.1 INTRODUCTION

When two metal surfaces moves against one another, there is a resistance to its motion, this resistance is called frictional resistance i.e. frictional resistance is that force which acts against two moving metal surfaces.

Causes of frictional resistance : All the metal surfaces posses many irregularities in the form of peaks (asperities) and valleys (no matter how smooth they are appearing) when such a metal surfaces move over each other, these peaks and vallies comes in contact to each other and the peaks get welded due to local melting and some energy has to be spent to break welded junction.

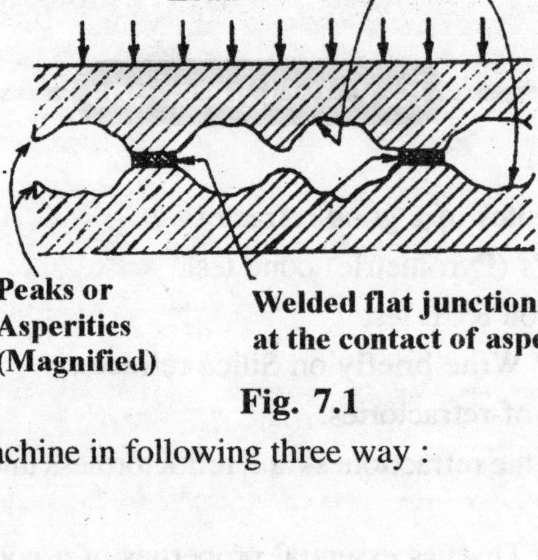

Fig. 7.1

Friction can affect the machine in following three way :

(i) Material Loss

(ii) Energy Loss

(iii) Heat generation

So lubricants may be define as any substance, which is introduced between two sliding/moving surfaces with a view to reduce frictional resistance between them, and the process of reducing frictional resistance between moving surfaces by introduction of lubricants in between them is called lubrication.

Roles of lubricants :

1. It reduce wear and tear and surface deformation of machine.

2. It acts as a collent between two surfaces and reduce energy loss in form of heat.

3. It reduce the frictional resistance.

4. It reduce the maintenance and running cost of the machine and increase its efficiency.

5. It can also acts as a seal between piston and cylinder wall of IC engine and prevent leakage of gases.

6. It provide protection against corrosion.

7. It also carries away contaminated product.

7.2 MECHANISM OF LUBRICATION

Three types of mechanism are given to explain lubrication in any machine. These are :

(i) Fluid film lubrication (Hydrodynamic lubrication)

(ii) Boundary lubrication (thin film lubrication)

(iii) Extreme pressure lubrication.

(i) Fluid film lubrication : It is also called hydrodynamics lubrication. According to this theory a film of lubricant fills the annular space between two moving surfaces. The thickness of film is about 100 nm and coefficient of friction is of the order of 0.001 - 0.03. The resistance to movement of moving or sliding parts is only due to the internal resistance between the particles of lubricants moving over each other. So, for this mechanism, lubricant should have minimum viscosity under working condition and simultaneously, it should remain in place and separate the surfaces.

Hydrocarbons are considered to be satisfactory lubricants for fluid film lubrication.

Hydrodynamic lubrication occurs in the case of a junior (shoft) running in a well lubricated bearing. At beginning the shaft rest on the bottom of the bearing. When shaft starts rotating its pumping action drouls oil under it, the shaft is forced to the other side by the "oil wedge".

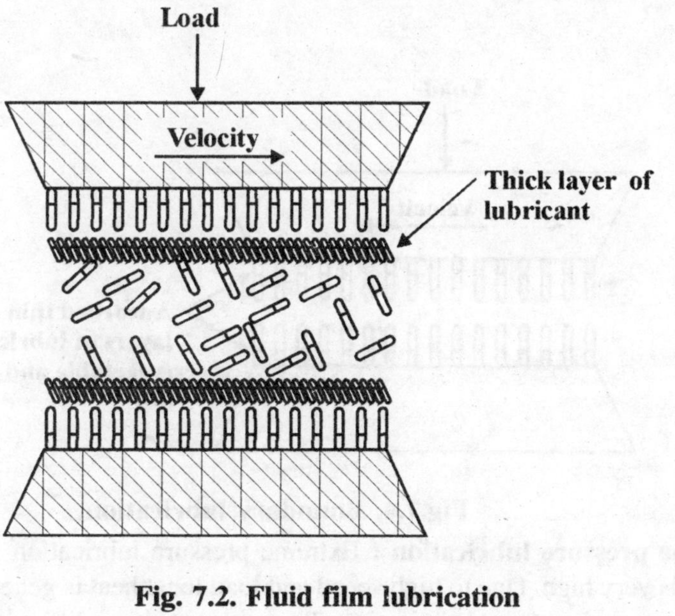

Fig. 7.2. Fluid film lubrication

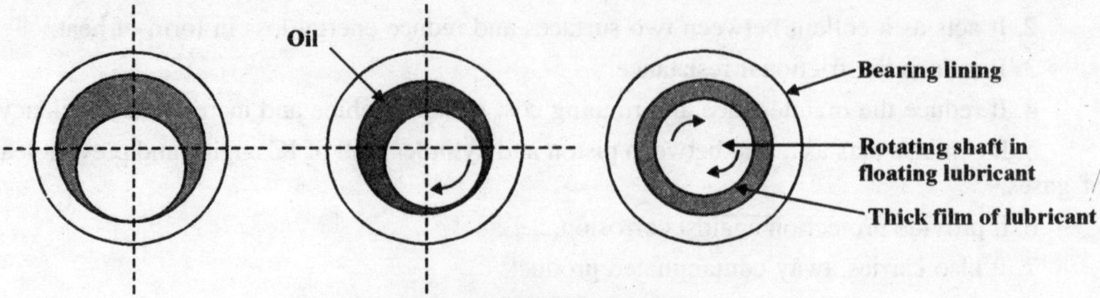

Fig. 7.3. Hydrodynamic.

Under these circumstances, after sometime, hydrodynamic theory predicts development of a sufficient pressure to keep shaft and bearing apart and the shaft "floats" in the lubricant.

(ii) Boundary film or thin film lubrication : Boundary film lubrication is done when (a) speed is very low (b) load is very high (c) viscosity of the oil is very low.

In all the above condition a continuous film of lubricant can not persist by hydrodynamic lubrication and metal contact become possible. In such condition boundary film lubrication is favorable in which a thin film of lubricant is absorbed by physical or chemical forces or both on the metallic surfaces.

Boundary lubrication depends on the applied load, oiliness of lubricants and concern metal surface and does not depend on the viscosity of lubricating oil.

The friction coefficient for boundary lubrication is ranged from 0.05 - 0.15 for good boundary lubrication. The lubricant should have long chain hydrocarbon, lateral attraction between the chains, active groups which can react chemically with the metal surface and polar groups to promote spreading and orientation over the metal surfaces at high pressure. E.g., vegetable oil, animal oils and their soaps, graphite and molybdenum disulphide are good boundary lubricants.

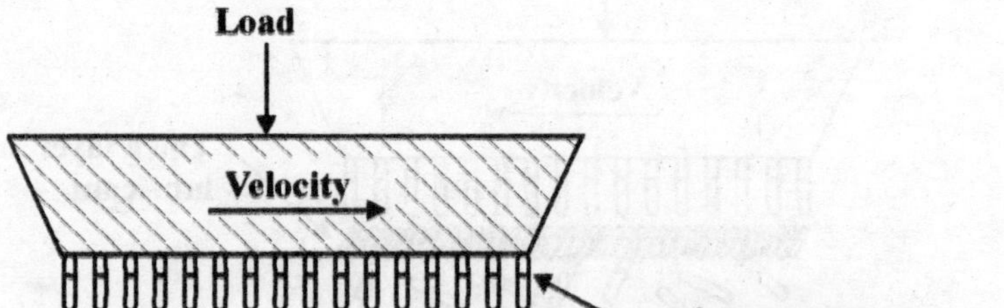

Fig.7.4. Boundary lubrication.

(iii) Extreme pressure lubrication : Extreme pressure lubrication is done when load and speed of machine is very high. Due to high speed and load local heat is generated, and this heat may decompose lubricants and surface deformation. To overcome these difficulties high pressure lubricants are to be employed. Extreme pressure additives may also added to these lubricants. Organic compounds having active radicals or group such as chlorinated esters, sulphurized fats and oils etc. are used as additives. These compounds react with metallic surfaces at prevailing high temperature to form durable film of metallic chloride or sulphide and able to withstand extreme pressure and temperature condition (due to high m.p. of itself).

7.3 CLASSIFICATION OF LUBRICANTS

Lubricants are classified in three - groups on the basis of their physical state.

(1) Liquid lubricants : These are further classified as follow :

(a) Mineral or petroleum oil : This is heavier fraction of petroleum obtain during fractional distillation of petroleum. These are cheap but have poor oiliness. Mineral oils are the most widely used lubricants and commonly used in ordinary machinery, steam cylinder, watches, clocks etc.

(b) Animal and vegetable oil : These are available from natural sources. These lubricants are costly but have good oiliness. Most of these undergo deterioration with time therefore are usually blended with appropriate blending agent. Because of good oiliness these are added to mineral oils and also used in preparation of greases and cutting emulsions. These oil are generally used in lubrication of light parts of machinery.

(c) Blended oil : These are prepared by adding specific substances called "additives" to raw lubricants to get desired properties in lubricants. The resultant oil is called blended oil or compounded oil. Oiliness carrier, pour point, depressant, viscosity index improver, antifoaming agent, emulsifiers, antioxidant, corrosion inhibiter, extreme pressure additives etc. are generally use to improve the functioning of lubricating oil.

(d) Synthetic lubricating oils : Synthetic lubricating oils are used in specific condition where normal lubricating oils are failed to perform like in hot rolling mills, oils craft turbines etc. Synthetic oil have high flash point, high viscosity index and relatively more stable at high temperature. Polyethylene glycol and silicon oil are important classes of synthetic lubricants.

(2) Semi-solid lubricants or greases : Semi-solid lubricants or greases can be prepared by mixing soap to hot lubricating oil or in synthetic siloxanes, fluorocarbons etc. Greases may be calcium based, soda based, lithium based (according to the base used during soap formation.)

The useful mechanical property of greases is to maintain consistency in viscosity when temperature changes abruptly. Greases are stable towards oxidation and resistant towards H_2O. Grease may be used as sealing agent against entry of dirt, dust etc.

(3) Solid lubricants : Liquid lubricants are generally best suited but under certain conditions including decomposition and oxidation at high temperature, liquid lubricants can not be employed. In such conditions solid lubricants like graphite, molybdenum disulphide, talcum etc. are used.

(a) Graphite : It is very soapy to touch, non - inflammable and not oxidised by air below 375°C. It consists of multitude of one atom thick flat plates, made up of network of hexagons. Which are held together by only weak bonds. So that force to shear the crystals parallel to the layer is low. This results in sliding of parallel layers over one another easily. It acts through boundary lubrication.

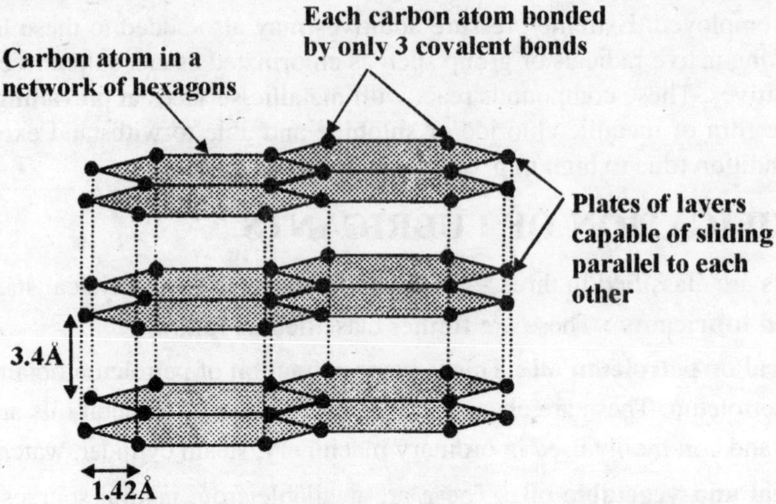

Fig.7.5. Multiple layered Structure of graphite

When graphite is dispersed in oil, it is called 'oil dag' and when it is dispersed in it water, it is called aquadag.

(b) Molybdenum disulphide : It has a sandwich like structure in which a layer of Mo-atoms lies between two layers of S-atoms. It has very low co-efficient of friction and is stable in air upto 400°C. It may be used alone or with solvents and greases.

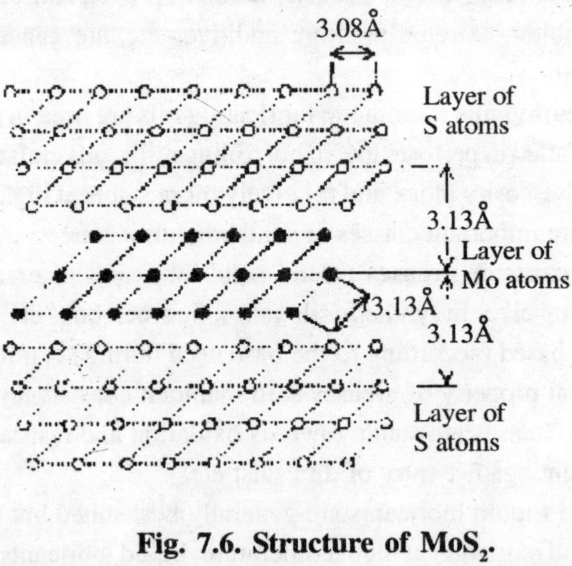

Fig. 7.6. Structure of MoS_2.

7.4 PROPERTIES OF LUBRICANTS

The important properties of the lubricants are as follow :

7.4.1 Viscosity

Viscosity is the property of a liquid or a fluid by virtue of which it offers resistance to its own flow. When a liquid flows on a surface at a steady rate, its flow actually consists of a flow of series of parallel layers moving one above the other. Each layer moves with different velocity, the top layer moves faster than the next lower layer due to internal friction. Force per unit area (F) required to maintain velocity difference (V) between the two parallel layers is expressed as follows.

$$F = \frac{\eta V}{d}$$

Where, d = distance between two layers of a liquid,

η = proportionality constant known as coefficient of viscosity η is characteristic of a particular liquid at a given temperature.

When d = 1 cm, V = cm/sec. then

$$F = \eta$$

Hence, coefficient of viscosity may be defined as "the force per unit area required to maintain a difference of unit in two adjacent layers of a liquid separated by 1cm".

If viscosity of a lubricating oil is too low, a liquid oil film can not be maintained between two surfaces and if viscosity is too high, excessive friction due the shearing of oil itself would result and heat would be generated in the system.

Viscosity index or effect of temperature on viscosity : Viscosity of lubricating oil is inversely proportional to temperature. This is due to decrease in intermolecular attraction. A good lubricant should show minimum variation in viscosity with temperature change, so that it can be used under varying condition of temperature. The rate at which the viscosity of an oil changes with temperature is measured by an arbitrary scale, known as 'viscosity index'.

If the viscosity of lubricating oils falls rapidly with increasing temperature, it has low viscosity index and oil is of poor quality in view of viscosity.

If viscosity of an oil is slightly change on rising the temperature its viscosity index will be high. Good lubricants show high viscosity index.

Determination of viscosity index : The viscosity index represent average decrease in viscosity of an oil per degree rise in temperature range of 100°F - 210°F (38°C - 99°C). To determine the viscosity index the viscosity of lubricating oil is first determined at 100°F and then at 210°F. Now compare it with two standard oil, out of which one have viscosity index of 100 and other have viscosity index of zero. Paraffinic base Pennsylvanian oils have viscosity index 100 and called high viscosity index standard while naphthionic base gulf oil have viscosity index zero and called low viscosity index standard. Viscosity index of oil under test is given by formula :

$$\text{Viscosity index} = \frac{L-U}{L-H} \times 100$$

U = viscosity of sample oil at 100°F(38°c)

L = viscosity of gulf oil at 100°F.

H = viscosity of Pennsylvanian oil at 100°F.

Viscosity of both the standard is same as that of sample oil at 210°F.

In case of good lubricating oil under test, the difference between the two values of viscosity should be minimum. If difference is large, the oil is of poor quality.

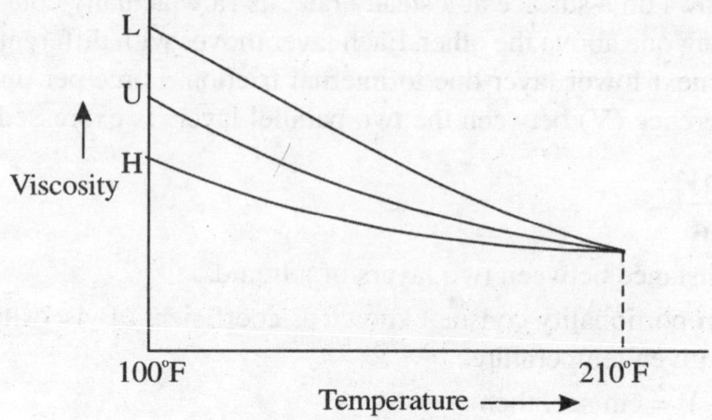

Fig. 7.7 : Curve.

The slope of viscosity index curve is high for L i.e. viscosity of low viscosity index oil changes rapidly with temperature, so it has low viscosity index and marked 0 at 100°F while viscosity index curve is comparatively flatter for high viscosity index standard, so, its viscosity changes only slightly with temperature.

Determination of Viscosity of a Lubricating Oil : Viscosity of a lubricating oil can be determined with the help of Redwood viscometer.

Principle : In Redwood viscometer a fixed volume of oil is allowed to flow through a standard hole (orifice) at fixed height and the time of flow in second is noted to determine the viscosity of an oil.

Redwood viscometer construction : Two types of Redwood viscometer are available which are differ from one-another only in respect of dimensions of discharge capillary (orifice).

Viscometer	Dimension of orifice	length of jet	lubricant tested light oil
RW - 1	1.62 mm	10 mm.	Light oil (kerosine)
RW - 2	3.8 mm	50 mm	Heavy oil (fuel oil)

Both Redwood viscometer have following parts :

(i) Oil cup : This is a silver plated brass cylinder having about 90 mm height and 46.5 mm diameter. Lid of the cup is fitted with a thermometer to indicate the oil temperature. The bottom of cylinder is fitted with an agate jet. The jet is opened or closed by a "valve rod". Which is a small silver plated brass ball fixed to a stout wire.

(ii) Heating bath : Oil cup is surrounded by a cylindrical copper bath containing water. It is heated electrically or by burner and provided with a tap on other side for water outlet. A thermometer indicates the temperature of water.

(iii) Stirrer : Stirrer is provided to maintain a uniform temperature inside the heating bath.

(iv) Kohlrausch flask : It is specially designed flask of 50 ml. It is placed inside below the jet outlet to collect the oil drops.

(v) Legs with leveling screw : The entire apparatus stands on these legs provided with leveling screw.

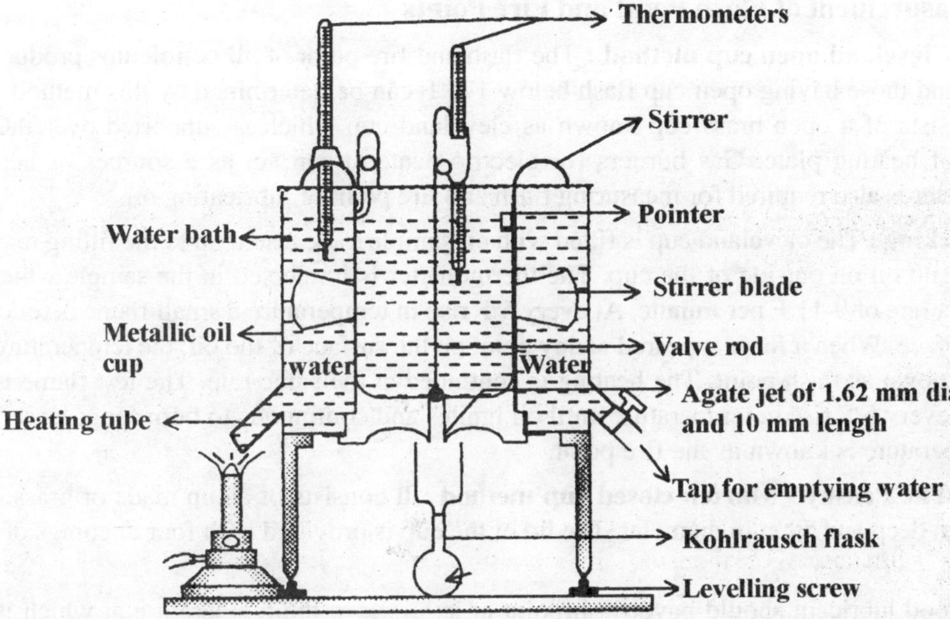

Fig. 7.8. Redwood viscometer No.1.

Working : First level the screw and clean the oil cup with suitable solvent. Now fill the water bath with water and keep the brass ball in position to seal the orifice. Fill the test oil in oil cups and heat the water bath and maintain the desired temperature of oil. Keep the empty Kohlausch flask just below the jet. Remove the ball of valve rod from ajate jet and allow to flow oil through orifice. Start the stop watch. Note the time taken for 50 ml of the oil to collect is the flask and close the ajate jet to prevent any overflow of oil. The result in reported is "Redwood" seconds at a particular temperature.

Significance of viscosity measurement : Viscosity values are used in

(i) Evaluating load carrying capacity

(ii) In denoting the effect of temperature change.

(iii) For determining the presence of contaminants is used oil during service.

7.4.2 Flash point and fire point

"Flash point is the lowest temperature at which the lubricating oil gives off enough vapours that is ignited for a moment, when a test flame is brought near it. A good lubricant should have flash point at least above the temperature at which it is to be used.

Fire point is the lowest temperature at which sufficient vapours are given off by an oil so that it burns continuously for at least five seconds on being lighted by a test flame. In general practice, the fire points are 5 to 40°C higher than the flash point.

The flash point and fire points are used to indicate the fire hazards of petroleum products and evaporation losses under high temperature condition.

Measurement of Flash Point and Fire Points

(a) Cleveland open cup method : The flash and fire point of all petroleums products except fuel oils and those having open cup flash below 175°F can be determined by this method. It essentially consists of a open brass cup known as cleveland cup which is supported over the circular opening of heating plate. Gas burners (or electric heaters) can act as a sources of heat and of thermometer is also required for measuring flash and fire point of lubricating oil.

Working : The cleveland cup is filled with oil sample to be tested up to the filling mark. There should be no oil on outside of the cup. The thermometer is immersed in the sample which is then heated at a rate of 9-11°F per minute. At every 5°F rise in temperature a small flame is touched over the oil surface. When a flash appeared at any point on the surface of the oil, the temperature reading shall be known as flash point. The heating is continued at the same rate. The test flame is applied again for every 5°F rise in temperature until oil ignites and continuous to burn for at least 5 second. This temperature is known as the fire point.

(b) The Pensky - Marten closed cup method : It consists of a cup made of brass, which is about 6 cm deep and 5 cm in diameter. The lid of the cup is provided with four openings of standard size.

A good lubricant should have flash point at least above the temperature at which it is to be used. The flash point and fire point are usually determined by using Pensky Marten's apparatus (fig. 7.9). It consist of :

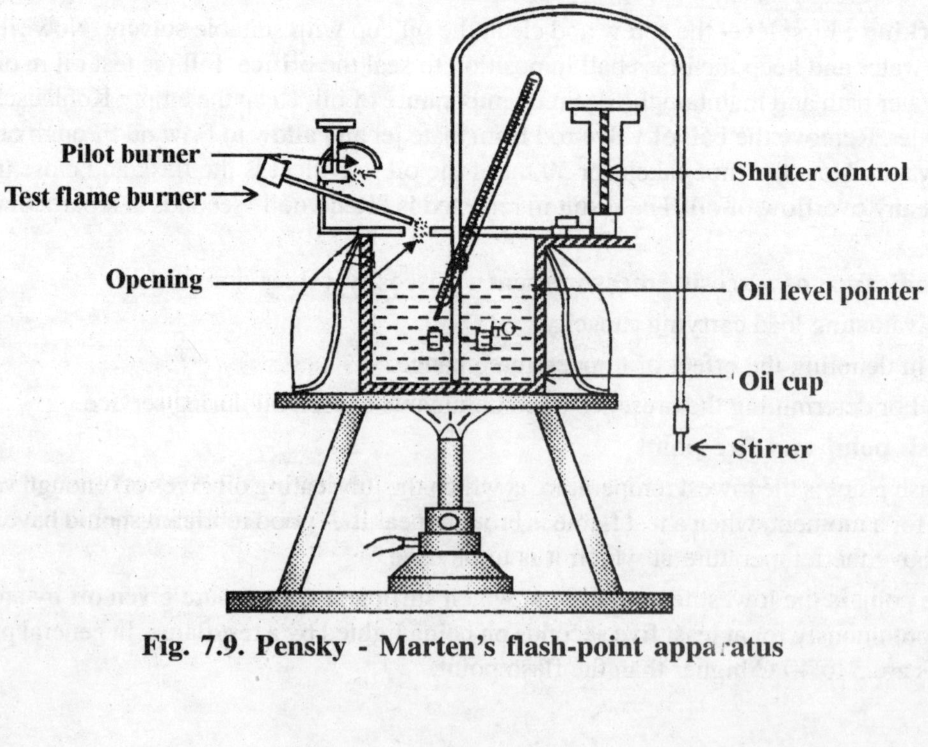

Fig. 7.9. Pensky - Marten's flash-point apparatus

(i) Oil cup : This oil cup is 5 cm is diameter and 5.5 cm deep. There is a mark inside the cup to check the level of the oil. The cup lid is provided with four openings of standard sizes. One of which is used for thermometer, second for introducing the test flame, third for stirrer and fourth is for entrance of oils.

(ii) Shutter : It is provided at the top of the cup. By moving the shutter, opening of the lid opens and flame is dipped into this opening, thereby bringing the flame over the oil surface.

(iii) Flame exposure device : It is a tiny flame, connected to the shutters.

(iv) Air bath : There is an air bath also, which is heated by a gas burner.

(v) Pilot burner : When test flame is introduced in the opening, it gets extinguished, but when the test flame is returned to its original position, it is lighted by the pilot burner automatically.

Working : Test oil is filled upto the mark in the oil cup and heated by heating oil bath by a burner. Stir the oil by stirrer. Heat is applied to increase the temperature of oil by about 5°C per minimum. At every degree centigrade increase test flame is introduced momentarily with the help of shutter. The temperature at which a distinct flash (weak sound and light) appears inside the cup is recorded as the flash point. The heating is continued and the test flame is introduced as above. When the oil ignites continuously for at least 5 sec, the temperature is noted. This is the fire point of the oil.

7.4.3 Cloud and Pour Point

When oil is cooled under some specific conditions, it first gets cloudy and then solidifies. The temperature at which a cloudy or hazzy appearance is noticed is called the cloud point of the oil. The temperature at which the oil ceases to pour or flow is called its pour point. Cloud and pour points indicate the suitability of lubricants in cold conditions. Lubricant used in a machine working at low temperature should pour low power point otherwise lubricant becomes solid and will cause jamming of the machine.

The cloud point of a petroleum oil is the temperature at which solidified compounds, like paraffin wax, present is oil begin to crystalize or separate from solution.

Pour point is important in establishing the lowest temperature at which a diesel fuel is still sufficiently fluid to be plumed (or transferred). An oil with a low pour point should be selected whenever the oil must remain at low temperature.

Determination of cloud and pour points : The apparatus (fig.7.10) consists of a flat-bottomed tube (about 12 cm height and 3 cm diameter) enclosed in an air jacket. The jacket is surrounded by freezing mixture (ice + NaCl). The tube is half - filled with oil. A thermometer is introduced in the oil.

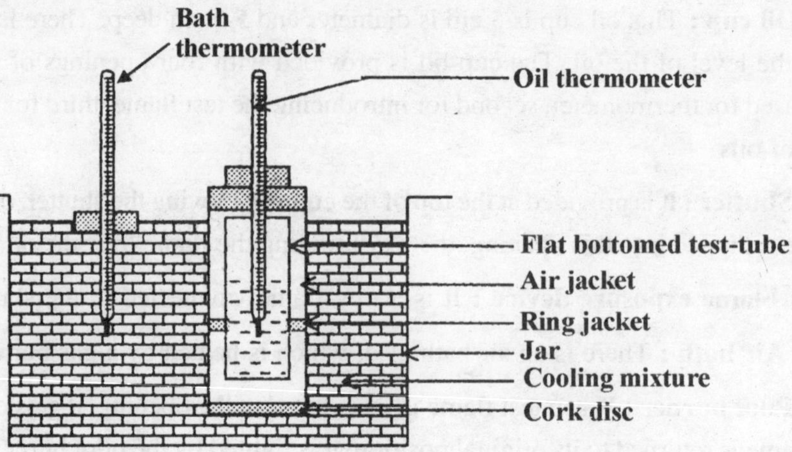

Fig. 7.10 : Cloud and pour-point apparatus

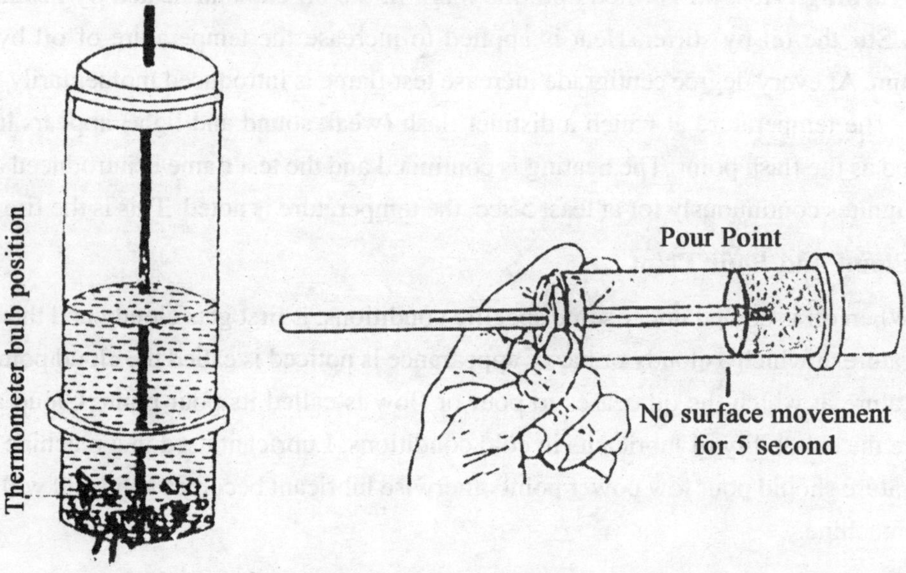

Fig. 7.11 : Observation of Cloud and Pour Point

Working : On cooling via air jacket, the temperature of oil falls continuously. Withdraw the tube with fall in each degree centigrate of oil and check for cloudiness. The temperature at which cloudiness is noticed, is recorded as the cloud - point. Continue the cooling and withdraw the test tube after every 3°C fall of temperature and tilted to observe the flow of the oil. The temperature at which the oil does not flow in the test tube, is taken as the pour point.

7.4.4 Steam Emulsion Number

The oil when thoroughly mixed with water, forms thick fluffy mass called emulsion and this process is called emulsification. Emulsion have a tendency to collect dirt, grit, dust, foreign matter etc., thereby causing abrasion and wearing out of the lubricated parts of the machinery. So a good lubricating oil should form a emulsion with water, which can break off quickly.

The tendency of lubricant - water emulsion to break is determined by ASTM test. In this test

20 ml of oil is taken in a test tube and steam at 100ºC is bubbled through it till the temperature of emulsion increases to 90ºC. The tube is then placed into bath maintained at 90ºC and the time in seconds is noted, when the oil and water seperate out in distinct layers, is called "Steam Emulsion Number" (S.E.N.) or densification number. A good lubricant should possess a low steam emulsion number.

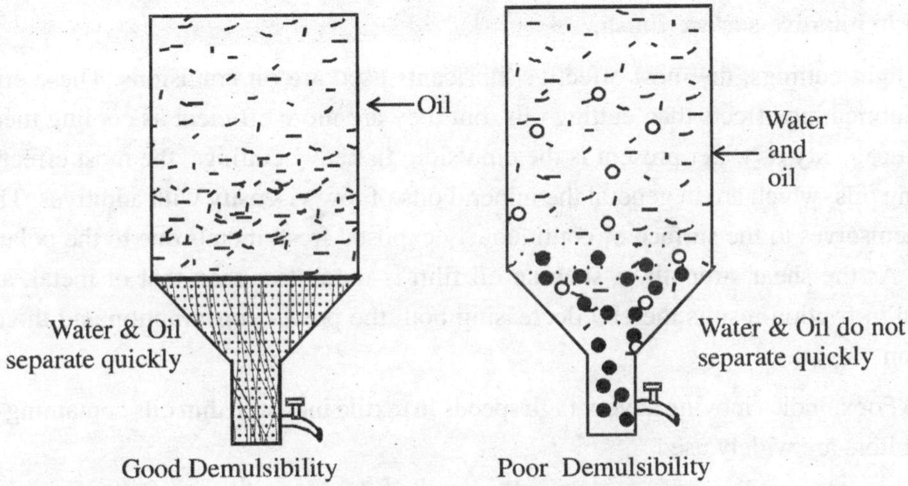

Fig. 7.12 : Demulsibility

7.4.5 Precipitation Number

It shows the percentage of asphalt present in the oil. To determine the precipitation number of an oil, a known weight of the oil is dissolved in petroleum either and centrifuged. The centrifuged asphalt, if any, is separated by filtration and then is washed, dried and weighed. It is then reported as weight percentage of the oil taken.

7.4.6 Neutralization Number

The acidity or alkalinity of a lubricating oil is determined in terms of neutralization number. The neutralization number represents either total acid number (TAN) or total base number (TBN). Total acid value is the number of milligrams of KOH required to neutralize acid present in 1 gm of oil. The number of milligrams of HCl required to neutralize any base present is one gram of oil is known as total base value[TBS]. Test of acidity is more important because presence of acid in the lubricant may lead to corrosion or may form gum and sludge. The higher acid value shows that the oil may oxidized, which may create problems. (gum formation, corrosion).

7.5 SELECTION OF LUBRICANTS

While selecting a lubricant for a particular job, the service condition requirements are to be related to the properties of the lubricant. The properties of a selected lubricant should not change much under service condition. Selection of lubricants for certain typical jobs and their functions are as below :

(i) For cutting tools : In cutting, grinding, turning operations, the friction is very high because of close contact between the work price and the tool and this generates a large amount of local heat.

Heat so liberated may overheat the tool and may lower its temper and hardness. The main functions of lubricants used as cutting fluids are :

(a) To cool the metal piece and to prevent distortion and dimensional inaccuracies.

(b) To reduce power consumption

(c) In improve surface finish.

In light cuttings, the most effective lubricants used are oil emulsions. These emulsions have smaller lubricating effects than cutting oils, but they are more efficient as cooling media due to the high heat capacity of water present is the emulsion. In heavy cuttings, the most effective lubricants are cutting oils, which are in general the mineral oils of low viscosity with additives. These additives attach themselves to the surface of continuously exposed fresh metals due to the polar gaps present in them. As the shear strength of such an oil film is much less than that of metal, a considerable reduction in friction results thereby decreasing both the power consumption and the extent of heat generation.

(ii) For spindles moving at very high speeds in textile industry, thin oils containing oxidation and rust inhibitors are widely used.

(iii) In internal combustion engines, the lubricant has to be exposed to high temperature conditions. So lubricant used in internal combustion should have high VI and thermal stability. Petroleum oils containing additives are generally used for this purpose.

(iv) In high pressure devices, the lubricants are subjected to very high pressure. Hence for such type of application, the lubricants must posses good oiliness, good load carrying capacity, good resistance to oxidation and should not be removed from the applied place. Thick mineral oils having extreme pressure additives are employed for this purpose.

(v) In high pressure and low speed device, (like rail axle boxes, wire ropes etc.) greases and blended thick oils are most suitable.

(vi) For refrigeration system, the lubricants with low pour point, low viscosity and low cloud point are used. E.g.. naphthalene based oils.

(vii) For electrical transformers, the lubricants should possess low viscosity good dielectric properties, optimum oxidation resistance and high chemical stability. Moreover transformer oil is also exposed to air to a very small extent and so when the transformer is on load, such exposure to air, high temperature electric stress and catalytic effect of upper etc. cause various chemical changes in oil leading to acid and sludge formation, that's why applied lubricating oil should have high chemical stability and optimum oxidation resistance.

Review Questions

1. What are lubricants. Write function and properties of lubricants. ***[RTU 2009]***
2. Define viscosity and viscosity index. How are these properties of lubricating oil improved? ***[Raj. Univ. 1994]***
3. Write short notes on flash and fire point and their determination. ***[RTU - 2010, 2001, Raj. Univ., 1995, 2001]***
4. Write short notes on :
   (a) Cloud and pour point ***[RTU - 2010]***
   (b) Emulsification factor ***[RTU - 2005]***
5. What are lubricants? How are they classified? Explain the following properties of lubricants and give their significance :
   (1) Viscosity (2) Viscosity index (3) Pour point ***[Raj. Univ. 1997, RTU - 2008]***
6. Explain thin layer mechanism of lubrication. ***[Raj. Univ. 2004]***
7. Discuss the types of mechanism of lubrication. ***[RTU June 2008]***
8. What is viscosity ? How it changes with temperature? Give method of its determination.
9. Write a brief note on :
   (i) Neutralization number
   (ii) Stem Emulsion number
   (iii) Precipitation number.
10. What are greases ? Mention their specific uses.
11. Discuss the various types of lubrication. ***[RTU 2010]***

❑❑❑

EXPERIMENT - 1

Object : To determine the hardness of water by HCl method.

Apparatus : Burette, pipette, conical flask, funnel, volumetric (250 ml), Beaker.

Reagents : Water sample, HCl $\frac{N}{50}$, standard Na_2CO_3, methyl orange.

Theory : Hardness of water is characteristic property of water which prevent the lathering of soap due to presence of soluble bicarbonates of calcium and magnesium and formation of insoluble PPT due to dissolved some chloride and sulphets of calcium and magnecium.

Temporary hardness is removed by simply boiling of water because its decomposed to carbonate and hydroxide of calcium and magnicium.

$$Ca(HCO_3)_2 \xrightarrow{\text{Boiling}} CaCO_3 \downarrow + CO_2 \uparrow + H_2O$$

$$Mg(HCO_3)_2 \xrightarrow{\text{Boiling}} Mg(OH)_2 \downarrow + 2CO_2 \uparrow$$

The Temporary Hardness can be determined by estimating the alkalinity of water sample before and after boiling by titrating with $\frac{N}{50}$ HCl solution.

$$Ca(HCO_3)_2 + 2HCl \longrightarrow CaCl_2 + 2CO_2 + 2H_2O$$

$$Mg(HCO_3)_2 + 2HCl \longrightarrow MgCl_2 + 2CO_2 + 2H_2O$$

Indicator : Methyl orange with P^H 3.1 to 4.5 acting in acidic medium

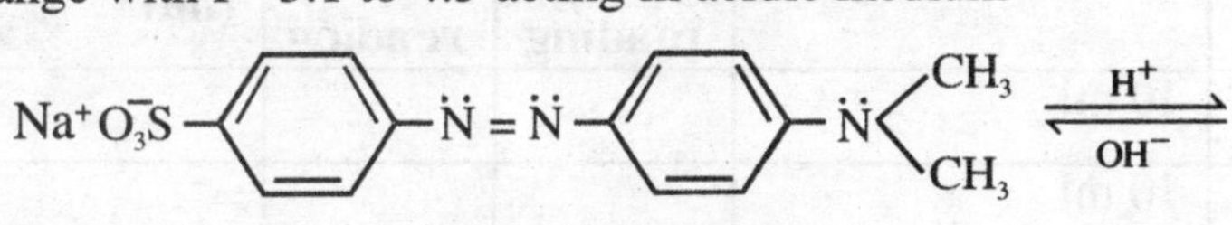

(Yellow in basic medium)

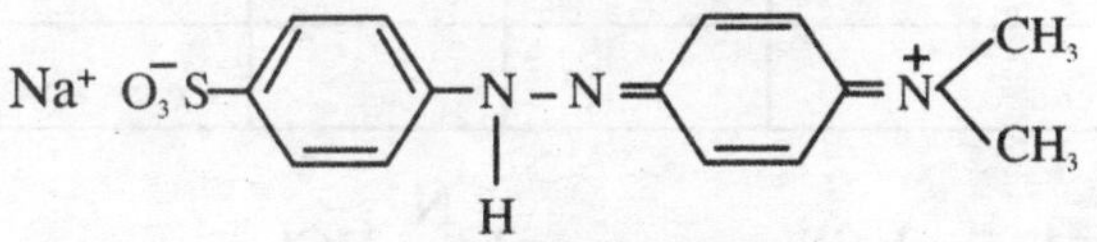

(Red in acidic medium)

Procedure :

(1) Wash all the apparatus with distill water.

(2) Fill the burette with $\frac{N}{50}$ standard HCl solution and note the initial reading.

(3) Take pipette out 10 ml of Na_2CO_3 solution is conical flask and add 2-3 drops of methyl - orange indicator.

(4) Titrate it against standard HCl from buretter drop by drop and shaking till the colour changes from yellow to red. This is end point and note the final reading.

(5) Repeat the titration two concordant reading are obtained.

(6) Repeat the titration till two reading.

(7) Take 250 ml of water sample and boiled half an hour because all bicarbonates are completely decomposed and filter it.

(8) Take pipette out 10 ml of filtrate water in conical flask and add 2-3 drops of indicator.

(9)Titrate it against HCl till colour changes from yellow to red.

(10) Repeat the titration for finding concordant reading.

Observation Table :

(A) Titration between $Na_2CO_3 + \frac{N}{50}$ HCl standard

S.NO.	Volume of Na_2CO_3	Burette reading		Volume of HCL solution used (ml)	Concordant reading
		Initial reading	Final reading		
1.	10 ml				
2.	10 ml				
3.	10 ml				
					V_1

(B) Titration between sample of water and $\frac{N}{50}$ HCl solution (before boiling)

S.NO.	Volume of Na_2CO_3	Burette reading		Volume of HCL solution used (ml)	Concordant reading
		Initial reading	Final reading		
1.	10 ml				
2.	10 ml				
3.	10 ml				
					V_2

(C) Titration between boiling water and $\frac{N}{50}$ HCl

S.NO.	Volume of Na_2CO_3	Burette reading		Volume of HCL solution used (ml)	Concordant reading
		Initial reading	Final reading		
1.	10 ml				
2.	10 ml				
3.	10 ml				
					V_3

Calculation :

(A) Standardization of HCl solution

$$N_1V_1 = N_2V_2$$

$$N_1 = \frac{N_2V_2}{V_1}$$

Where, N_1 = Normality of HCl solution
V_1 = Volume of HCl consumed
N_2 = Normality of Na_2CO_3 solution
V_2 = Volume of Na_2CO_3 solution

(B) Determination of temporary hardness

$$N_3V_3 = N_4V_4$$

$$N_3 = \frac{N_4V_4}{V_3}$$

Where, N_3 = Normality of water sample
V_3 = Volume of water sample
N_4 = Normality of HCl solution
V_4 = Volume of HCl used by water

$V_4 = [V_2 - V_3]$ = [Vol. of HCl used by sample water] **(Before boiling)**
– [Vol. of HCl used by boiled water] **(After boiling)**

Strength of Hardness : = N_3 × gm equivalent weight of $CaCO_3$
= N_3 × 50 gm of $CaCO_3$
= N_3 × 50 × 1000 mg of $CaCO_3$
= N_3 × 5/50 × 1000 ppm

Result :

Hardness of given water sample is = ...ppm

Precautions :

(i) Wash all the apparatus with distill water.
(ii) All solutions should be freshly prepared.
(iii) The amount of indicator should be used same.
(iv) End point should be observed carefully finding the correct concordant - reading.

❑❑❑

EXPERIMENT - 2

Object : To determine the temporary and permanent hardness of a given water sample by EDTA method.

Apparatus and Reagents : Burette (50 ml), pipette (10 ml), Conical flask, Volumetric flask (100 ml), $CaCO_3$ (1 PPM), EDTA Solution, Ammonia buffer (PH = 10) Erichrome Black - T Indicator.

Theory : Hardness is that property of water which prevents lather formation with soap temporary or carbonate hardness is due to carbonates and bicorbonates of Ca^{2+}, Mg^{2+}. It can be removed by boiling of water. The permanent hardness or non carbonate hardness, cannot be removed by simple methods hence it is termed as permanent hardness. The salts responsible for causing this type hardness are $MgSO_4$, $CaSO_4$, $CaCl_2$ and $MgCl_2$ apart from Ca^{2+} and Mg^{2+} which are hardness causing salts, other ions such as fe^{2+}, fe^{3+}, Mn^{2+}, Sr^{2+} and Al^{3+} also cause hardness but they are in negligible quantity.

The complexometric method is supposed to be a most accurate method for determining the hardness of water. In this method Ethylene diamine tetra acetic acid (EDTA) and Eriochrome Black - T (EBT) are used EDTA (ethylene diamine tetra acetic acid) is used asa complexing agent.

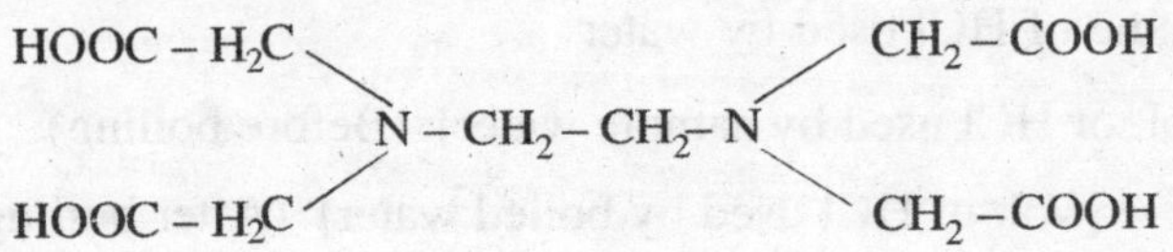

As it is not very soluble in water and hence EDTA in the form of its disodium salt is normally used in all complexometric titrations.

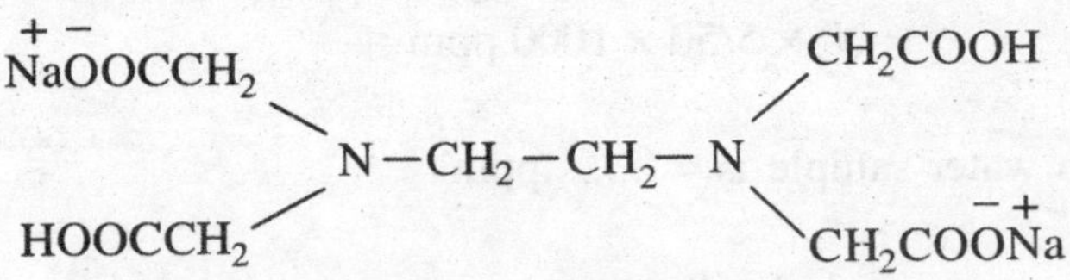

Disodium salt of EDTA

Eriochrome black - T is the metal ion indicator used in the determination of hardness by complexometric method of EDTA.

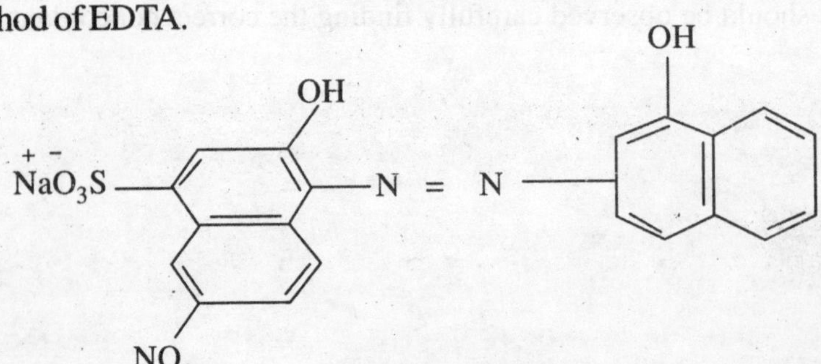

This indicator is effective at a PH of about 10. When EBT is added to hard water buffered to a PH of about 10 (by employing NH_4OH - NH_4CL buffer), a wine - red unstable complex isformed. Thus

$$\left(Ca^{2} + \text{or } Mg^{2+} \text{ of hard water}\right) + EBT \xrightarrow{PH=10} [M-EBT]\text{Complex Wine} - \text{Red}$$

So initially a wine - red coloured is obtained. During the course of titration against EDTA solution EDTA combines with Mg^{2+} [or Ca^{2+} or Mg^{2+}] ions from stable complexM-EDTA and Relesing free EBT, which instantaneously combines with M^{2+} ions still present in the solution there by win - red colour is retained. Thus

$$[M-EBT]\text{ Complex} + EDTA \xrightarrow{\text{Titration}} \underset{\text{Complex}}{[M-EDTA]} + \underset{\text{(blue)}}{EBT}$$

$$\left[Ca^{2+}\text{or } Mg^{2+} \text{ still present}\right] + \underset{\text{(Blue)}}{EBT} \rightarrow \underset{\text{wine - red}}{[M-EBT]\text{Complex}}$$

However, when nearly all $M^{2+}\left[Ca^{2+} \text{ or } Mg^{2+}\right]$ ions have formed [M-EDTA] complex, then next drop to EDTA - added displaces the EBT indicator form [M-EBT] complex and wine - red colour changes to blue colour (due to EBT). Thus at equivalent point.

$$[M-EBT]\text{ Complex} + EDTA \rightarrow [M-EBT]$$

$$\text{Complex} + EBT\text{(blue)}$$

Thus change of wine - red colour to blue marks the end - point of titration.

Procedure :

Preparation of standard water : 1 gm of pure and dry $CaCO_3$ is dissolved in a minimum quantity of HCl and the solution isevaporated to dryness over a hot water both. The Residue left behind is dissolved the distilled water and the solution is made - up to one litre.

Preparation of EDTA Solution : 3.78 gm of disodium salt of EDTA is dissolved in distilled water and made upto 1 litre.

Preparation of Eriochrome Black - T Indicator : 0.5 gm of Erichrome Black - T indicator is dissolved in 100 ml of ethanol.

Preparation of Buffer Solution ($P^H \simeq 10$) : 70 gm of NH_4Cl and 568 ml of ammonia solution is mixed and make-up to 1 litre with distilled water.

Step 1 : Standaridzation of EDTA Solution : First of all Rinese the burette with EDTA solution and fill it with EDTA solution.

Rinese with pipette with standard $CaCO_3$ solution and take 10 ml $CaCO_3$ solution in a 250 ml conical flask. Now add 2-3 ml of buffer solution and 2 - 3 drops of EBT indicator.

The colour of solution turn wine red. Titrate the solution against standard EDTA solution (filled in burette) the colour changes from wine red to clear blue.

This is the end point and note down the burette readings. Repeat the process atleast three times and to get concordant reading obtained. Let the volume of EDTA used be V_1 ml.

Step II : Determination of Total hardness of water : Take 10 ml ofhard water sample and titrate it against EDTA solution. Let the volume of EDTA consumed be V_2 ml.

Determination of permanent hardness of water : Take 10 ml of boil water sample into a conical flask. Add 2-3 ml of buffer solution and 2-3 drops of EBT indicator to it.

Titrate it against EDTA solution untill the end point is appears. Let the volume of EDTA consumed be V_3 ml.

Observations :

Volume of water sample taken = 10 ml

Table I : Titration of standard hard water v/s EDTA

S.NO.	Volume of SHW in ml	Volume of EDTA solution in ml		Volume of EDTA Consumed (ml)	Concordant Reading
		Initial	Final		
1.	10 ml	0.0			
2.	10 ml	0.0			V_1 ml
3.	10 ml	0.0			

Table II : Titration of hardwater sample v/s EDTA

S.NO.	Volume of H.W in ml	Volume of EDTA solution in ml		Volume of EDTA Consumed (ml)	Concordant Reading
		Initial	Final		
1.	10 ml	0.0			
2.	10 ml	0.0			V_2 ml
3.	10 ml	0.0			

Table III : Titration of boiled water sample v/s EDTA

S.NO.	Volume of B.W in ml	Volume of EDTA solution in ml		Volume of EDTA Consumed (ml)	Concordant Reading
		Initial	Final		
1.	10 ml	0.0			
2.	10 ml	0.0			V_3 ml
3.	10 ml	0.0			

Calculations :

$$\text{Total hardness} = \frac{V_2}{V_1} \times 1000 \text{ mg./litre}$$

$$\text{or total hardness} = \left(\frac{V_2}{V_1}\right) \times 1000 \text{ PPm}$$

$$\text{similarly permanent hardness} = \left(\frac{V_3}{V_1}\right) \times 1000 \text{ PPm}$$

Temporary hardness = Total hardness – Permanent hardnes

$$= \left(\frac{V_2}{V_1}\right) \times 1000 - \left(\frac{V_3}{V_1}\right) \times 1000 \text{ PPm}$$

$$= \left(\frac{V_2 - V_3}{V_1}\right) \times 1000 \text{ PPm}$$

Result :

The hardness of a given water sample is

(i) Total hardness = ...ppm

(ii) Permanent hardness = ...pPm

(iii) Temporary hardness = ...pPm

Precautions :

(i) The glass wares used should be thoroughly washed with distilled water and dried.

(ii) All the solutions should be freshly prepared.

(iii) Same quantity of EBT indicator should be used every time.

(iv) Add standard EDTA dropwise to observe the end point correctly.

(v) P^H of the medium should be kept around 10.

❑❑❑

EXPERIMENT - 3

Object : To determine the dissolved carbon dioxide (CO_2) of a given sample of water.

Apparatus and reagents : Burette (25ml); conical flask, volumetric flask (100ml) Na_2CO_3 solution $\left(\frac{N}{50}\right)$, phenolphthalein.

Theory : Natural water contains dissolved carbon dioxide (CO_2). It may enter in water by absorption from atmosphere or liberated by biological oxidation of organic matter with which water has been in contact.

The dissolved carbon dioxide content of water sample is important as it contribute to the corrosion. The dissolved CO_2 is often the sole contributor to the acidity of potable natural water sample. On this account CO_2 determination bears a close resemblance to acidity titration.

Either Na_2CO_3 or NaOH standard solution is acceptable, though Na_2CO_3 is preferred. The completion of reaction is indicated by appearance of pink colour by phenolphthalein as indicator.

$$CO_2 + 2OH^- \rightarrow CO^{2-} + H_2O$$

$$CO_2 + CO_3^{2-} + H_2O \rightarrow 2HCO_3^-$$

Procedure :

1. Wash the apparatus with distilled water.

2. Rinse the burette with standard (N/50) Na_2CO_3 solution and then fill it in burette. Note down the initial burette reading.

3. Rinse the pipette with water sample. Pipette out 10 ml of water sample, transfer it to conical flask.

4. Add 2-3 drops of phenolphthalein indicator.

5. Titrate the water sample in conical flask by adding Na_2CO_3 solution from burette. The appearance of pink colour indicates the presence of end point. Note down the burette reading and find out the volume of Na_2CO_3 consumed.

6. Repeat the titration to get concordant reading.

5. Observation and Calculations :

Volume of water sample taken for each titration = 25ml.

Concordant volume of n/50 Na_2CO_3 used = V ml.

$$N_1V_1 = N_2V_2$$

$$(CO_2)\,(Na_2CO_3)$$

$$N_1 \times 25 = N/50 \times V$$

Therefore, normality of the CO_2 sample $= \dfrac{V}{50 \times 25}$

$$\text{Strength} = \frac{V \times 22}{50 \times 25} \text{ gm/lit}$$

$$= \frac{V \times 22 \times 1000}{50 \times 25} \text{ mg/lit}$$

$$= 17.6 \times V \text{mg/lit.}$$

Result :

Amount of dissolved CO_2 in given sample of water = 17.6 mg./Lit.

Precaution :

(i) The glass wares used should be washed with distilled water.

(ii) All the solution should be freshly prepared.

(iii) Indicator should be used proper time.

❑❑❑

EXPERIMENT - 4

Object : To determine the amount of free chlorine in a given water sample.

Apparatus and Reagents : Burette (50ml), pipette (10ml), conical flask (250ml), sodium thiosulphate $\frac{N}{40}$, glacial acetic acid, KI (10%) starch indicator (freshly prepared), dill H_2SO_4.

Theory : Purified water is used for drinking purposes, usually chlorine gas is used for complete removal of bacteria, fungicides and other micro organisms. The germicide action of Cl_2 gas depends upon its reaction with water producing hypochlorous acid (HOCl) and nascent oxygen [O] both of which are powerful germicides.

$$CaOCl_2 + 2CH_2COOH \rightarrow (CH_3COO)_2\,Ca + Cl_2 + H_2O$$

$$Cl_2 + H_2O \rightarrow HOCL + HCL$$

$$HOCl + Cl_2 \rightarrow HCL + [O] \text{ Nascent oxygen}$$

If chlorine in water is beyond a certain limit it will make municipal water unfit for drinking purposes because chlorine gas injurious to human metabolism process. It is therefore, necessary to determine the amount of free chlorine in municipal water to adjust its quantities prior to the use of water for domestic drinking purpose.

The analysis is based on the oxidation of KI by the free chlorine present in water. The liberated iodine is estimated by titrating against standard hypo solution, using starch as an indicator.

$$Cl_2 + 2KI \rightarrow 2KCl + I_2 \text{ liberated iodine}$$

$$\underset{\text{sodium thiosulphate}}{I_2 + 2Na_2S_2O_3} \rightarrow \underset{\text{sodium tetra thionate}}{Na_2S_4O_6} + NaI$$

Procedure :

(1) First of all wash all the apparatus with distilled water.

(2) Rinse the burette with hypo solution and fill it with standardized hypo solution. Not down the initial reading of burette.

3. Take 10 ml of given water sample in conical flask and 3-4 ml glacial acetic acid to maintain 3-4 P^H, shake the solution and than add 10 ml of KI(10%) solution.

4. Titrate the water sample with standardized hypo solution.

Add hypo solution from burette fill the solution in the conical flask becomes faint yellow. Now add few drops of freshly prepared starch indicator, a blue colour appears.

Continue to add hypo solution drop wise with constant shaking fill the blue colour disappears. It indicates the end point note down the burette reading.

Repeat the titration till the concordant reading obtained.

Observation Table :

Normality of standard sodium thiosulphate used $=\frac{N}{40}$ volume of water sample taken for each titration = 10 ml

S.NO.	Volume of water sample in ml	Burette reading volume of hypo solution in ml		Volume of hypo consumed (ml)	Concordant Reading (ml)
		Initial	Final		
1.	10 ml	0.0			
2.	10 ml	0.0			V
3.	10 ml	0.0			

Calculations :

[A] Calculation of normality of free chlorine in the given water sample :

Water sample Sodium thiosulphate solution

$$N_1 V_1 = N_2 V_2$$

$$N_1 = \frac{N_2 V_2}{V_1}$$

$$N_1 = \frac{N}{40} \times \frac{V}{10}$$

[B] Calculation of amount of free chlorine :

Strength of free chlorine = Normality × equivalent weight of chlorine

$$= \frac{N}{40} \times \frac{V}{10} \times 35.5 \text{ gm/lit}$$

$$= \frac{V \times 35.5 \times 1000}{400} \text{ mg/lit}$$

$$= 88.75 \text{ V mg/lit}$$

$$= 88.75 \text{ ppm}$$

Result :

The amount of free chlorine in a given water sample is ....ppm.

Precautions :

(1) All the reagents should be freshly prepared.

(2) Only 10 ml of KI solution is used carefully.

(3) Starch indicator should be same used in whole titration.

(4) Use distilled water throughout the titration.

❑❑❑

EXPERIMENT - 5

Object : To determine the viscosity of a given sample of lubricating oil using redwood viscometer.

Apparatus and Reagents Required : Redwood viscometer No. 1, stopwatch, thermometer, lubricating oil.

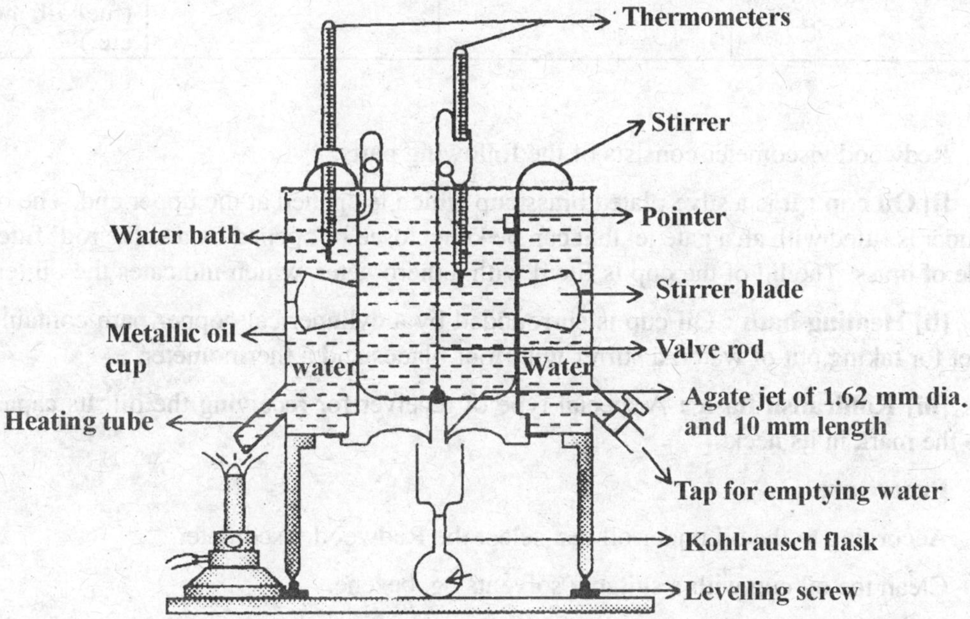

Theory : The viscosity of a fluid oil can be defined as the tangential force per unit area required to maintain a unit velocity gradient between two adjacent layers in the fluid which are unit distance apart. (Resistance to flow between two layers)

For academica purposes viscosity is usually expressed in centipoise (1/100 poise) or centistoke

$$V = \frac{\eta}{\rho}$$

where V = viscosity of fluid

η = coefficient of viscosity

ρ = density of the fluid

Viscosity of an oil can be measured in terms of the time (or seconds) taken by the oil to flow through the particular standard apparatus used.

Redwood viscometer is available in two sizes

[A] Redwood viscometer no. 1.

[B] Redwood viscometer no. 2.

Both viscometers are identical in principle shape and working. They differ only in dimensions of the discharge capillary (yet/orifice).

Viscometer	Dimension of orifice	Length of the orifice	Useful for the lubricants
RW 1	1.62 mm	10 mm	Light oils
RW 2	3.8 mm	50 mm	Highly viscous oils (fuel oil, mobile oil etc.)

Redwood viscometer consists of the following parts.

[i] Oil cup : It is a silve plated brass cup which is opened at the upper end. The bottom of the cylinder is fitted with an a gate jet that can be kept closed or opened by a valve rod' fitted with a ball made of brass. The lid of the cup is fitted with a therometer, which indicates the oil temperature.

[ii] Heating bath : Oil cup is surrounded by a cylinderical copper path containing water an outlet for taking out of water, a stirrer with four blades and a thermometer.

[iii] Kohiraush flask : A special type of receiver for receiving the oil. Its capacity is 50 ml upto the mark in its neck.

Procedure :

According to the oil under oil test select the Redwood viscometer.

Clean the oil cup with a suitable solvents eg. bezene.

Fill the heating bath with and oil cup with oil upto the tip of the indicator.

Agate jet is closed by ploacing the ball of valve rod on it.

Put the Kohlvausch flask below the jet.

Heat the water in heating bath with the help of burner placed below the long side tube.

Maintain the desired temperature by stirring the water in heating bath and oil in oil cup.

As soon as the desired temperature achieved, lift the ball valve and start the stop watch. Note the time for collecting the oilcup the 50 ml, mark in the receiver.

Replace the ball valve in position to seal the cup and refill the oil upto indicator mark perform the experiment to get reproducible results.

Repeat the experiment at five different temperatures and note the respective times.

Observation Table :

S.No.	Temperature (°C)	Time (Seconds) Trial-1	Trial-2	Trial-3	Viscosity average in Redwood seconds
1.	40	a_1	a_2	a_3	$\frac{a_1+a_2+a_3}{3}=a$
2.	50	b_1	b_2	b_3	$\frac{b_1+b_2+b_3}{3}=b$
3.	60	c_1	c_2	c_3	$\frac{c_1+c_2+c_3}{3}=c$
4.	70	-	-	-	-
5.	80	-	-	-	-

Calculation :

$$V = At - \frac{B}{t}$$

where V = viscosity of liquid

t = time of flow in seconds

A and B are instrument constants the value of

(A) = 0.264 (B) = 190 when t = 40 to 85 sec.

(A) = 0.247 (B) = 65 when t = 85 to 2000 sec.

100 centistoke = 1 stoke

$$\frac{1}{\text{poise}} = \text{centipoise}$$

Result :

The viscosity of given sample of oil at T°C is ....Redwood seconds.

Precautions :

(i) Before starting the experiment and after each reading, the cup and receiver should be properly washed.

(ii) The receiver is so kept that the oil jet touches inside layer of the flask and does not cause foaming.

(iii) Filter the oil through a mesh wire seive before testing for its viscosity.

(iv) The temperature of bath and oil cup should be maintained identical throughout the experiment.

EXPERIMENT - 6

Object : To determine the residual chlorine in a given water sample.

Apparatus and Reagents : Burette (50ml), pipette (10ml), volumetric flask (100ml), measuring cylinder, conical flask, watch glass, bleaching powder, sodium thiosulphate N/40, KI (10%) solution, glacial acetic acid, starch solution (freshly prepared).

Theory : Available chlorine which is a measure of quality of bleaching powder. It is liberated by the action of dilute acid, oxidizes KI and liborates iodine in equal amount which may be titrated against standardized hypo solution.

$$CaOCl_2 + 2CH_3COOH \rightarrow (CH_3COO)_2 Ca + H_2O + Cl_2$$

$$Cl_2 + 2KI \rightarrow 2KCl + \underset{\text{(liberated iodine)}}{I_2}$$

$$I_2 + 2Na_2S_2O_3 \rightarrow \underset{\text{Sodium tetra thionate}}{Na_2S_4O_6} + 2NaI$$

$$Starch + I_2 \rightarrow \underset{\text{(Deep blue colour)}}{\text{do starch Complex}}$$

Procedure :

- Wash the burette, pipette and conical flask with distilled water thoroughly.
- Rinse the burette with standardized hypo solution and fill the burette with hyposolution.
- Note down the initial reading of burette.
- Rinse the pipette with homogenous solution of bleaching powder. Pipette out 10 ml of homogenous solution, transfer it to conical flask.
- Add 10 ml of KI (10%) solution and 3-4 ml of glacial acetic acid solution becomes brown colour.
- Titrate the liberated iodine against the hypo (thiosulphate) solution untill the solution in conical flask turns to pale yellow colour.
- Now add 2-3 drops of freshly prepared starch solution. Solution turns to blue colour.
- Add continuously hyposolution till the blue colour disappears. This blue colour indicates the end point.
- Repeat the procedure at least three times and to get concordant readings.

Observation :

Titration of bleaching powder sample with intermediate hypo solution.

S.NO.	Volume of water sample solution (ml)	Burette reading volume of hypo solution (ml)		Volume of hypo solution (ml)	Concordant Reading
		Initial	Final		
1.	10 ml	0.0			
2.	10 ml	0.0			V ml
3.	10 ml	0.0			

Calculation :

[A] Calculate of normality of chlorine water sample

Water sample Hypo solution

$$N_1V_1 = N_2V_2$$

$$N_1 = \frac{N_2V_2}{V_1}$$

[B] Calculate the strength of available chlorine

Strength of available chlorine = Normality × equivalent weight of chlorine

$$= N_1 \times 35.5 \text{ gm/lit}$$

$$\% \text{ of availble chlorine} = \text{strength} \times \frac{100}{5}$$

Result :

The percentage of availble chlorine in a given sample of bleaching powder is .....%.

Precautions :

(i) Clean glass apparatus should be used in experiment.

(ii) All the reagents should be freshly prepared.

(iii) End point should be observe carefully.

(iv) Use distilled water to prepared the solution.

❑❑❑

EXPERIMENT - 7

Object : To determine the flash and fire point of lubricating oil by Pensky - Marten's apparatus.

Apparatus and Reagents : Pensky - Marten's apparatus thermometer, lubricating oil.

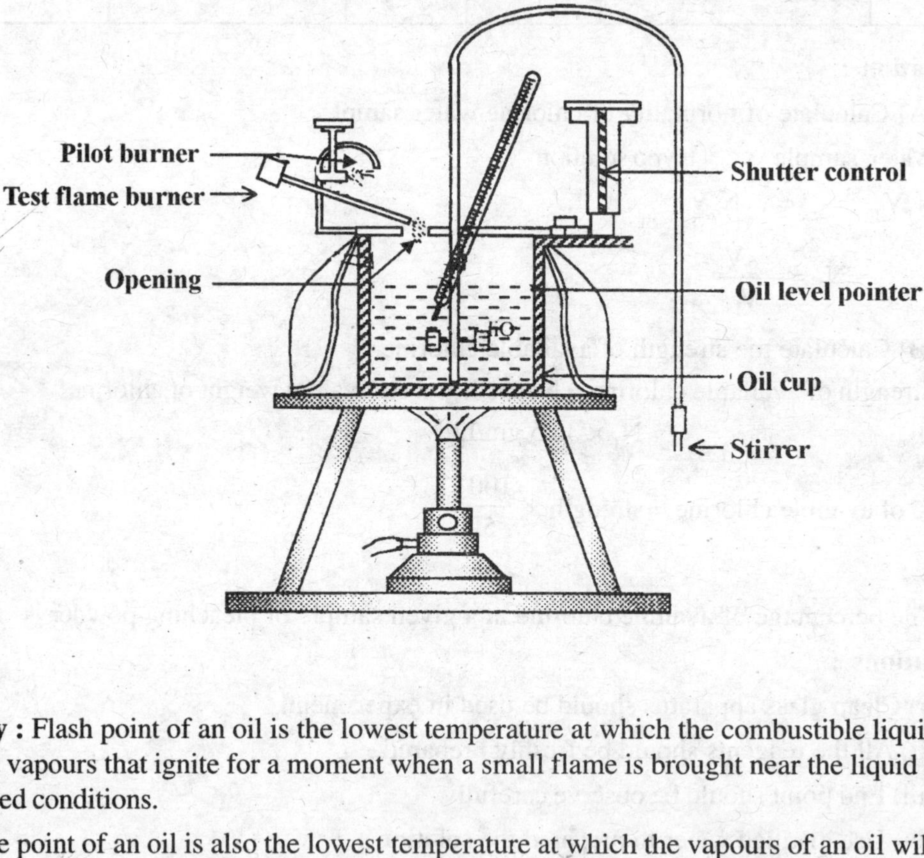

Theory : Flash point of an oil is the lowest temperature at which the combustible liquid gives off sufficient vapours that ignite for a moment when a small flame is brought near the liquid surface under specified conditions.

The fire point of an oil is also the lowest temperature at which the vapours of an oil will begin to produce a continuous flame above the oil for atleast 5 seconds.

If a liquids is having flash point less than 140° F is called flammable liquid and those with flash point above 140° F are called combustible liquids. Normally, the fire point of an oil is 5 to 40°C higher than its flash point.

Flash and fire point apparatus :

Flash and fire point of a lubricating oil can be determined with

1. Abel's apparatus
2. Cleveland's open cup apparatus
3. Pensky - Morten's closed cup apparatus

Pensky-Morten's apparatus is the most commonly used apparatus for determination of flash point of oils. This apparatus consists following features.

1. Oil cup : It consists of brass cup having 5 cm diameter and 5.5 cm depth and a mark up to which the oil has to be filled.

2. Lid of the oil cup : The cover lid of the cup has four openings one for special type of stirrer second for thermometer third for an air inlet and fourth a device for introducing the standard flame. at the top of the cup a shutter is provided which has a lever mechanism.

3. Electrical Heater : The heat up the complete assembly in a controlled manner.

Procedure :

1. Clean the oil cup and other parts throughly experiment.
2. Put the apparatus on a level steady table to avoid any damage or accident.
3. Fill the oil to be tested in the cup to the level of mark.
4. Cover the lid and insert the thermometer stirrer device and flame exposure device carefully in its openings.
5. Heat the appratus homogenously by using the air bath with the help of burner or hot plate and stirrer (approx. 60 revolution per minute).
6. When the temperature with in the range of anticipated flash point at every 1°C rise flame is introduced for a moment with the help of shutter.
7. Record the flash point at the temperature at which a flash appears in the form of weak sound and light. This temperature is flash point. Allow to cool the oil for some time, heat again and test the flame for a distinct flash. Repeat the process 3-4 times.
8. The procedure is continued as before until oil vapour catches fire which stays minimum for seconds. The temperature at which this ignition taken place is recorded as fire point of the oil.

Observation Table :

S.No.	Temperature °C	Flash point	Fire point
1.	40		
2.	50		
3.	60		
4.	70		
5.	80		

Result :

The flash point of given oil sample is .....°C.

The fire point of given oil sample is ....°C.

Precautions :

(i) The oil cup and apparatus should be cleaned and dried properly.

(ii) Stirring of oil and heating should be stopped at the time of the application of test flame.

(iii) The bulb of the thermometer should be in touch properly with the oil surface.

(iv) Breathing over the surface of the oil should be avoided.

(v) For each experiment the fresh oil has to be used to get correct value of flash and fire points.

❑❑❑

EXPERIMENT - 8

Object : To determine the dissolved oxygen (D.O.) contents of given water sample.

Apparatus and Reagents : Burette (50ml), pipette (10ml), glass rods, glass bottles, conical flask, measuring flask, manganous sulphate solution, alkaline potassium iodide, sodium thiosulphate (N/40), con. H_2SO_4, starch indicator, water sample.

Theory : The determination of dissolved oxygen is based on the estimation of iodine liberated during Kl reactionwith dissolved oxygen. When solution having dissolved oxygen react with manganese sulphate it oxidise int. higher oxidation state, if we add NaOH and Kl solution to it, we get brown colour precipitate of minimum on adding con. H_2SO_4, the precipitate get dissolved which oxidised iodide of KI into iodine. This liberated iodine is than estimated with sodium thiosulphate using starch as indicator. Disappearance of blue colour of iodo starch complex indicates end point.

$$MnSO_4 + 2NaOH \rightarrow Mn(OH)_2 + Na_2SO_4$$

$$2Mn(OH)_2 + O_2 \rightarrow 2MnO(OH)_2$$

Dissolved oxygen oxidised brown colour ppt.

$$MnO(OH)_2 \xrightarrow{+H_2SO_4} MnSO_4 + 2H_2O + [0]$$

$$2KI + H_2SO_4 + [0] \rightarrow K_2SO_4 + H_2O + I_2$$

$$2Na_2S_2O_3 + I_2 \rightarrow Na_2S_4O_6 + 2NaI$$

Procedure : First of take 50 ml standard sodium thiosulphate solution $\left(\frac{N}{40}\right)$ fill - up in burette and note down the initial reading. Pipette out 10 ml of water sample into a conical flask.

Now titrate it against sodium thiosulphate solution (filled in burette). When brown colour fades the faint yellow colour appears, add 2-3 drops of starch indicator and shake the conical flask throughly, the solution will turn blue, continue the titration till the blue colour disappears. This is the end point repeat the titration at least three times and to get concordant reading.

Observations :

S.NO.	Volume of sample	Burett reading Hypo consumed		Difference (ml) Used Hypo solution	Concordant Reading (ml)
		Initial	Final		
1.	10 ml	0.0			
2.	10 ml	0.0			
3.	10 ml	0.0			

Calculations :

D.O. Sample Hypo solution

$N_1V_1 = N_2V_2$

$$N_1 = \frac{N_2V_2}{V_1}$$

The strength of oxygen = normality × equivalent weight of oxygen

$$= \frac{N}{40} \times \frac{V_2}{10} \times 8 \text{ gm/lit}$$

The strength is also expressed in parts per million as ppm

$$= \frac{N}{40} \times \frac{V_2}{10} \times \frac{8}{1000} \times 10^6 \text{ ppm}$$

$$= x \text{ ppm}$$

Result :

The amount of dissolved oxygen in given water

sampel = ...ppm or mg/lit.

Precautions :

(i) The glass wares used should be thoroughly washed with distilled water and dried.

(ii) All the solutions should be freshly prepared.

(iii) Special care should be taken in sampling.

(iv) The reagents should be added inside the bottle with the help of pipette to avoid air contact with the sample.

(v) Same volume of indicator should be used every time.

❑❑❑

EXPERIMENT - 9

Object : To determine the cloud and pour point of a given lubricating oil.

Apparatus and Reagents : Clould and pour point apparatus, thermometer, lubricating oil sample, freezing mixture.

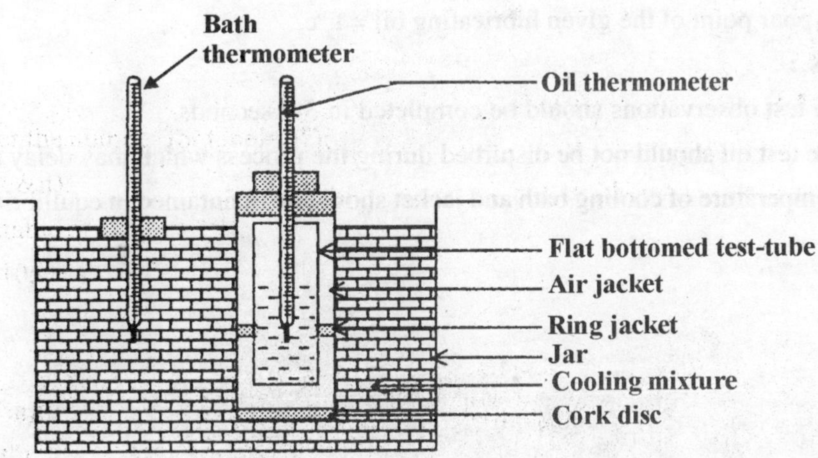

Theory : Lubricating oils obtained from crude oil usually contains dissolved paraffin wax and other such substances which have tendency to crystallize and separate out at lower temperature effecting the lubricating properties.

Cloud point : It is the lowest temperature at which lubricating oil becomes cloudy or hazy in appearance and crystallization takes place.

Pour point : It is the lowest temperature at which the oil just ceases to flow on cooling.

The cloud point determination helps in identifying the temperature at which separation of way crystals which may clog the filter screens in fuel in take system. A high pour point may cause jamming of machines. Cloud and pour point apparatus is used for the determination of cloud and four points of oil. It consists of following parts :

(i) Test tube : It is glass tube having flat bottom and standard dimensions (3cm diameter 12 cm height).

(ii) Cooling bath : It consists of an insulated jackets of glass or copper containing cooling mixture. (here it is ice)

(iii) Thermometers : In given sample and cooling mixture, two thermometer are fitted.

Observation Table :

S.No.	Temperature (°C)	Observation
1.	t_1	No cloud point
2.	t_2	Cloud point
3.	t_3	No pour point
4.	t_4	Pour point

Results :

1. The cloud point of given lubricating oil = t_1°c.

2. The pour point of the given lubricating oil = t_2°c.

Precautions :

(i) The test observations should be completed in 3-5 seconds.

(ii) The test oil should not be disturbed during the process which may delay the observation.

(iii) Temperature of cooling bath and jacket should be maintained in equilibrium.

❑❑❑

EXPERIMENT - 10

Object : To determine the measurement of nitrate in water.

Apparatus : UV-vis spectrophotometer, quantz cuvette, pipette, measuring cylinder.

Reagent : Potessium nitrate (KNO_3) 1N HCl acid, $CHCl_3$, zistilled water.

Theory : Nitrates in water are determined by UV absorption at 220nm. It is observed that organic matters present in the water have absorption at 220 and 275 nm but nitrate not absorb at 275nm and 1N acid of the sample is done to prevent from noun or corborate concentration upto 1000mg $CaCO_3$/l. Chloride and sulphate has no effect on the measurement of nitrates.

Absorbance reading 220nm – 2 × (Absorbance reading at 275 nm)

$$3NO_3^- + 8Al + 5OH^- + 2H_2 \rightleftharpoons 8AlO_2^- + 3NH_3$$

Procedure :

(1) First off taken 500 ml sample water in NH_3 distillation apparatus and add 20 ml of 10% naon and evaporate to about 200 ml.

(2) Cool the solution and add 3gm zevarda's alloy and 30 ml of 10% naon and connect the flask to a vertical candensor.

(3) Zistill at 50-80°C for one hour.

(4) Add 2 ml Nessler's reagent (70 gm KI + 160 gm HgI_2 + 160 gm naon) anddiluted to 1 litre and estimate the obserbance.

(5) Calibration of spectrophotometer.

(6) Determination of the concentration of nitrates.

(7) Note (O.D.) optical density of series of solution prepared.

(8) Plot a graph between O.D. and concentration this is the calibration curve.

(9) This curve should be straight line.

Observation :

S.No.	Concentration (moles/lit)	Absorbance (O.D.)

Calculation :

The concentration of the sample solution can be found out.

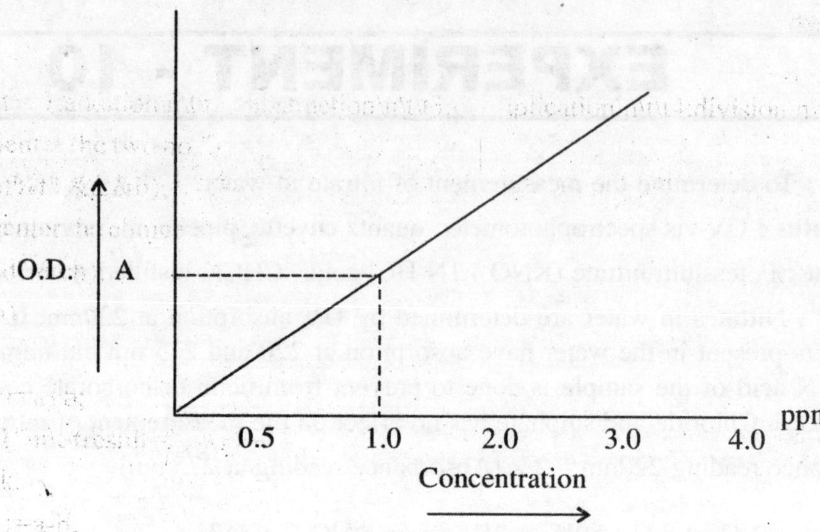

Fig. if A is the O.D. of sample solution then its concentration will 1 ppm.

One mole of NH_3 = one molecular of NO_3^-

$\therefore$ 17 mg of NH_3 = 63 mg of NO_3^-

$\therefore$ 1 ppm of NH_3 the concentration of $NO_3^- = \frac{63}{17} =$ ....ppm

Result = Nitrate context of a given water sample is .... ppm.

Precautions :

(1) Cuvette should be cleaned properly with distilled water and should be wiped with tissue paper.

(2) End point should be observed carefully.

(3) Prepare standard solution.

(4) Only use dilute solution for getting caliberation curve.

(5) The glass wares used should be washed with distileld water.

❑❑❑

Total hardness = 350 ppm

Step (iii) Determination of permanent hardness

100 ml of boiled water = 10 ml of EDTA

$= 10 \times 1 = 10$ mg of $CaCO_3$ eq. hardness

$\therefore$ 1000 ml (or 1 litre) of boiled water $= \frac{10}{100} \times 1000 = 100$ mg of $CaCO_3$ eq. hardness

Permanent hardness = 100 ppm

APPENDIX

Appendix I

Molecular and Equivalent weight of some Chemical Reagent

S. No.	Chemical reagents	Molecular Formula (mw) (gm)	Molecular weight weight (mw/n)	Equivalent (gm)
1.	Aluminium hydroxide	$Al(OH)_3$	78	mw/3 = 29
2.	Ammonium acetate	CH_3COONH_4	77	mw/1 = 77
3.	Ammonium carbonate	$(NH_4)_2CO_3$	96	mw/2 = 48
4.	Ammonium chloride	NH_4Cl	54	mw/1 = 54
5.	Ammonium nitrate	NH_4NO_3	80	mw/1 = 80
6.	Ammonium oxalate	$(NH_4)_2C_2O_4.2H_2O$	142	mw/2 = 71
7.	Ammonium sulphate	$(NH_4)_2SO_4$	132	mw/2 = 61
8.	Ammonium thiocyanate	NH_4CNS	76.10	mw/1 = 76.10
9.	Barium chloride	$BaCl_2.2H_2O$	244	mw/2 = 122
10.	Barium hydroxide	$Ba(OH)_2.8H_2O$	315.50	mw/2 = 157.75
11.	Bleaching powder	$Ca(OCl)_2$	143	mw/2 = 71.50
12.	Borax	$Na_2B_4O_{10}.10H_2O$	381.38	mw/2 = 190.69
13.	Calcium chloride	$CaCl_2.6H_2O$	219	mw/2 = 109.5
14.	Calcium carbonate	$CaCO_3$	100	mw/2 = 50
15.	Calcium hydroxide (lime water)	$Ca(OH)_2$	74	mw/2 = 37
16.	Calcium sulphate	$CaSO_4$	136	mw/2 = 68
17.	Cupper sulphate	$CuSO_4.5H_2O$	249.60	mw/1 = 249.60
18.	Di sodium hydrogen phosphate	$Na_2HPO_4.12H_2O$	360	mw/3 = 120
19.	EDTA	$C_{10}H_{14}N_2Na_2O_8.2H_2O$	372.24	mw/1 = 372.24
20.	Ferrous ammonium sulphate	$FeSO_4(NH_4)_2SO_4.6H_2O$	392.10	mw/1 = 392.10
21.	Ferrous ammonium sulphate (Anhydrous)	$FeSO_4.(NH_4)_2SO_4.6H_2O$	284	mw/1 = 284
22.	Ferric chloride	$FeCl_3.6H_2O$	270.50	mw/1 = 270.50
23.	Ferric chloride (Anhydrous)	$FeCl_3$	162.12	mw/1 = 162.12
24.	Ferric nitrate	$Fe(NO_3)_3.9H_2O$	404	mw/1 = 404
25.	Ferrous sulphate	$FeSO_4.7H_2O$	278	mw/1 = 278
26.	Iodic acid	HIO_3	176	mw/7 = 29.33
27.	Lead acetate	$(CH_3COO)_2Pb.3H_2O$	379	mw/2 = 189.50
28.	Manganese sulphate	$MnSO_4.4H_2O$	480	mw/2 = 240
29.	Magnesium sulphate	$MgSO_4.7H_2O$	246.48	mw/2 = 123.24

Appendix II

Equivalent Weights of substance used in Volumetric Analysis

Titration and substances used	Formula	Eq. Weights
Acid - Alkali Titrations :		
Sodium bicarbonate	$NaHCO_3$	M.W/1 = 84.00
Sodium carbonate	Na_2CO_3	MW/2 = 53.06
Potassium bicarbonate	$KHCO_3$	M.W/1 = 100.00
Potassium carbonate	K_2CO_3	M.W/2 = 69.00
Sodium hydroxide	$NaOH$	M.W/1 = 40.00
Barium hydroxide	$Ba(OH)_2.8H_2O$	M.W/1 = 157.75
Oxalic acid (hydrated)	$H_2C_2O_4.2H_2O$	M.W/2 = 63.03
Sulphuric acid	H_2SO_4	M.W/2 = 49.04
Hydrochloric acid	HCl	M.W/1 = 36.46
Redox Tritration :		
Potassium permanganate	$KMnO_4$	M.W/5 = 31.606
Potassium dichromate	$K_2Cr_2O_7$	M.W/6 = 49.03
Ferrous sulphate (hydratd)	$FeSO_4.7H_2O$	M.W/1 = 278.00
Ferrous sulphate (anhydrous)	$FeSO_4$	M.W/1 = 152.00
Ferrous Ammonium sulphate	$FeSO_4.(NH_4)_2SO_4.6H_2O$	M.W/1 = 392.1
Iodine Titrations :		
Iodine	I_2	M.W/2 = 126.92
Anhydrous sodium thiosulphate	$Na_2S_2O_3$	M.W/1 = 158.09
Hypo (Sodium thisulphate Hydrated)	$Na_2S_2O_3 5H_2O$	M.W/1 = 248.19
Copper sulphate (hydrated)	$CuSO_4.5H_2O$	M.W/1 = 249.68
Arsenious Oxide	As_2O_3	M.W/1 = 49.45
Argentometric Titrations :		
Silver	Ag	M.W/1 = 107.88
Silver nitrate	$AgNO_3$	M.W/1 = 169.89
Sodium chloride	$NaCl$	M.W/1 = 58.45
Chloride ion	Cl^-	At.W/1 = 35.46
Potassium sulphocyanide	$KCNS$	M.W/1 = 97.17
Ammonium sulphocyanide	NH_4CNS	M.W/1 = 76.12

Appendix III

COOLING MIXTURES

S.No.	Mixture	Temperature obtained
1.	Finally crushed Ice	$0 - 5^{\circ}C$
2.	$CaCl_2.6H_2O$ (Crystalline) + Ice	$- 40^{\circ} - 50^{\circ}C$
	(5 parts of $CaCl_2.6H_2O$ + 4 parts of Ice)	
	[If Ice is not available the following mixtures can be used].	
3.	Common salt + crushed Ice	Below $0^{\circ}C$
	(1 part common salt + 3 parts of Ice)	
4.	H_4Cl (1 part) + $NaNO_3$ (1 part) (2 parts)	$- 15^{\circ}C$ to $- 30^{\circ}C$
5.	NH_4Cl (3 parts) + water (10 parts)	13 to $- 15^{\circ}C$
6.	$Na_2S_2O_3.5H_2O$ (11 parts) + water (10 parts)	11 to $- 8^{\circ}C$

Appendix IV

DRYING AGENTS

Substance	Remarks
1. $CaSO_4$	Very efficient drying agent and is converted to its hydrate $2CaSO_4.H_2O$
2. $CaCl_2$	Fairly good capacity of dehydrating, cannot be used to dry amines, alcohols and phenols.
3. $MgSO_4$	Forms heptahydrate $MgSO_4.7H_2O$.
4. Na_2SO_4	Its capacity as drying agent is quite high but it possesses low action and efficiency.
5. Metallic sodium	It is used in the form of wire for drying some organic solvents.

Appendix – V

ATOMIC MASSES OF THE ELEMENTS

Element	Symbol	At. No.	At wt.
Aluminium	Al	13	26.98
Barium	Ba	56	137.34
Calcium	Ca	20	40.08
Carbon	C	6	12.011
Chlorine	Cl	17	35.453
Chromium	Cr	24	51.996
Copper	Cu	29	63.54
Flourine	F	9	18.998
Gold	Au	79	196.967
Iodine	I	53	126.904
Iron	Fe	26	55.847
Lead	Pb	82	207.19
Magnesium	Mg	12	24.312
Mercury	Hg	80	200.59
Nitrogen	N	7	14.007
Phosphorus	P	15	30.974
Potassium	K	19	39.102
Silver	Ag	47	107.870
Sodium	Na	11	22.990
Sulphur	S	16	32.064
Zinc	Zn	30	65.37

Appendix VI

ATOMIC NUMBER AND ATOMIC MASSES

Elements	Symbol	At. No.	At. Mass	Elements	Symbol	At. No.	At. Mass
Actinium	Ac	89	227.0278	Helium	He	2	4.00260
Aluminum	Al	13	26.98154	Holmiun	Ho	67	164.9304
Antimony	Sb	51	121.75	Hydrogen	H	1	1.0079
Argon	Ar	18	39.948	Indium	In	49	114.82
Arsenic	As	33	74.9216	Iodine	I	53	26.9045
Astatine	At	85	(210)	Iridium	Ir	77	192.22
Barium	Ba	56	137.33	Iron	Fe	26	55.847
Beryllium	Be	4	9.01218	Krypton	Kr	36	83.80
Bismuth	Bi	83	208.9804	Lanthanum	La	57	138.9055
Boron	B	5	10.81	Lead	Pb	82	207.2
Bromine	Br	35	79.904	Lithium	Li	3	6.941
Cadium	Cd	48	112.41	Lutetium	Lu	71	174.97
Calcium	Ca	20	40.08	Magnesium	Mg	12	24.305
Carbon	C	6	12.011	Manganese	Mn	25	54.9380
Cerium	Ce	58	140.12	Mandelevium	Md	101	(258)
Cesium	Cs	55	132.9054	Mercury	Hg	80	200.59
Chlorine	Cl	17	35.453	Molybdenum	Mo	42	95.94
Chromium	Cr	24	51.996	Neodymiun	Nd	60	144.24
Cobalt	Co	27	58.9332	Neon	Ne	10	20.179
Copper	Cu	29	63.546	Neptunium	Np	93	237.0482
Dysprosium	Dy	66	162.50	Nickel	Ni	28	58.70

Elements	Symbol	At. No.	At. Mass	Elements	Symbol	At. No.	At. Mass
Einsteinium	Es	99	(254)	Niobium	Nb	41	92.9064
Erbium	Er	68	167.26	Nobelium	No	102	(259)
Europium	Eu	63	151.96	Osmium	Os	76	190.2
Fluorine	F	9	18.99840	Oxygen	O	8	15.9994
Francium	Fr	87	(223)	Palladium	Pd	46	106.4
Gadolinium	Gd	64	157.25	Phosphorus	P	15	30.97376
Gallium	Ga	31	69.72	Platinum	Pt	78	195.09
Germanium	Ge	32	72.59	Plutonium	Pu	94	(244)
Gold	Au	79	196.9665	Polonium	Po	84	(209)
Hafnium	Hf	72	178.49	Potassium	K	19	39.0983
Radium	Ra	88	226.0254	Praseodymium	Pr	59	140.9077
Rhenium	Re	75	186.207	Promethium	Pr	61	(145)
Rhodium	Rh	45	102.9055	Protactinium	Pa	91	231.0359
Rubidium	Rb	37	85.4678	Tellurium	Te	52	127.60
Ruthenium	Ru	44	101.07	Terbium	Tb	65	158.9254
Scandium	Sc	21	44.9559	Thallium	Ti	81	204.37
Selenium	Se	34	78.96	Thulium	Tm	69	168.9342
Silicon	Si	14	28.0855	Tin	Sn	50	118.89
Silver	Ag	47	107.868	Titanium	Ti	22	47.90
Sodium	Na	11	22.98977	Tungsten	W	74	183.85
Sulfur	S	16	32.06	Uranium	U	92	238.029
Tantatium	Ta	73	180.9479	Xenon	Xe	54	131.30
Technetium	Te	43	(97)	Ytterbium	Yb	70	173.04
				Yttrium	Y	39	88.9059
				Zinc	Zn	30	65.38
				Zirconium	Zr	40	91.22

Appendix VII

LIST OF INDICATORS

(A) Acid- base Indicators

S. No.	Indicator	pH Range	Colour in acidic Medium	Colour in Basic Medium
1.	Alizarin yellow	10.1-11.1	Yellow	lilac
2.	Bromothymol blue	3.8 – 5.4	Yellow	blue
3.	Litmus	4.5 – 8.3	Red	Blue
4.	Methyl orange	3.1 – 4.4	Red	Yellow
5.	Methyl red	4.2 – 6.3	Red	Yellow
6.	Phenophthalein	8.0 – 7.6	Colourless	Pink
7.	Eriochrome Black-T	7.0 – 11.0	Blue	Wine red
8.	Calcon	7.4 – 13.5	Pink	Blue

(B) Redox Indicators

S. No.	Indicator	Colour in reduced state	Colour in oxidized state
1.	Di phenyl amine in Conc. H_2SO_4	Colourless	Violet
2.	Di phenyl benzidine in Conc. H_2SO_4	Colourless	Violet
3.	Ferroin in Conc. H_2SO_4	Red	Faint blue
4.	N-Phenylanthranillic acid	Green	Violet red

(C) Argentometric Indicator

S. No.	Indicator	Colour in reduced state	Colour in oxidized state
1.	Potassium chromate	Orange	Brick red
2.	Ferric alum	Colourless	Reddish brown

Appendix VIII

INTERNATIONAL SYSTEM OF UNITS (SI UNITS)

Base Units

Quantity	Unit	Symbol
Length	Meter	M
Mass	Kilogram	Kg
Time	Second	S
Electric current	Ampere	A
Thermodynamic temperature	Kelvin	K
Luminous intensity	Candela	Cd
Amount of substance	Mole	Mol

Supplementary Units

Quantity	Unit	Symbol
Plane angle	radian	Rad
Solid angle	steradian	sr

Derived Units

Quantity	Unit	Symbol	Definition
Force	Newton	N	1 N = 1 kgm/s^2
Energy	joule	J	1 j = 1 N, m
Power	watt	W	1 w = 1 J/s
Flux	Weber	Wb	1Wb = 1 V.s
Flux density	tesla	T	1 T = 1 h/m^2
Frequency	hertz	Hz	1 Hz = 1 c/s (s^{-1})
Electric conductance	siemens	S	1 S = 1 A/V
Electromotive force	volt	V	1 V = 1 W/A
Pressure stress	Pascal	Pa	1 Pa = 1 N/m^2

Appendix IX
PHYSICAL PROPERTIES OF WATER(SI Units)

	Specific weight,	Density	Modulus of elastic-	Dynamic viscosity	Kinematic viscosity	Surface tension+	Vapor pressure,
Temperature,	γ	ρ	$E/10^6$	$\mu\times10^3$	$\nu\times10^6$	σ	p_v
°C	kN/m^3	kg/m^3	kN/m^2	$N\cdot s/m^2$	m^2/s	N/m	kN/m^2
0	9.805	999.8	1.98	1.781	1.785	0.0765	0.61
10	9.804	999.7	2.10	1.307	1.306	0.0742	1.23
20	9.789	998.2	2.17	1.002	1.003	0.0728	2.34
30	9.764	995.7	2.25	0.798	0.800	0.0712	4.24
40	9.730	992.2	2.28	0.653	0.658	0.0696	7.38
50	9.689	988.0	2.29	0.547	0.553	0.0679	12.33
60	9.642	983.2	2.28	0.466	0.474	0.0662	19.92
70	9.589	977.8	2.25	0.404	0.413	0.0644	31.16
80	9.530	971.8	2.20	0.354	0.364	0.0626	47.34
90	9.466	965.3	2.14	0.315	0.326	0.0608	70.10
100	9.399	958.4	2.07	0.282	0.294	0.0589	101.33

* At atmospheric pressure.

+ In contact with air.

Appendix X

TEMPERATURE CONVERSION FORMULA

°C	F-32/1.8
°C	°K-273.15
°F	1.8 × C + 32
°F	°R -459.67
°K	°C + 273.15
°R	°F +459.67
°C	Degree Celsius
°F	Degree Fahrenheit
°K	Degree Kelvin
°R	Degree Rankine

Appendix XI

VISCOSITIES OF LIQUIDS (MILLIPOISE)

Substance	0°C	10°C	15°C	20°C	25°C	30°C	40°C	50°C
1. Aniline	122.0	64.5	53.3	42.7	36.4	31.1	23.6	18.6
2. Ethyl alcohol	17.72	14.66	13.0	12.00	10.78	10.03	8.34	7.02
3. Methyl alcohol	8.08	6.90	6.23	5.92	5.44	5.15	4.49	3.95
4. Carbon tetra-chloride	13.51	11.38	10.40	9.75	9.03	8.48	7.46	6.62
5. Chloroform	6.99	6.25	5.96	5.63	–	5.10	4.64	4.24
6. Benzene	9.00	7.57	6.96	6.47	5.96	5.61	4.92	4.36
7. Toluene	7.72	6.71	6.23	5.90	–	5.25	4.71	4.26
8. Water	17.865	13.04	11.37	10.02	8.9	8.01	6.54	5.477

Appendix XII

HEAT OF SOLUTION OF SOME SALTS

Substance	Moles of H_2O per mole of salt	Δ H solution kcal mole	Substance	Moles of H_2O per moles of salt	Δ H solution kcal/ mole
1. NaCl	200	+1.28	$MgSO_4 7H_2O$	400	+23.80
2. NH_4Cl	200	+3.88	$Na_2SO_4 10H_2O$	400	– 0.55
3. $BaCl_2 2H_2O$	400	+4.93	KCl	200	+ 18.90
4. $CuSO_4$ (anhydrous)	400	– 15.80	H_2SO_4 (l)	200	– 17.91
5. KNO_3	200	+ 8.52	Na_2SO_4	400	– 0.55
6. $CuSO_4 5H_2O$	400	+ 2.75	KOH(s)	5	– 11.53
7. NH_4NO_2 (s)	5	+ 4.24		–	–

Periodic Table of the Elements

- hydrogen
- alkali metals
- alkali earth metals
- transition metals
- poor metals
- nonmetals
- noble gases
- rare earth metals

1 H																	2 He
3 Li	4 Be											5 B	6 C	7 N	8 O	9 F	10 Ne
11 Na	12 Mg											13 Al	14 Si	15 P	16 S	17 Cl	18 Ar
19 K	20 Ca	21 Sc	22 Ti	23 V	24 Cr	25 Mn	26 Fe	27 Co	28 Ni	29 Cu	30 Zn	31 Ga	32 Ge	33 As	34 Se	35 Br	36 Kr
37 Rb	38 Sr	39 Y	40 Zr	41 Nb	42 Mo	43 Tc	44 Ru	45 Rh	46 Pd	47 Ag	48 Cd	49 In	50 Sn	51 Sb	52 Te	53 I	54 Xe
55 Cs	56 Ba	57 La	72 Hf	73 Ta	74 W	75 Re	76 Os	77 Ir	78 Pt	79 Au	80 Hg	81 Ti	82 Pb	83 Bi	84 Po	85 At	86 Rn
87 Fr	88 Ra	89 Ac	104 Unq	105 Unp	106 Unh	107 Uns	108 Uno	109 Une	110 Unn								

58 Ce	59 Pr	60 Nd	61 Pm	62 Sm	63 Eu	64 Gd	65 Tb	66 Dy	67 Ho	68 Er	69 Tm	70 Yb	71 Lu
90 Th	91 Pa	92 U	93 Np	94 Pu	95 Am	96 Cm	97 Bk	98 Cf	99 Es	100 Fm	101 Md	102 No	103 Lr

INDEX

F

G

H

I

J

L

M

N

O

P

Q

R

S

T

U

V

W

Z

S

T

U

V

W

Z

and biotechnology (an example is the **COVID-19 pandemic**) will have a significant impact in the New World Order. The United States has already come out with '**5G Clean Network Initiative**' to secure its critical communication infrastructure from Chinese vendors describing them as 'malign actors'.

The **New Globalism** – the global interdependence – has given a boost to worldwide cooperation leading to a huge increase in world trade and consequent material prosperity. Despite this general prosperity, the bulk of humanity still suffers from an inadequate supply of food, water and medical facilities. The income gaps between the poor and the rich within the nations and between the nations have greatly widened. Pollution of environment and the dwindling physical resources of the earth have set the danger alarm ringing for the first time in human history. There is also a clash between the old and the new. While the fundamentalists yearn to go back to the traditional past (**Afghanistan** is an example, where the **Taliban** recaptured power recently), others look for reordering the world on modern values. Amidst all these, the Global Order is undergoing tremendous changes and historical evidence shows that globalism will be accompanied by continuing uncertainty and will continue to expose us to the differences that surround us.

SUMMARY

Non-Aligned Movement – The Non-Alignment was a foreign policy initiative of retaining autonomy of policy between the two superpowers and the Non-Aligned Movement was a platform for the newly independent countries to move in this direction. The 'Panchsheel' and the 'Ten Principles of Bandung' formed the basic spirit of this movement. It was formed in the background of two international developments – Decolonisation and Cold War and hence uphold some basic elements such as the right of independent judgement in international affairs, opposition against neo-colonialism, use of moderation in relation with all big powers and restructuring of the international economic order.

European Union – The EU is a political and economic union of large number of European countries whose people share a common market, enjoy guaranteed rights and possess a common history under the slogan 'United in Diversity'. The European Coal and Steel Community (ECSC), the European Economic Community (EEC), the European Community (EC) and the European Union (EU) were different landmark developments of it. Though it faces certain crisis, with its geographical size, population strength, economic might, social standards and as a single market and as the largest trade bloc the EU is trying for a major role in a world dominated by the United States.

QUESTIONS OF PREVIOUS YEARS CIVIL SERVICES EXAMINATION

1. "The supremacy of the USA after the end of Cold War had its challenges as well". Critically examine. (2023)
2. Discuss the launching of Non-Alignment Movement. Why the small nations wanted to remain aloof from the powerful nations? (2022)

3. During the Cold War, some important leaders of the Non-Aligned Movement wanted to keep the movement away from the military blocs. Critically examine. (2021)
4. The impact of the end of the Cold War and the emergence of the US as the lone superpower has been both, good and bad. Discuss. (2021)
5. 'The multitude of newly independent countries came to be known as the "Third World", belonging neither to the First World of capitalist democracies, nor the Communist Second World'. Critically examine. (2020)
6. A new configuration of power emerged in world politics after the end of the Cold War. Analyse how USA managed to become the sole superpower. (2020)
7. 'Non-alignment came to symbolize the struggle of India and other newly independent nations to retain and strengthen their independence from colonialism and imperialism'. Critically examine. (2019)
8. 'The collapse of Berlin Wall on 9 November 1989 brought new meaning to idea of cooperation in Europe'. Critically examine. (2017)
9. What factors contributed to the emergence of a unipolar world? (2016)
10. 'The European Union, a diplomatic marvel, continues to grapple with international fissures arising out of economic contentious issues that pose a challenge to an effective integration of the Union'. Critically examine. (2015)
11. 'The European Union is the new sick of Europe'. Critically evaluate. (2013)
12. Would you argue that the Non-Aligned Movement played a crucial role in promoting a climate of peace? (2011)
13. 'The collapse of the Berlin Wall in 1989 brought new ideas of co-operation in Europe'. Critically examine. (2011)
14. Explain the circumstances leading to emergence of Third World and analyze its impact on world affairs. (2010)